Praise for
For the Love of Russian Gold

"Ludmila Melnikoff's *For the Love of Russian Gold* is a captivating memoir about a business-savvy young woman navigating the treacherous world of Russian gold mining. She has inside knowledge on the ins and outs of Russian society and commerce, and because of this she faces manipulation from the men around her. She recounts harrowing tales from her past, including kidnapping, encounters with brown bears, sandstorms, bribery, and bugged devices, highlighting the pervasive dangers of her pursuit in mining for Russian gold. I am surprised she made it out alive. Melnikoff's descriptive writing makes this book a compelling read for anyone interested in adventure, drama, and ethical quandaries."

—Holly Mayes, author of *Dream, Girl*

"A fervent true story of corruption, betrayal, and deceit at the highest echelons of the Russian government, narrated with unblinking directness by Melnikoff. A captivating memoir that reads more like a fast-paced political/romantic thriller. An eye-opening, brave exposé of Russia and how business is conducted in a country where Western ethics do not exist. This could almost be a prequel to Bill Browder's bestseller *Red Notice*. Absolutely thrilling, considering every word is true, backed by records and documents!"

—Stasija Moyle, graphic designer

"If you are a forever learner or just a curious person, this fascinating tale of deceit and grift is an eye-opener on recent Russian history. Timely and a cautionary tale. Highly recommended."
—Marie Newman, author of *A Life Made from Scratch*, and former congresswoman

"This fast-moving, page-turning book is by a woman who does not know the word 'no' and like a Spanish toreador goes into the arena of high-stakes, high-finance deals and waves the red cape at the storming bull—in this case, none other than Russia's leaders, Gorbachev and Yeltsin."
—Laurinel Owen, author of *Strings Attached*

"When Russia opened its doors to foreign investment in the 1990s, the author decided to explore emerging business opportunities in Moscow. It was a gutsy move for someone who had yet to see her thirtieth birthday. Australian by birth, with an aristocratic Russian family background that offered powerful political connections, the author gets swept up in the excitement of a high-risk gold mining venture. Her memoir of what ultimately transpired has all the elements of a spy novel—political tension, ruthless billionaires, mafia hit men, government corruption, and personal betrayal. Allured by the prospect of mega-millions, it's no surprise that virtually everyone involved was playing a double game. When the dust eventually settles, Melnikoff realizes which promises are truly worth banking on. Based on her diary, business meeting reports, and company records, Melnikoff's memoir is a detailed account of the events that took place over that ten-year period.

This book is for anyone who wants proof of the saying 'Behind every great fortune lies a great crime.'"
—Jennifer E. Hassel, author of
Badass Grief: Changing Gears, Moving Forward

"This book has all the twists and turns of a compelling spy novel, but with the added personal connection that Melnikoff brings to the story. Her resolve and tenacity make for an inspiring memoir. I learned so many interesting details about the history of Russia after the collapse of the Soviet Union. *For the Love of Russian Gold* is a compelling read that makes you want to keep turning the pages right from the start."
—Ward V. B. Lassoe, author of *Diane: True Survivor*, psychotherapist, and former TV reporter

"A wonderful tale and exposé of the evolution of Russia from the 'tsar wars' in the early twentieth century to freedom from the Berlin Wall as Russia, broke, begins enticing capital investments. Written from actual experience and a matter of record, the content could only have been exposed by someone with an incredible in-depth knowledge of actual events. What amazes the reader is the realization that this is not a fictional drama. It reads like a novel with all the thrills interwoven of love, power, adventure, corruption, and life-and-death scenarios as each page unfolds. It's a 'can't put down' read and highly recommended."
—Ric Lawes, author and movie producer

"Truly exposes the events of Russia's transformation into a young democracy under Yeltsin and the rise of Putin to the power he wields today in 2025. All against a backdrop of intrigue and an amazing love story, adding spice! Completely engrossing. I loved it!"

—Dr. Amy Ho, medical doctor

"A real eye-opener into Russia's first wild days of democracy, involving former Australian Prime Minister Malcolm Turnbull (the one who just attacked Trump, calling him a rude, chaotic bully and a threat to global economy and security), Russia's Boris Yeltsin; a multimillionaire international mining magnate, the world's largest secret gold mine in Siberia, affairs, mafia, corruption—all making this a thrilling true story!"

—Michael Kretch, IT manager

For The Love of Russian Gold
by Ludmila Melnikoff

© Copyright 2025 Ludmila Melnikoff

ISBN 979-8-88824-669-6

All rights reserved. No part of this publication may be reproduced, stored in a retrieval system, or transmitted in any form or by any means—electronic, mechanical, photocopy, recording, or any other—except for brief quotations in printed reviews, without the prior written permission of the author.

Edited by Hannah Woodlan
Cover design by Catherine Herold

Published by

3705 Shore Drive
Virginia Beach, VA 23455
800-435-4811
www.koehlerbooks.com

For The Love of Russian Gold

LUDMILA MELNIKOFF

VIRGINIA BEACH
CAPE CHARLES

Contents

Introduction 14
Preface 15
Prologue 24
My Early Years 30
Moscow at Last 40
Can I Ever Return? 46
Back to Russia 55
The Birth of Star 62
Katya to the Rescue 71
A Journey to Bodaibo 81
Sukhoi Log Unveiled 88
Blood in the Streets 97
Falling in Love 106
Ordinance #693-p 117
The Birth of Lenzoloto JSC 129
Drug Money? 138
Among the Shadows 146
Argy-Bargy 158
Start of an Affair and a New Enemy 165
A Pregnancy and a Betrayal 180
Australia's First President? 187
The Miracle of Conversion 198
A Baby Is Born 203
Meeting Malcolm 213
A Lovers' Spat 224
Altercations and Explosions 232
Malcolm Opens Up 244
Changing Sides 246
A Drunken Hero 251

Held Over a Barrel	257
Dissension	260
A Birthday Celebration	263
Another Hurdle Overcome with Help from a PM	266
Dare We Hope?	271
A New CEO and an A-List Party	275
Turmoil in Star	279
World's Greatest Mining Company	290
Must Get Rid of Malcolm	293
Yatskevich in Australia and More Bribery	301
War in Bodaibo	309
Knives Are Out	315
Liquidity—Dividing Up the Spoils	320
Broken Record	325
Collateral Damage and a Trip to New York	330
The Biggest Sting of All	335
More Smoke and a Lifeline	345
Rats and Sinking Ships	351
Ripped Off by One, Dumped by the Other	358
Could It Be?	365
Court—and Finally the Whole Truth About Ian	372
The Secret Life of a Sociopath	384
To Catch a Thief	400
Epilogue	405
After Notes	408

Introduction

This memoir depicts the particular period of my entry to Russia, home of my ancestors, and events that took place to secure what was reputed to be the largest gold deposit in the world. It exposes a corrupt land and follows how Putin came to power.

The following record is based on my recollections and comprehensive diary notes, minutes of meetings, reports, tape recordings, faxes, emails, travel logs, court notes, and all hard copies in my possession, totaling hundreds of documents. Some names and identifiable information have been changed where necessary.

Reliving the journey has been difficult: the emotional cruelty, the disappointments, the hardships, the triumph, and the final outcome. I have laughed and cried, perhaps too many times, but I do not regret a moment of my life, for life is a journey, and we must play the hand we are dealt to the best of our ability. I hope readers will find my journey inspirational.

Preface

The Berlin Wall has come down. East meets West, and Gorbachev's Soviet Union is bankrupt. Yeltsin becomes president, introducing democracy. Desperate for cash, Russia opens its doors to foreign companies; and Australian-born Ludmila is lured to the homeland of her ancestors.

Sukhoi Log, alleged to be the largest gold reserve in the world at a value of US$30 billion, belongs to Lenzoloto—a government-owned mining enterprise in Siberia—and is the jewel in Russia's crown. With Yeltsin's apparent backing, Ludmila forms a joint venture between her company, Star, and Lenzoloto to mine Sukhoi Log. She is aided by a charismatic mining magnate, Ian MacNee, and Australia's future twenty-ninth prime minister, Malcolm Turnbull. The two men share a passion for gold, and for Ludmila.

Business in Russia, the land of smoke and mirrors, is done over cognac and vodka. Millions of dollars raised by merchant bankers in London, New York, and Australia flow into Siberia as the mining world eagerly watches. The stakes are high, and the game of gold begins. The hard-line Communists and the FSB, the successor to the KGB (the Soviet Union's security agency from

1954 to 1991), will never accept Yeltsin's plans to control Russian gold and use every possible pawn to prevent a checkmate.

One question will remain when the smoke clears: How much gold is really in Sukhoi Log—and did Star ever have a chance to mine it, or was it Russia's greatest grift?

◆ ◆ ◆

MAIN RUSSIAN CHARACTERS IN MOSCOW

Alexei: A KGB informant, employed by Star as a consultant and later company secretary of the Lenzoloto Joint Stock Company (JSC) board.

Azarova: A lawyer in the president's legal department, reporting to Ruslan Orehov, the first deputy head of President Yeltsin's legal department.

Mikhail Barsukov: The head of FSB (Russia's main security agency, formed in 1995) under Yeltsin from July 1995 until he was fired during the June 1996 elections to increase Yeltsin's chances of winning. Barsukov appointed his close confidant Alexander Korzhakov as Yeltsin's chief of security, and together they pushed the president toward authoritarian rule while blocking further steps toward a free-market economy, so they were unpopular with the Russian people. They also tried to expose Yeltsin's election corruption scandal, known as the "Xerox Affair."

Boris Berezovsky: An oligarch and Yeltsin's private adviser.

Bychkov: The head of Komdragmet, the Committee for Precious Metals from 1991 until 1996. He was fired by Yeltsin for alleged links to a shadowy deal that siphoned US$88 million in uncut gems through a San Francisco company called Golden ADA. Komdragmet shipped the rough diamonds to the company for cutting, but Russia got neither the stones nor the money in return.[1]

Borisov: An official from the Department of Foreign Economic Relations in Yeltsin's administration.

Viktor Chernomyrdin: The prime minister of Russia from December 1992 to March 1998. He died in November 2010 after a long illness.

Anatoly Chubais: The chairman of the Government Committee for Property (GKI), i.e., the head of privatization, starting in November 1991 and architect of Russia's privatization program. From June 1992, he was the deputy prime minister for economic and financial policy, and he was the first deputy prime minister from November 1994 until his resignation in January 1996 to run Yeltsin's reelection campaign. In July 1996 he was appointed by Yeltsin as chief of the president's administration.

Chugaevsky: One of Russia's first successful entrepreneurs.

Yegor Gaidar: A brilliant Russian economist who was deputy prime minister for finance from November 1991 until March 1992, when Yeltsin promoted him to first deputy prime minister. He served as acting prime minister of Russia from June 1992 to December 1992, but the parliament (composed of the Congress of People's Deputies and the Supreme Soviet) refused to confirm him as PM. Gaidar returned to government in September 1993 as first deputy prime minister, resigning in January 1994. He died unexpectedly in 2009 at the age of fifty-three from a cardiogenic pulmonary edema (heart failure).

Grigoriev: The head of the Gold Committee of the Russian Federation.

Ruslan Khasbulatov: The Speaker of the Supreme Soviet from

---

1 "International Business: Yeltsin Fires Top Russian Diamond Official," February 22, 1996, from Associated Press.

July 1991 until October 1993. At first, he was Yeltsin's strong ally, but by 1993 he had become the second most powerful man in Russia and a sworn enemy of Yeltsin. He attempted to overthrow Yeltsin during the 1993 constitutional crisis, which ended in Yeltsin's bloody assault on the White House (the house of the Russian parliament) and the parliament's dissolution. He was subsequently imprisoned for treason.

Kuranov: An adviser to the minister of atomic energy and a director of Lenzoloto JSC.

Lebedev: Russia's leading nuclear scientist at the Ministry of Atomic Energy.

Viktor Mikhaylov: A nuclear bomb maker and Russia's nuclear tsar, overseeing thirty nuclear reactors. He was the minister of atomic energy from March 1992 until March 1998, when he was fired abruptly by Yeltsin on the eve of negotiating the sale of US$13 billion worth of Russian uranium to the US. The American broker involved in the deal was Mikhaylov's personal friend.

Mostovoy: The first deputy chairman of the GKI from 1992 to 1997; the chairman of Lenzoloto JSC until 1996.

Golovnin: Gaidar's first aide.

Mikhail Poltoranin: The minister for information and mass media and Yeltsin's best friend.

Vladimir Putin: Russia's president after Yeltsin.

Alexander Rutskoy: The vice president of Russia from 1991 to 1993. During the 1993 constitutional crisis, the Russian parliament proclaimed him acting president in opposition to Yeltsin, but Yeltsin dissolved the parliament and imprisoned Rutskoy for treason.

Rudakov: The chairman of GlavGold (in charge of gold mining in the Soviet Union) and also a KGB general and fierce opponent of Star.

Ekaterina ("Katya") Shevelova: A veteran journalist, poet, presidential translator, childhood playmate of Yuri Andropov (the Soviet Union's feared KGB chief cum

Soviet leader), and Star's political adviser.

Alexander Shokhin: The deputy prime minister for foreign economic relations in May 1992 and then prime minister for economics in March 1994.

Vladimir: The chief economist at GlavGold who later worked as an agent for Star.

Weinberg: The chairman of Russia's Bank of Development and Reconstruction; a member of Yeltsin's advisory council; and later chairman of Bam Credit Bank, Siberia. He was imprisoned briefly in August 1994 for bribing a customs official with a US$500 gold chain.

Boris Yatskevich: The first deputy head (in fact, head honcho) of Geolkom (the federal Committee for Geology) from late 1991. He replaced Mostovoy as chairman of Lenzoloto in 1996. Later he became the first deputy minister of the newly formed Ministry for Natural Resources, and in August 1999 he was promoted by Yeltsin to minister of natural resources. He was sacked by Putin in June 2001, soon after Putin became Russia's president, for corruption.

Boris Yeltsin: The first president of the Russian Federation, serving from 1991 to 1999. He died in April 2007 from cardiac arrest, having previously had a quadruple bypass. He was survived by his wife, Naina, and daughters, Tanya and Elena.

IN SIBERIA

Avlov: The general director of Lenzoloto.
Yury Nozhikov: The governor of the Irkutsk region.
Varenikov: The director of the Lenzoloto Artels and then president of the newly formed Siberian Association of

Artels.

Yakovenko: The first deputy governor of the Irkutsk region and director of Lenzoloto JSC.

* * *

MAIN AUSTRALIAN CHARACTERS

Brian Croser: An Australian winemaker and owner of Australia's Petaluma Wines and, together with Ian, owner of Argyle Winery in Oregon.

Rob Hampshire: An Australian celebrity psychiatrist.

John Helmer: An Australian journalist based in Moscow who reported on Australia's *60 Minutes* in 1995 as "Socrates"; it was alleged that he was a Russian/American double agent.

Paul Keating: The prime minister of Australia from 1991 to 1996.

Angus MacNee: son of Ian and Bobby, Ian's second wife.

Chris MacNee: A director of Star Technology; director of Star Mining; director of Lenzoloto JSC; and son of Ian and Jan, Ian's first wife.

Ian MacNee: A founder and director of Star Technology; director of Star Mining NL; and director of Lenzoloto JSC.

Ludmila Melnikoff: A founder and director of Star Technology and director of Lenzoloto JSC.

Greg Moore: A founder and director of Star Technology and Ludmila's husband until 1992.

Bill O'Neill: Ian MacNee's financial adviser and director of Coherent Resources.

Gerard Seeber: The trade commissioner at the Australian Embassy in Moscow.

Dr. John Thomas: Star's mining engineer.

Malcolm Turnbull: The main partner at Turnbull & Partners, an Australian investment bank; director of Star Technology (British Virgin Islands); and director of Star Mining NL.

Tess: Ian's personal assistant in the USA.

Dr. Bruce Wood: Star's chief geologist.

Australian side

CORPORATE AND GOVERNMENT ENTITIES

Artels: Independent contractors and miners of alluvial gold (gold extracted from rivers and streams).

Central Mining NL: A shell company, 80 percent owned by Ian MacNee, listed on the Australian Stock Exchange in January 1986. Its directors were Ian MacNee, Graeme Ellis (MacNee's best friend), and KPMG corporate adviser Bill O'Neill. In 1993 Central Mining acquired all the issued capital of Star Technology (Star) from its owners and changed its name to Star Mining NL. Bill resigned promptly to make way for Malcolm Turnbull, Star's new banker.

Crusader Investments Ltd.: Ian MacNee's company in Hong Kong, a listed offshoot of the Lee Ming Group.

GKI: The Government Committee for Property.

GlavGold: The Russian government agency that oversaw gold production in the Soviet Union. In August 1991 GlavGold was dissolved and transformed into two departments: the Committee for Geology (known as Geolkom) and Committee for Precious Metals (known as Komdragmet).

Lenzoloto Association: A government-owned gold mining enterprise from the 1890s until 1991, when it was privatized into the Lenzoloto Joint Stock Company. It was named after the Lena River, the hub of its alluvial gold mining operations (*zoloto* means "gold"). The Lenzoloto Association was near the town of Bodaibo in the Irkutsk region, northeast of Lake Baikal, and had mining rights to develop the world's largest proven gold deposit: Sukhoi Log ("Dry Gulch").

Lenzoloto JSC: The joint stock company formed in 1991. Under the founding agreement, the shareholders were Star,

GKI, and the Lenzoloto workers. It had rights to 106 gold deposits, including Sukhoi Log.

Star Technology Ltd. (Star): A company set up by Ian MacNee in 1991 in the British Virgin Islands do business in Russia. Crusader Investments Ltd. held 80 percent of Star, and Greg Moore (Ludmila's husband at the time) and Ludmila held 10 percent each.

PROLOGUE

Three powerful men dominated my life in the 1990s: the Russian president Boris Yeltsin, Australia's future prime minister Malcolm Turnbull, and an elusive Australian multimillionaire named Ian MacNee.

We all had one thing in common: Russian gold. You might say that Ian and Malcolm had me in common as well. Yeltsin was purely business.

I met Yeltsin in December 1990, when he was Speaker of the Russian parliament. Twelve months later, the Communist flag was lowered over the Kremlin, and Boris Yeltsin became the first president of a newly independent Russia.

Of all the reasons to cross paths with the future Australian prime minister, the lure of Sukhoi Log in the remote Siberian taiga would seem the least likely of all possibilities. Back then, the Russians put the undeveloped gold deposit's value at $21 billion American. We—Ian MacNee, Malcolm, and I—wanted the license to mine it.

I worked hard to pave the way for us, and I had firsthand experience in trying to do business in Russia long before the men came along for the ride. When Boris Yeltsin's predecessor, Gorbachev, opened Russia to the West, capitalists like me couldn't get there fast enough. Gorbachev talked about openness, and

Westerners took him at his word. The old Union of Soviet Socialist Republics (USSR) had been one monstrous, inefficient public service machine wrapped up in masses of red tape. This machine had been paralyzed by bankruptcy and had come to a grinding halt. In 1986, Gorbachev pledged a free economy, freedom of speech, and equality for all. And everything rolled on from there.

The 1990s were tumultuous. The rest of the world watched with amazement as the former Soviet Union converted into a lawless "democracy," one driven by an insatiable hunger for money, with politicians and the mafia the main beneficiaries. It was no place for the weak.

When I met Malcolm, he was a successful investment banker, possessed of great charm and an explosive temper. As a banker, his enthusiasm for the Sukhoi Log project was understandable. But Malcolm was also a romantic. "Mining gold in the middle of Siberia is very sexy," he said. He was not exceptional in this. Westerners have always romanticized Siberia, and Russia itself. Like Winston Churchill once famously said, "Russia is a riddle, wrapped in a mystery, inside an enigma."

Among Russians, Malcolm became very "Russian." I think his new skin excited him. And as a young, entrepreneurial, Russian-speaking Australian businesswoman with an aristocratic Russian family background, I became part of that excitement. There was chemistry between Malcolm and me.

I first went to Moscow as a nineteen-year-old university student on a one-year scholarship to study Russian at Moscow University. I fell in love, stayed on illegally, and was incarcerated in a grisly Russian prison as a result. Ten years later, in 1989, I went back very nervously, accompanied by my then husband Greg, to explore the business opportunities emerging under Gorbachev. Our marriage didn't last long. Indeed, we were on our honeymoon when I realized I'd married the wrong man.

We spent part of the honeymoon in Moscow, returning to Sydney with what we believed was a great business proposition. I hired a consultant to find a prospective equity investor. The candidate he came up with was Ian MacNee, a self-made, Australian-born millionaire who'd earned his money as a mining entrepreneur. He was interested in doing something in Russia but didn't know how to go about it. I spoke the language and, through my mother, had powerful connections in Moscow. Best of all, I had a business proposition that looked good.

Ultimately, we abandoned the initial proposition, since it had the fingerprints of the Chechen mafia all over it. However, only seven months after I met Ian, the two of us would walk into Yeltsin's office, and Boris would make us a stunning offer. He also left us in no doubt that he intended to control all the gold in Russia.

To have powerful political connections was vital in Russia at that time. The great danger was to bet on the wrong side, which could be fatal. On the other hand, the advantage of operating in an extremely unstable political atmosphere was that high-risk business deals could result in high rewards, with the astute making millions and even billions of dollars.

The key to everything was having the money to bribe the right people in government. That's why most publicly listed Western companies struggled to succeed in Russia. They couldn't hand out millions of dollars in bribes without accounting for it.

We could.

But we were the little guy. Our company, Star Technology Ltd., was unknown. We needed investors who could raise the sort of capital needed to develop Sukhoi Log, automatically giving us credibility as businesspeople.

Malcolm Turnbull, of the investment bank Turnbull & Partners in Sydney, became one of those people. In time, other powerful investors, such as County National Westminster in London,

Barclays, and big players in the British business world like Sir Rudolph Agnew, came on board.

I thought that with my Russian background and connections and a personal endorsement from Boris Yeltsin, the road to riches would be easy. But almost immediately, there emerged a cast of characters with their own agendas who made the going bewildering at best and downright dangerous at worst.

Some, like Yegor Gaidar, the economist who was Russia's acting prime minister in our time and whom I disliked intensely, came with powerful political affiliations. A few, like the mysterious M, who apparently ran Moscow's most elite hospital, offered to kill our enemies for us. Others were simply there to make sure we never succeeded. The KGB (officially renamed FSK in 1991 but still referred to as KGB) waited and watched in the wings. Even our amazingly influential Russian adviser, Katya, was playing a double game.

Every time we thought we'd finally reached the end of the tortuous process to win the Sukhoi Log tender (an invitation to bid for a project with a deadline to submit the bid), the rules would change yet again. "We're being screwed over by the Russians!" Malcolm yelled at me on one occasion, frustrated beyond belief at how Sukhoi Log had become the glittering prize lying always just beyond our grasp. All the same, right to the end I really thought we'd do it.

Early in May 2016, the Panama Papers scandal created international headlines. A massive leak of files from the database of Mossack Fonseca—the world's biggest offshore law firm, based in Panama—revealed how the world's most powerful people could exploit secretive tax havens. One of those named was Malcolm Turnbull. The Panama Papers showed him to be the former director of a British Virgin Islands company set up and administered by Mossack Fonseca.

Neil Chenoweth, a leading financial journalist from Australia's most prestigious paper, the *Australian Financial Review*, covered the story.[2] He wrote that in October 1993, Malcolm had joined the board of Star Mining NL, an Australian-listed company hoping to develop a $21 billion American–Siberian gold mine called Sukhoi Log. Five weeks later, they were appointed directors of Star Mining's subsidiary in the British Virgin Islands, Star Technology Limited. One of the key people who had helped obtain Star's Siberian mining leases, Chenoweth added, was a Russian Australian named Ludmila Melnikoff.

The prime minister's spokesman told the media that Malcolm Turnbull wasn't aware that the company had been administered by Mossack Fonseca as the registered agent in Road Town, Tortola (the largest of the British Virgin Islands). And Chenoweth emphasized in his article that there was no suggestion the PM had acted improperly.

But a few weeks after the first flurry of articles in the Australian media, Chenoweth wrote a detailed letter to John Garnaut, one of the prime minister's media advisers (and former China correspondent for Fairfax Media), to say that the picture had become a little more complicated. I was given access to the letter and the detailed questions Chenoweth asked regarding Malcolm's business involvement with Star Mining.

At the end, he included one further question:

> There have been suggestions dating over a long period and from a number of sources, that Mr. Turnbull was romantically linked in some form with Ms. Melnikoff. I should be clear that I am not suggesting a sexual relationship. But for the record I'm bound to ask about the nature of the working relationship between Mr. Turnbull

---

2   Neil Chenoweth, "PM's Road to Siberia via Panama," *The Australian Financial Review*, June 14, 2016.

and Ms. Melnikoff, whether this could be characterized as a warm friendship; and whether at any time this could be described as a romantic attachment or even infatuation, on the part of either or both parties.

No answer was forthcoming from the prime minister.

Exactly eleven years after we walked into Boris Yeltsin's office, I found out why Ian MacNee had been so keen to do business in Russia. In all our time together, chasing Sukhoi Log, I never suspected that something else might be going on, not even on the occasion when our car was intercepted on the way to the airport by a stretch limousine with blacked-out windows.

After our driver pulled over to the side of the road, the door of the limousine opened, and a voluptuous blond woman in her early forties emerged. She was wearing heavy black eyeliner, bright-red lipstick, and a brown tweed skirt suit with knee-high brown leather boots.

Ian told me her name was Nadya. She was Ukrainian, and he had some documents to give her. He got out of the car, and the two of them spoke briefly before he passed her a large yellow envelope. Not once did Nadya glance my way as I sat in the back seat, watching this scene with bemusement.

When Ian returned, I asked curiously: "All good?"

"Yes, little girl," he replied as the limousine sped off in the opposite direction.

He took my hand and held it for the rest of the journey.

CHAPTER ONE

My Early Years

My name is Ludmila Melnikoff. The only child of Oleg and Nataly, I was born in 1960 in Adelaide, the city of churches and the capital of South Australia.

Both my parents were Russian émigrés who ended up in Adelaide in the 1950s. My mother was born in 1938 in Harbin, capital of Manchuria in China. The city became an enclave for aristocratic Russians following the 1917 Russian Revolution.

The tiny one-bedroom house where Mum would begin her married life was a far cry from the ten-bedroom blue-and-white timber mansion on the outskirts of Ekaterinburg in the Ural Mountains where her grandfather and grandmother, Victor and Sonya, once lived. The opulent country estate had been tended by an army of serfs.

Victor, my great-grandfather, was a nobleman with an interesting story: He was a descendant of Sergei Bukhvostov—Peter the Great's "first soldier," a major of artillery in the navy, and hence part of the royal court in St. Petersburg. Peter the Great was Russia's tsar from 1682 to 1721 and founded St. Petersburg.

Victor was tall and debonair, with thick, jet-black hair and a bushy moustache. Sonya, a blond beauty from an extremely wealthy German family, had piercing emerald-green eyes and an hourglass figure.

Victor was a surgeon. He met Sonya in the richly gilded ballroom of the Grand Palace of St. Petersburg and fell in love. They married and had three children, two beautiful girls and a very handsome boy, and for a time they led a charmed existence on Victor's beautiful estate.

Then came the revolution. Victor joined the Royalist "White Army" and went off to fight the Bolshevik Red Army in Siberia. The following year, he and his troops advanced toward Ekaterinburg, but by the time they arrived, the Bolsheviks had moved on—having slaughtered Tsar Nicholas II and his family. There were no bodies, just one bloody finger still adorned with an enameled gold Fabergé ring. Realizing that the death of the tsar meant the defeat of the White Army, Victor decided to retreat across the border into China. He made his way back to the family estate at Ekaterinburg, only to find that Sonya and their children, like thousands of others, had fled for Harbin in China.

So Victor took the dangerous journey to Harbin with his men, with the Bolsheviks hot in pursuit. They managed to board the very last train leaving Russia. But the Red Army had already reached the station when Victor's train stopped at the border. Desperately hungry, he stepped out onto the platform in a split-second decision right before the train departed, drawn to a frail, elderly woman in rags selling hot buns from a basket.

From their carriage, his men heard the shot. The train had started moving. They looked back to see Victor's body on the platform where he'd been killed.

Sonya was heartbroken. She mourned for a year, dressing in black every day. My grandmother, Marianna, was two years old at the time. Sonya raised her children as best as she could, and when they reached adulthood, she was understandably keen to marry them off. Both girls had grown into lovely young women.

At seventeen, Marianna reluctantly accepted a marriage proposal from Anatoly, a wealthy mining engineer who'd graduated from the mining academy in Germany and had overseen the construction of the Trans-Siberian railway across Manchuria. He was exactly twice my grandma's age. Their marriage produced just one child: my mother, Nataly. Thereafter, Anatoly proved to be a womanizer.

Nina, Marianna's sister, married a Russian Cossack named Taras. Like many Cossacks, he had settled on a farm outside of Darwin, the capital of the Northern Territory in Australia, in the early 1920s. Darwin is located at the top end of Australia, where the weather is unbearably hot and humid all year round. The Cossacks wanted Russian wives, who could not be found in Australia, so many made their way to Harbin in search of a Russian wife.

One day Taras rode his horse into the city and saw Nina in the street. It was love at first sight for him, and he grabbed her, flung her onto his horse, and galloped away. But she also fell in love with him, and the pair wed in a Russian church in Harbin and then boarded a ship to Australia. As Taras only knew farming, they returned to his desolate farm outside of Darwin. Nina had four children with her husband but couldn't bear the heat, or his beatings, so in 1955, she fled to Adelaide to join the rest of the Russians who'd come there from Harbin.

Meanwhile, Harbin had become a thriving cosmopolitan center full of Russian shops, schools, restaurants, churches, cathedrals, museums, monuments, and gold- and pastel-colored palaces in the lavish, imperial St. Petersburg style. It was known as the "Paris of the East" and was almost like home. The local Chinese embraced the Russians, and all lived together in perfect harmony. My mother became very fond of the Chinese people and learned how to speak Mandarin to communicate and discover more about their culture and history.

However, China experienced its own Communist revolution in 1949, and in 1957 Chairman Mao Zedong ordered all "white faces" out of China. Once again, my family became homeless. Half the Russian population returned to what was now called the Soviet Union, only to be persecuted by Stalin—either shot or imprisoned in the Siberian gulags as traitors. The other half, including my family, made their way to Adelaide by ship, as Australia was promoted as the "Golden Country of Opportunity."

My mother was seventeen when she and the family left Harbin. The long sea journey was difficult, and there was an outbreak of typhoid. Tragically, Sonya's only son died, and the increasingly frail Sonya passed away soon after, their bodies buried at sea.

So, when the ship docked in Adelaide, only my mother and grandmother disembarked. They had no money and did not speak a word of English. Luckily, they were met by Nina, my grandmother's sister, and settled in with her, quickly becoming part of the close Russian community there.

Shortly after arriving in Adelaide, my mother, a keen volleyball player, fell in love with my father, Oleg, on the volleyball court during a mixed match. Oleg and his family had emigrated to Adelaide from Germany in 1954.

My father was born in 1937 in Crimea, Russia. His father, who also came from an aristocratic background, moved the family to Germany in 1942; he was anti-Communist and fought with the Germans against his own country in World War I. My mother, who loved the home of her ancestors, would regard Oleg's father as a murderer of the Russian people and vow never to step into his home.

My mother, Nataly, was a beautiful twenty-one-year-old virgin with a stunning figure, dark-brown eyes, and long dark hair that she always wore in a fashionable high bun. Oleg was a blond, tanned twenty-two-year-old hunk with dreamy blue eyes. They made a striking couple on their wedding day.

They and my grandmother moved into a small one-bedroom house with a small backyard garden together. It was Russian tradition for a young married couple to live with their grandparents, who held a very respected position in society. My grandmother did all the cooking and cleaning and slept on a fold-up bed in the kitchen. Then I was born, and my grandmother became the main babysitter.

But my parents' marriage didn't last long. Nataly found life with Oleg, and life in Adelaide in general, stultifying. She was an intellectual, whereas my father was illiterate. It was a total mismatch. When I was two, my mother and grandmother bundled me up, and the three of us fled to Sydney, a vibrant city on the east coast of Australia, where we moved into a terrace house owned by relatives in Elizabeth St. Paddington, a very fashionable suburb in Sydney.

Although most Russians from Harbin had settled in Adelaide, some ended up living on farms in tropical Queensland, the northeastern state of Australia, and at one stage, my mother went there for a holiday. At the local Russian club, she ran into an old school friend from Harbin who'd always had a crush on her: Alex Melnikoff.

Alex was a rugged, handsome, tanned farmer who loved riding motorbikes and fishing. He was happy to move to Sydney, so they married in 1965 and, together with my grandmother, bought a lovely four-bedroom house in Bronte. I was five. They had two daughters: my beautiful sisters, Marina and Veronica.

The house was a five-minute walk from Bronte Beach, a classic Australian surf spot with golden sand, crystal-clear crashing waves, a rock pool, a park with gazebos, and a lush gully with a creek. I loved Bronte Beach so much that in 1989 I bought an apartment almost directly across the road from our family home. It cost A$285,000—and I sold it a few years later for A$460,000.

I mention this here because, right from the beginning, it has always been important to me to make my own way financially. Perhaps this determination to stand on my own two feet came from my grandma, who said if I didn't finish university and start a stellar career, I would end up a prostitute on the streets of Kings Cross, Australia's notorious red-light district. It was mainly my grandma who raised me, and she was very strict. I was only allowed to socialize with Russian kids as she thought that all Australians were promiscuous and would corrupt me.

On Saturdays, I was sent to Russian Saturday school, where I learned Russian history, literature, geography, and culture, as well as the Russian language. My social life revolved around Russian school concerts, dances, and functions at the Russian club—a great venue for vodka, food, and dancing.

At "ordinary" school, I was an outsider. The other kids called me "wog," "teacher's pet," and "square." I tried not to care. Compared with other teenage girls, I was unsophisticated. I didn't even wear makeup. Only tarts did that, said grandma.

"You will remain a virgin until you are married, my dear. Otherwise, no man will want you," she warned me.

I loved my grandma very much. When she died from cancer just after my sixteenth birthday, I grieved terribly for a very long time, as if I had lost my mother.

CHAPTER TWO

Two Universities

At seventeen, I started studying at the University of New South Wales (UNSW) in Sydney, majoring in biochemistry and biotechnology. We had to do one arts subject, and I chose Russian. My mother had joined the Russian faculty at UNSW as a lecturer.

After my closeted upbringing, life on campus was like one big party. I soon met a young woman who became my best friend, Fran, and we partied like there was no tomorrow.

Halfway through my second year at university, my mother burst into my bedroom in great excitement one night and told me I'd been offered a one-year scholarship to study Russian language and literature at Moscow University. The scholarship had been set up by the Russian-Australian Friendship Society and the Russian faculty at UNSW, she explained. I was sure Mum had pulled a few strings to make sure I was selected.

I'd wanted to visit Russia for as long as I could remember. I tried not to think of it as a Communist country. I preferred the tsarist

Russia I'd always imagined from my grandmother's tales: troikas (three-horse sleighs) galloping through snowstorms; dazzling high-society balls; summer picnics in lush private gardens; parties in gilded palaces; and boisterous Cossack dancing.

I had absolutely no idea what to expect. I'd never been away from home and was full of trepidation as I made the bookings for the trip. Because money was tight, I would fly to Belgrade with JAT airlines, the cheapest way to get to Europe, and then catch a train to Moscow. I was due to depart on September 6, 1979.

At the airport on the day I left, I hugged my family and friends—even my dad, who'd come to see me off—and then walked through the departure gates, sobbing while tightly holding the huge stuffed koala my friends had given me. I'd always loved bears and grew up playing with bears instead of dolls. The koala bear was my security blanket.

But I lost the koala bear in Belgrade. I might have come close to losing my life too. I was only in the Serbian capital for a day, but when I fled the city that evening, I no longer cared about anything except getting away.

The naive nineteen-year-old Australian girl who walked out of Belgrade International Airport in a bright-pink tracksuit with her bear and climbed into a taxi had the sunny disposition of a first-time traveler. Everyone was a friend.

The taxi driver smiled and told me his name was Goran. He looked about twenty, not much older than me, and had a hypnotic smile. He suggested I sit in the front seat. We had little trouble communicating, as a lot of Serbian words are similar to Russian ones. I told him I was catching a train from Belgrade's main station that evening and needed to store my luggage. Then I wanted to play tourist.

I should have realized Goran was trouble when he put his hand on my knee as we drove off. I froze. He removed his hand. I said nothing.

Eventually the two of us ended up having lunch at an outdoor café on a busy street just across from the station. The bear was with us, sitting on the table. As my only link with home, it was a prized possession. Then, suddenly, a stranger came up to our table, snatched the bear, and ran off. I was devastated.

Goran chased the thief but came back empty-handed. However, he claimed that he knew the guy. He had friends, he said, who would get the bear back. The café was their hangout. He guaranteed that the bear would be returned to me at 7:30 p.m.

Still woebegone at its loss, I shrugged when Goran suggested going to his friend's party as a way of cheering me up. I wasn't that interested, but I thought it would fill in the afternoon.

I grew uneasy when we drove for a long time to the outskirts of the city and then wound up in a small village in front of an uninviting five-story building with dirty windows and a flickering neon sign that read *Hotel*.

Against all my instincts, I followed Goran inside. He told me the party was in the bar. He asked me to give him my passport—claiming that as a foreigner, I had to be registered—and handed the passport to a fat middle-aged woman sitting behind a desk.

Of course, there was no party. How had I fallen for such a story? Instead, I found myself screaming and banging my fists against the door of a room that Goran had pushed me into. There was no furniture except for two bunk beds. And there was no one else in the room. Just Goran—who'd locked the door.

No one came to rescue me. When Goran ordered me to undress, I screamed louder. Then he hit me hard across the face, and blood trickled from my mouth.

I had no idea if he was capable of worse violence. He still had my passport. All I wanted was to stay alive, get back to the station, and catch my train. I had no choice: I removed my clothes.

The nightmare continued. After he finished raping me, Goran got dressed, knelt in front of me, and announced that I now belonged to him. He said he loved me. And anyway, no other man would want me now. We would get married, he said. Then he started to count off on his fingers the number of children we would have.

I had an urge to burst out laughing, but as calmly as I could, I explained that I had to leave Belgrade that night, as planned, because I was expected in Moscow. I was committed to studying at university there for a year. After that, I'd come back.

"Will you marry me?" he demanded.

"Yes, of course," I replied.

After retrieving my passport, we left the hotel and drove back to the café where we'd had lunch earlier on. There was no one there with the bear. But at least the station was right across the road. Still speaking carefully, I said that since the train was departing at 8:30 p.m., we should make our way there and pick up my luggage from the locker I'd rented.

Goran didn't argue. But on the platform, when I said goodbye, he started to weep. I heard a whistle blowing and scrambled onto the train before he could kiss me. As we pulled out of the station, I saw him sobbing on the platform.

For the next few hours, I sat in my cabin. I needed solitude. I tried hard not to dwell on what had happened. As the train sped through Yugoslavia (as it was called then), passing through an autumn landscape filled with fluttering red and gold leaves, I started writing the diary that years later would become the basis for this book.

We stopped at the Russian border, and to my surprise, soldiers boarded and ordered everyone off. We were ushered into a hall for processing, then lined up in front of a window where a large lady examined our passports, banging each one with a stamp. Back in my cabin, I found my big green suitcase on the bunk with all its contents scattered next to it, although nothing seemed to be missing.

As we crossed the border, I suddenly realized: *I'm in the Soviet Union!*

CHAPTER THREE

Moscow at Last

The next morning, the train pulled into Moscow's central railway station. My first impression of the Russian capital wasn't good. The city looked gray, drab, polluted, and uninviting. The falling snow became instant slush, and the people trudging through it looked hostile. Even the babushkas, the old women in their headscarves, had scowls on their faces.

Two men in suits holding a sign that read "Moscow University" were waiting for me on the platform. They waved me into a van and began reeling off patriotic speeches about the Soviet Union the moment we'd set off. We passed run-down concrete apartment blocks, shops with dirty windows, and long queues of Russians waiting to buy food. Closer to the city center, I noticed a few hotels and buildings from the tsars' era that had obviously been very beautiful once but were now dirty and neglected. Most of the city seemed taken up with Soviet architectural monstrosities, creating a vast, grim concrete panorama.

Even so, I felt only excitement as we headed for Lenin Hills and was thrilled when I spotted the famous, majestic silver spire of Moscow University shimmering in the haze. We pulled up at the main campus of the university, a striking tall building edged by four massive wings of student accommodation.

I couldn't quite believe that I was there and about to become a student at Moscow University.

I wasn't quite so thrilled when I discovered that the special dormitory on campus for foreign students was a long way from the dormitories where the Russian students lived—and that foreign students were forbidden to leave their dormitory without a special permit. All the entrances to the West Wing, as our section was called, were guarded.

At least I had a private room, which was a luxury. It was small, with light-green walls and an old timber floor, and contained a single bed, a wardrobe, a desk, and a sink in the corner with a mirror above it.

I was determined to meet some Russian students, and so the following day at dusk, I tied my hair up into a high ponytail, applied black mascara and bright-red lipstick, and marched through the checkpoint into the main campus by pretending to be a Soviet student from Estonia, where they spoke Russian with an accent similar to my Australian accent. As I looked Russian and spoke Russian, the guards didn't ask questions.

A poster on the wall in the corridors advertised a dance party that evening in the main hall. I made my way there. The hall was a massive structure of white-and-brown marble floors, white marble walls, black granite columns, and a high, ornate ceiling. I had only just arrived and was watching everyone mill about in clouds of white smoke in front of the band when a boy with dark, curly hair, dark eyes, freckles, and luscious lips walked out of the crowd. He was wearing tight jeans and a white shirt with pale-blue stripes. I went weak at the knees.

"Would you like to dance?" he asked.

"Yes, I would!" I answered with a grin.

He held me close as we swayed to the disco beat. I hung on to him, wishing the moment would never end. Eventually the music stopped, and bright lights illuminated the hall, indicating the dance was over. My new beau offered to escort me back to my dormitory. Along the way, I discovered this dashing young man was Artyr, a medical student. We kissed goodbye, a short kiss but enough to whet our appetites.

I saw him again the following week at the Friday-night dance, and the following Friday, after which we started getting together during the week as well. We would meet on the stairs outside my room and talk, kiss, and cuddle.

I was truly enjoying university life, and because I had already studied most of the subjects at Russian school at home, I excelled at my studies. The only subject I struggled with was phonetics, as no matter how hard I tried, I could not master the Moscow drawl.

Weeks flew by. One day, Artyr grabbed my hand, pressing it to his flaming cheek.

"Ludmila, I have to have you. You consume me. I love you, my darling Ludmila, like I have loved no other!"

Finally ready to surrender to him, I exclaimed, "I love you too! My answer is yes."

"Oh, that's wonderful. Till tomorrow, then."

"My darling, unfortunately I am going to Uzbekistan tomorrow on a field trip for a week with all the other foreign students, so let's meet next Saturday night in my room."

He looked sad but replied, "Okay, I shall come to your room next Saturday at exactly 8 p.m."

He embraced me and kissed me passionately.

"Until then, my love," he yelled out as he ran down the stairs and disappeared through the door.

I was in love for the first time in my life and couldn't wait to spend the night with him. I cursed the untimely trip away.

We left at midnight to catch a plane to Tashkent, the capital of Uzbekistan. The country was parched, infertile, and very hot, yet exotic and beautiful.

Tashkent had been extensively rebuilt following a major earthquake in 1917, but luckily much of the Old Town had survived, and we walked along its narrow, winding alleys, past adobe houses and ancient mosques and mausoleums. That night, we dined at the popular Afsona Restaurant, known for its signature Uzbek dish *plov*, a delicious, aromatic mixture of rice, lamb, onions, carrots, sultanas, and spices. The next day, we traveled by coach to Samarkand, the second-largest city in Uzbekistan and the same age as Babylon.

Samarkand turned out to be a majestic Muslim city, its skyline studded with mosques and minarets covered in gilded turquoise and purple mosaics that sparkled in the sun and glowed in the moonlight.

We visited the Samarkand markets where local farmers sold fruit, vegetables, pastries, and meats. I stocked up on tomatoes, watermelons, grapes, apricots, pomegranates, figs, apples, and exotic fruits I had never seen before. Fresh produce was scarce in Moscow; you could only buy fresh fruit and vegetables at the black markets for exorbitant prices.

I made my way back to the coach followed by a long line of zealous Uzbek boys carrying my goods in their arms and on their heads. My fellow students yelled out, laughing, "Ludmila, you look like an Arabic princess being trailed by an entourage of adoring slaves." I laughed back, basking in the moment.

Later, we departed for the airport and arrived back in Moscow on Saturday afternoon. I was beside myself with excitement at the thought of seeing my beautiful Artyr that evening.

I covered the desk in my room with a colorful Uzbek tablecloth I'd purchased, laid out an array of fruit from the Samarkand markets, and lit two candles, completing the romantic setting. Eight o'clock came and went, yet there was no sign of Artyr. Another hour passed, then another. By midnight, I was distraught, as it was obvious he wasn't coming. Could he have forgotten, or did something happen to him? I was shattered. Finally, I climbed into bed, tears streaking my cheeks and soaking my pillow.

The next day, I went to our usual meeting place by the stairs. He was not there. I checked all the other floors, rooms of friends, the cafeteria, the pool where he trained, but Artyr was nowhere to be found. No one knew where he was. I ran back to the stairs and sat on the bottom step to catch my breath.

Suddenly his friend Yuri appeared. He walked along, reading a newspaper, totally ignoring my hellos. As he neared, he whispered softly but very distinctly, "Do not look for him. He is gone," and kept walking.

Hurt and confused, I ran after him, tears blurring my vision.

"Yuri, why?" I yelled, but Yuri didn't turn around.

To this day, I don't know whether it was the Soviet rules forbidding Russians to socialize with foreigners that undid us, though it seems the most likely reason.

Artyr was my first great love—and my first lost love.

The following morning, the director of the graduate course for foreigners called a snap meeting of all the foreign students. Dressed in a suit and tie, he seemed to be on edge. I stood staring at him with red, swollen eyes from crying all night. He glanced at me briefly, then avoided my gaze from then on.

There were going to be some changes, he said. The reason for this was the Olympic Games, due to start in Moscow shortly. The university campus had to be renovated to house Olympic guests. Consequently, all the foreign students were being moved to a hotel. We would be sitting our exams earlier than scheduled—and most of us would be going home in April 1980, three months before the games began.

It was startling news for all of us. Nothing had been said about Olympic guests before this. The next morning, I packed my things in a melancholy mood. A bus took us to our new home on the outskirts of Moscow.

The hotel was a tall, ugly concrete apartment block in the middle of a huge grass field. Each morning, we had to catch public transport to the university to attend our lessons, and we were packed in like sardines for two hours each way—first on a crowded bus and then on a more crowded train. We were so far from the city that it was almost impossible to go out at night. Then winter set in, and the grass turned into deep snow.

One night, though, I decided to brave the weather and return to the university, to the Friday-night dance, in my hopeless search for Artyr. He wasn't there.

Close to midnight, I made my way forlornly back to the hotel. It was minus twenty degrees. I waited an hour and had to stand in the unheated bus for another hour. By the time it arrived at my bus stop opposite the hotel, my feet and hands were numb. I began walking across the field toward the hotel and at one point fell backward onto the soft, fluffy white snow and was so tempted to lie there, close my eyes, and simply go to sleep. But I knew that I'd freeze to death.

When I eventually staggered through the doors of the hotel, I had to be helped to my room by some of my fellow students, while others rushed to bring pans of hot water for my hands and feet. I was screaming in pain as my body began to thaw.

It was the last time I tried to go out that winter. The bleakness matched my mood. I felt only sadness.

CHAPTER FOUR

Can I Ever Return?

Spring 1980 came. Moscow in sunshine was a dramatically different city, and finally my spirits started to lift.

One April day on the train, a handsome, blue-eyed *militsioner* (a Russian policeman) started chatting me up. He had the full, sensuous lips I love, and a great body. I thought he looked dashing in the smart gray uniform of the civilian police force, with its dark-gray blazer with red stitching, tie, and a military-style cap with a wide red ribbon and the gold Soviet hammer-and-sickle badge. Nikolai was his name. It turned out that he was studying a part-time psychology degree at Moscow University. We started dating.

Of course, sooner or later I had to tell Nikolai that I was due to leave Moscow shortly. When I did tell him, he begged me to stay. He said that he'd fallen in love with me. Naturally, I was tempted, but I needed more money. I sent a telegram to my dad, saying, "The boys are great here, Dad. Please send more money so I can stay longer." Dad kindly sent me A$200, so I decided to stay on illegally, without a visa.

My last days at Moscow University passed quickly. At the farewell party for foreign students, I made a series of toasts, hugged and kissed everyone, and then ostensibly left for Sheremetyevo International Airport to catch my flight home. I knew that by the time the director of the language department received an urgent phone call that I was a no-show, I'd be safely with Nikolai. I laughed in the taxi just thinking about it. Nikolai lived in the police barracks in the center of Moscow, right next to the Kremlin. No one would think of looking for me there!

What possessed me to take such a risk? The impetuousness of youth and my attraction to Nikolai—and my Russian blood and passionate nature! It was no laughing matter to be an illegal alien in a Communist country, but I convinced myself that if the KGB found me, I'd simply be deported back to Australia.

I threw myself into life as a Russian. I went to parties with Nikolai and met all his friends. I talked openly about life in Australia, read forbidden poems in the kitchens of their small apartments, and laughed at politically risqué jokes—for example, "Capitalism is rotting away, but what a wonderful smell!" One could get imprisoned for such behavior, but none of Nikolai's friends seemed to care.

Inevitably, Nikolai's police colleagues began questioning him about his "pretty girlfriend." None of them knew I was a foreigner, but since we all had to share the same toilet and wash basin, as there were no showers, their curiosity about me grew to the point where it became impossible for me to keep living with him in the barracks.

Nikolai found a rented room in a nearby apartment. I lived there temporarily, although I ended up moving three times. The apartments were grubby. Mostly, I had to share a bathroom and kitchen with other tenants. It was not uncommon for three Russian families to share a three-bedroom apartment. There was an acute housing shortage in Moscow, and the waiting list to be allocated an apartment by the Communist Party was years' long.

Money became a problem again too. I didn't want to burden Nikolai financially, so I started selling my clothes on the black market through taxi drivers. Red Marlboro cigarettes and denim jeans were the hottest items, and I managed to sell five pairs of my old jeans for US$1,000.

Then, out of the blue, Nikolai asked me to marry him. The two of us had grown close, and I could easily imagine becoming his wife. But I said that I needed to think about it. The truth was, Artyr's disappearance still haunted me. Whenever we made love, all I could think about was Artyr.

Summer came. Moscow in the heat was lovely. The glistening golden domes of its churches, the silvery white-and-green birch forests, and the shimmering rivers that bisected and encircled the city all helped make it an enchanting place.

One muggy August day, with thunder rumbling in the distance, Nikolai and I set off for a picnic in a luscious green pine forest with some friends. En route, I went into a small grocery store to pick up a bottle of vodka and some sandwiches. Suddenly, a policeman dressed in the all-too-familiar gray-and-red uniform that Nikolai wore materialized out of nowhere and grabbed my shoulder.

"*Devushka* [Miss], your passport, please."

"Here," I replied, handing over my passport. I was used to this happening because I stood out like a sore thumb in Moscow. I looked Russian but wore "Western" clothes, which, unfortunately, was the trademark of Russian prostitutes who were gifted Western clothes from their foreign admirers.

"Come with me. There is a warrant out for your arrest."

I went into shock. Within minutes, the policeman was forcing me into the back seat of a police car. A second officer was in the front, waiting to drive us away. The next minute, Nikolai came charging toward us. His friends grabbed his arms, pulling him back, and the car drove off with me looking frantically back at him through the window.

At the police station, I tried to put on a brave front: "I want to call my embassy, please."

"*Net.*" (No.)

I remonstrated with them: "Every foreigner has the legal right to call their embassy if arrested. I've seen it in the movies," I said with a half smile to lighten the situation.

"Not in Russia," came the menacing reply.

An hour later, a big black limousine, a Chaika, pulled up outside the police station. Three tough-looking characters emerged from it and came inside. Two of them grabbed my arms. "Come with us."

I was taken to the USSR Visa and Registration Directorate, the body for foreign visas, and led up long, narrow stairs to a dingy room with a desk and two chairs on opposite sides. There I was questioned for hours. The chief KGB interrogator was a Major Popovsky, who pulled out a chair and ordered me to sit down. He was massively built with broad shoulders and a large, square head and wore an old-style, well-worn gray suit. He sat in the chair across from mine while the rest of the interrogators stood behind him.

They demanded I write down the names of all the people I'd been in contact with in Moscow. I refused to do it. As if I was going to betray Nikolai and his friends! The air became thick from foul Belomor cigarettes, the cheap Soviet brand of unfiltered cigarettes they were all smoking. I was desperate for fresh air.

Major Popovsky asked me where I'd been living for the past five months.

"I lived wherever there was a room to let," I replied. "I can't remember the exact addresses. I moved around a lot and only remember the names of the streets."

"Where are all your clothes, Comrade Melnikova?"

"I sold almost everything so I could buy food. I once bought a dozen boxes of Soviet champagne in exchange for one pair of jeans," I boasted.

"That's a crime in the Soviet Union!" shouted Major Popovsky, stubbing out his cigarette. He demanded to know why I'd remained in Moscow when I didn't have a visa. Perhaps, he bellowed, I was a spy.

"Who advised you to stay? Write down their names!"

"I stayed because I fell in love with Moscow and wanted to experience the city and meet Russians, which I was prohibited from doing at the university," I replied, feeling exasperated.

"Oh, you wanted to discover Moscow! What about the rest of Russia?"

"I would love to visit Ekaterinburg in the Ural Mountains."

I told him about my family's history in Russia and the estate outside Ekaterinburg, where my great-grandparents had once lived, and how through my great-grandfather, I was related to Peter the Great.

Major Popovsky wasn't impressed. "Keep interrogating Peter the Great's fucking little princess!" he barked at his men and stormed out of the room.

A few hours later, I badly needed a toilet break so asked if I could use the bathroom. Two of the men escorted me down the corridor, but instead of taking me to the toilet, they guided me outside and into the back seat of the same black limousine.

Shaken, I asked where we were going but received no reply.

Eventually we reached a suburb on the outskirts of Moscow called Severny ("North"), where the car halted outside a squalid gray building next to a landfill on Dmitrovskoye Boulevard. The building's tall iron gates swung open. Horrified, I read the name on the wall: "Centre for Social Rehabilitation #1."

It was a prison.

I was rushed unceremoniously inside and then pushed into a pitch-black holding cell the size of a telephone booth. Within seconds, I became hysterical and started screaming at the top of my voice, banging on the door, realizing the severity of the situation.

Eventually, my captors returned, and I was marched down various dark corridors until we came to a small, damp cell with a concrete floor and cinder-block walls. The door was solid metal and had a rectangular slot at the bottom and a small open peephole for the guards. They pushed me inside—and then the cell door slammed shut.

I was alone in a tiny cell: a prisoner of the Soviet Union, a Communist country. A shallow cement trough in the corner functioned as a toilet. It reeked of urine and feces. A bare light bulb hung from the middle of the ceiling and stayed on all day and night. The glare from the naked bulb cut into my eyes. Wild dogs howled outside the barred window. It was freezing. I hardly slept. Three times a day, I was fed through the small slot in the door. The meals were all the same: black bread, milk, water, and *ooha*, normally a delicious Russian fish soup, but this one was just a fish head floating in boiled water. Within days, my clothes started hanging off me.

The only time I was allowed out of my cell was in the afternoon, when I could walk around on the roof of the jail for five minutes. That was my sole exercise.

I showered only once, on the day after I arrived. I was wearing the same clothes, jeans and a bright-pink sweater; to make matters worse, I got my period. I had to ask one of the guards if I could see a nurse. A few hours later, a female guard arrived and informed me there were no nurses. She asked me what my problem was. I told her and she left—returning with a roll of cotton wool.

As a chain-smoker, I was craving a cigarette. But worst of all was having absolutely nothing to do. The boredom drove me insane. The frightening part was that I had no idea when, or even if, I would be released, since the guards refused to give me any information.

Many people in Russian jails simply disappeared without a trace. I kept thinking that my family would never be able to find me here. Nor would the Australian embassy. I was completely at the mercy of my jailers. What if they really did believe I was a spy? What if they wanted me to become a spy—and I refused?

One day, one of the guards brought me a packet of Marlboro cigarettes and a box of matches. I can't even recall what he looked like.

"Thanks," I said gratefully. "Do you know when they are going to let me out of here?"

"No," he replied. "But I'll try to find out."

He started to kiss me. I didn't care: I desperately needed some tenderness. He began kissing me more urgently—then slid his hand down my top and fondled my breasts. I kissed him back. A few seconds later, we heard footsteps.

The guard got up instantly and fled, slamming the cell door behind him. In my state of mind, I thought I was falling in love with him. Only he could save me. I reached for the cigarettes and discovered the filters had been ripped off. I lit up regardless.

Each day I waited anxiously for "my" guard to come and visit me again. He turned up a few days later and said that someone from my embassy should arrive soon. He also told me he'd ripped the filters off the cigarettes because otherwise I could have burned one of the butts and turned it into a razor-sharp object.

If I'd been able to, I would have done it. I would have done anything to get out of there, even slash my wrists.

I asked if he could bring me paper and a pencil so I could write notes for my diary. He left and returned shortly with both. I expressed my gratitude by letting him fondle my breasts again. Later, I hid what I'd written in the pocket of my jeans.

On the eleventh day, a female guard built like a tank threw open the cell door. "You have a visitor from your embassy. Follow me."

She led me out of my cell and into the shower rooms. I had a long, glorious, piping-hot shower but unfortunately had to put my filthy clothes back on. I was then taken to a small conference room with white walls, a window, and a large brown desk with three wooden office chairs. A disheveled, nervous-looking man was waiting. He introduced himself as Richard, the Australian consul at the embassy, and said that he knew my mother. She had been his Russian lecturer at the University of New South Wales.

"We are truly sorry about this, Ludmila," he added. "It should never have happened. We didn't know you were in here. It took us all this time to find out."

"Eleven days!" I exclaimed.

"They should have allowed you to call the embassy," he added. "They violated all international protocol by refusing you that one call. It's in my report."

"What else is in your report?" I demanded, becoming emotional. "How they locked me up like a wild animal in a tiny, dirty, freezing cell and got their thrills by watching me pee?"

I was terrified that I'd be taken back to my cell. But then he told me that I was being put on an Aeroflot flight that night if there was an available seat.

"You better make sure I am on that plane, because I am not going back to that hellhole. I will kill myself!" I yelled frenziedly.

"Calm down. Let me make a phone call."

Thirty minutes later, Richard confirmed that the embassy had managed to book a seat for me.

The relief I felt was overwhelming—until Major Popovsky and his KGB thugs walked into the room. This time, though, they had come to escort me to Sheremetyevo Airport, and their attitude was completely different. In the car, the major pulled out a bottle of chilled vodka, which he poured into two glasses and offered me one. I was quite amazed but accepted it gladly and downed the soothing liquid.

"Ludmila, you are very Russian," the major commented, gazing at me.

"Yes, I know. I was brought up very Russian. Why did you keep me locked up for so long? How could you do that to one of your own?"

"My dear, it took us that long to locate your clothes. They were spread all over the city," he answered, grinning at me.

He then came up with an astonishing proposition. "Listen to me, Ludmila, you could stay here with us. I can arrange this. We have very interesting work lined up for you. Of course, you will have to give up your Australian passport, but you will be able to visit your family anytime you want."

I was intrigued and even a little flattered. "Tempting, but no thanks. I want to go home," I said flatly.

The KGB major shrugged, looking disappointed. The car drove right onto the tarmac, halting next to the plane, and the major escorted me up the stairs, holding my arm the whole way. "I have to hand your passport and air ticket to the pilot just in case you decide to jump out of the plane," he said with a slight smile. "Goodbye, Ludmila, and good luck."

"Will I ever be able to return?" I asked out of curiosity.

"In seven years, my dear. The KGB only keeps files for seven years, but even then, only on the condition you bring me a carton of Marlboro Reds. I will be in touch. Bye!"

"That's a deal," I said and waved goodbye.

Was there some prescience to my question? At that moment, all I wanted was to get home to Sydney.

And once I was safely back with my family in our home on Bronte Beach, I felt like never setting foot outside Australia again.

CHAPTER FIVE

Back to Russia

In March 1985, just over two years after graduating from the University of New South Wales with a science degree, I started Labstaff, the world's first scientific recruitment agency.

I loved owning my own business. I'd worked very briefly for a leading biotechnology research company but was unhappy and bored. Being stuck in a white lab coat in a stuffy laboratory all day for a mere A$16,000 per year was not my idea of a career.

I got the concept for Labstaff after watching my boss, a brilliant scientist, waste his time sifting through hundreds of résumés, looking for talented people to hire. A friend of mine, Thomas Keogh, a wealthy Irish entrepreneur, thought Labstaff an excellent idea. He backed me financially, and I put all the cash I had into the new company. Thomas was not attractive, but he was fun socially, and we became good friends as well as business partners.

In early 1986, Thomas sold his half of Labstaff to my best friend, Fran, who'd been backpacking around Europe until then. Financed by her mum, she became my partner. The two of us turned the company into an overwhelming success, with offices all around Australia. Eventually, in 1999, we would sell Labstaff for A$1 million.

Fran and I were based in Sydney and rented a modern space in Bondi Junction comprising two offices, one for me and the other for her, and a reception area where Judy, our receptionist, sat. The views across the city, sprawling all the way to the Harbour Bridge and Opera House, were spectacular. One day, a handsome superannuation insurance salesman called Greg knocked on our door and tried to sell us a superannuation scheme. For me—impulsive as ever—it was love at first sight. Greg was tanned, blond, sexy, and dressed in a designer suit. He drove a brand-new Land Cruiser and said that he owned the company he worked for.

We got married in September 1989 at the brand-new five-star Kirkton Park resort in the Hunter Valley, a three-hour drive from Sydney. The resort, surrounded by rolling wine country, was set on seventy acres of lawn with manicured rose gardens and a beautiful three-tiered stone fountain centerpiece. The rooms were decorated in opulent vintage country style. The resort was a magical locale for a lavish wedding.

We hired the entire resort and kept to the Russian tradition of a three-day wedding, starting with a formal wine tasting on Friday night, the wedding on Saturday night, and ending with a champagne brunch on Sunday. Our guests undoubtedly viewed us as a glamorous couple. However, I already knew when I married Greg that he wasn't the success he pretended to be. For a start, he was not only broke but A$20,000 in debt. He didn't own the company he worked for. The car he drove belonged to his boss.

Because I'd fallen head over heels in love with him, I'd paid off his debt, and we moved into my apartment in Bronte Beach. There was no way he could help pay the bill for our extravagant wedding, so I paid for that too.

My new husband hadn't always been broke, though. He'd spent much of his adult life in Saudi Arabia, earning big money working on oil rigs, before some Arab "friends" ripped him off to the tune of a million dollars. Or so he claimed. It was Greg who came up with the idea of exploring the opportunities rapidly opening up in Gorbachev's Russia. He wanted to be in the money again. Gorbachev was bringing down the "iron curtain" by dismantling the Soviet totalitarian state.

The very thought of returning to Russia frightened me. But I knew Greg's idea was a good one. Russia was changing under Gorbachev. Foreigners were flocking to Moscow in droves, hoping to strike it rich with joint ventures, the new buzzwords in the Russian capital. Greg kept trying to convince me to give Russia a try, and he finally succeeded. I agreed to visit Moscow for one week at the end of our honeymoon, which was to be a first-class trip around the world. Naturally, I paid for that too.

We started off in Santorini, a volcanic island located in the Aegean Sea, part of Greece. It was famous for its beautiful white-and-blue buildings, stunning sunsets, black-sand beaches, and romantic ambiance. We then flew to Paris. In Paris, I sent a postcard to Fran saying, "Hi from Paris. I'm really bored. I wish you were here instead of Greg!"

Already I had begun to suspect that I'd married the wrong man. I was tired of paying for everything, and my new husband and I had very little in common, just as my mother learned about my father shortly after their marriage. Greg wasn't well read, whereas I loved books and intellectual conversations, like my mum. It was history repeating itself! I only cheered up when we got to Italy. The scenery, the food, and the wine (and the Italian men!) put me in a good mood immediately.

We left Rome in early December 1989 and flew to London, then boarded an Aeroflot flight to Moscow. Three hours later, we landed. I saw a snowstorm raging outside the plane's windows and thick snow weighing down the branches of a long line of birch trees just visible beyond the dull lights illuminating the runway. It was early afternoon, yet it was as dark as night. As we waited to disembark, I started to hyperventilate from anxiety and forced myself to breathe deeply to calm down.

We were herded down various corridors to Passport Control, where I almost jumped out of my skin when someone suddenly tapped me on the shoulder.

"Citizen, it's your turn. Don't hold up the queue," muttered the man standing behind me. He had grayish skin and bags under his eyes—the typical Soviet look. I felt sorry for him.

Terrified, I approached the glass booth ahead, clutching my passport. The Passport Control officer stared at me through the glass window for what seemed an eternity. Then he banged down his stamp on my passport.

So, Major Boris Popovsky hadn't lied to me. My past had been wiped clean. I was in!

Moscow still looked like the old, gray Communist city I remembered from 1979. The same long, winding lines of people stood in the snow, hoping to buy something from mostly bare shops. The buildings were grimy and neglected. The whole city really needed a paint job.

After we checked into the Belgrade Hotel, a shabby, sixties-style skyscraper, I left Greg to unpack and went down to the lobby, desperate for what passed in Russia for coffee.

All around me, Russians were talking openly to foreigners—something that had been strictly prohibited in the pre-Gorbachev era.

I sat by a window, and within minutes, two handsome guys in smart designer suits approached me. "Devyshka, mozhno poznokomitsa?" said one of them. This was the standard pickup line. It meant "Miss, can we get to know you?"

"No, not really," I replied.

Ignoring this, they introduced themselves as Ica and Arbi. They were Chechens, they said, who had set up a base in Moscow, and the Belgrade Hotel was their hangout. I explained that I was in Moscow with my husband. We were looking to get involved in a business deal involving natural resources. "Either gold or platinum," I added. Ica and Arbi smiled and said they might be able to help.

That night, Greg and I had dinner with them in the hotel restaurant. Some of Ica and Arbi's Chechen friends joined us. Two beautiful Russian women, who I guessed were prostitutes, were part of the group. We had the best table in the place, right in front of the stage. A band pumped out "Western" songs—Kaoma's "Lambada" being the crowd favorite—as we worked our way through lashings of black caviar, a gourmet meat platter, smoked fish, crab salad, beefsteak, whole grilled fish, chicken Kiev (crumbed and fried chicken stuffed with melting garlic butter), and shish kebab, all washed down with cognac, champagne, and vodka.

At one stage, upon Ica's request, the band performed a compilation to accompany a traditional Chechen love dance that was performed on the floor in front of us. Ica's male friends formed a circle on the dance floor. With their arms stretched out horizontally, they circled each other with ferocious expressions, stomping their feet. Suddenly, a lone girl floated into the men's circle like a beautiful swan. They started dancing around her, faster and faster, panting and grunting and stomping harder, until finally she chose one of them. As the girl glided around her man, he made movements with his hands as if caressing her body and face, and the erotic ritual ended. The pair then vanished to thunderous applause. I will never forget the splendor and beauty of this fierce, erotic spectacle.

For the rest of our week in Moscow, Greg and I partied with Ica and Arbi at the Belgrade Hotel every night. I knew that ordinary

Russians couldn't afford to dine out more than once a month, and certainly not in the lavish style we were. But I was enjoying the company of our new Chechen friends. I loved their passion for life, even though the history of Chechnya and the volatility of the people made for sober reflection. I wondered how Ica and Arbi would fare in Gorbachev's new Russia—and how we would, too.

On our last night in Moscow, Ica and Arbi offered us a business deal involving a nickel and platinum mine called Norilsk Nickel, situated north of the Arctic Circle in Russia. Luckily, I'd taken geology as an elective subject at university, so when they handed me fifty pages of information about the mine, I understood the material I was reading. Fran and I had chosen geology because of the high ratio of male students in the class. Finally, it was paying off!

The situation, in a nutshell, was this. Russian law prohibited foreigners from mining primary ore. Foreign companies were only permitted to process secondary waste material, known as tailings. Norilsk Nickel, however, had millions of tons of tailings piled up, and these had concentrations of platinum higher than most Western mines because Russian mining equipment was too old and rusty to extract high percentages.

According to Ica and Arbi, a joint venture between Norilsk Nickel and a foreign investor—with the Russians contributing the tailings and the foreigners contributing the cash and new mining equipment—would potentially be worth US$500 million. Arbi swore that we were the first foreigners to be offered the project. He also showed me a document giving him authority to negotiate with foreign investors on behalf of Norilsk Nickel. He promised me total exclusivity for six months and said he'd send a copy of the protocol of intent by fax (email did exist yet).

As Greg and I would soon learn, a protocol of intent was regarded as an essential document in Russian business practice, even though it had no legal clout. Ostensibly it promised confidentiality and exclusivity to prevent the parties from dealing with others while the joint venture (a company between the Russian and foreign side) was formed. As soon as foreign investors and Russians decided to form a joint venture, a protocol of intent was ceremoniously signed, followed by many cognac and vodka toasts.

In the end, all fired up, I solemnly promised to return to Russia with an investor from Australia.

CHAPTER SIX

The Birth of Star

In Sydney in January 1990, I hired Kim Jacobs, CEO of Inteq Ltd., a mortgage broker that specialized in attracting investors for commercially viable projects or cutting-edge inventions. Jacobs, a shrewd businessman with a sharp wit, hailed Norilsk Nickel as the deal of the century. He immediately negotiated for himself a monthly fee of A$10,000, a commission of A$500,000, and a 5 percent profit share in the project. As I had no other option, I signed him up.

Four months later, he came through. There was a wealthy Australian international mining entrepreneur, he said, who lived in Hong Kong and wanted to do business in Russia. His name was Ian MacNee.

Jacobs organized a meeting at the Regent Hotel, the five-star hotel in Sydney where Ian was staying. He had flown in from Melbourne that morning. It turned out that he owned a vast country estate in Victoria called Lambruk, set on thirty-seven acres of gardens, with a majestic ornamental lake and cascading waterfall, an orchard, two pools, a spa and tennis court, three stone cottages, and a main sandstone residence with a stunning conservatory. The estate also housed his collection of eighty vintage cars. He had homes in Hong Kong, Aspen, and London as well. But his mailing address was "Seat 2C on United Airlines," his friends would joke, as he spent most of the time flying first-class around the world and doing business deals.

I was not sure what sort of man I expected to meet. What did a mining entrepreneur look like? Tanned, it turned out, with sandy-gray hair and striking blue eyes. He looked to be in his mid-fifties.

I was mesmerized by Ian from the moment we met, and quite startled by how low-key he was. He was obviously very sophisticated but came across as shy and even prudish. He was the first multimillionaire I'd ever met—and he intrigued me.

Ian took the documents on Norilsk Nickel that I'd brought for him, saying that he'd study them overnight, and suggested that Greg and I join him for breakfast at the Regent the next morning.

We must have looked nervous when we duly turned up, because he told us immediately that the answer was yes—and then said that he was prepared to invest US$500,000 to develop the Norilsk Nickel tailings project.

"I'm going to send both of you back to Moscow to set up a small office and work on the deal," he added. "I'll pay you a joint fee of twenty-five hundred US per month and offer you equity in the project as a bonus."

"What about Inteq?" I asked. "They have their hand out for a huge commission, a monthly fee, and a profit share that Greg and I can't afford to pay."

"They are piranhas. Don't worry. I will take care of them."

I was ecstatic, and very impressed at how quickly he'd made his decision. Ian flew back to Hong Kong that day, and on May 18, Greg and I received a letter confirming that we had a deal: "I will register a company called Star Technology P/L (Star) in the British Virgin Islands to carry on business in Russia," wrote Ian. He explained that his Hong Kong company, Crusader Investments Ltd., would hold 80 percent of Star, and Greg and I would hold 10 percent each. We were to travel to Hong Kong as soon as possible to work with him on business plans and cash flows for Star. Then we would fly directly to Russia from Hong Kong. Two business-class tickets would be provided for us.

Three days later, Greg and I flew to Hong Kong. My suitcase was full of clothes and bare necessities, including packaged dry food like instant noodles and biscuits. I'd also packed toilet paper and twelve months' supply of the pill, tampons, and deodorant. Essentials like these were simply unavailable where we were headed. As I knew well, Russians used old newspapers cut into squares in their bathrooms for toilet paper and powder under their arms instead of deodorant. Women used cotton wool or cloths instead of sanitary pads. Contraception items were also nonexistent. In fact, the only form of birth control was abortion, which was DIY more often than not.

I was also armed with the names of two contacts in Moscow that my mother had given me. One was Izumov, a die-hard Communist and publisher of a popular Communist newspaper, *Izvestia*. He'd also published some of Mum's poems.

The other contact was sixty-eight-year-old Russian journalist Katya Shevelova. She was a famous poet and had once been a personal translator of Russia's former First Secretary Nikita Khrushchev, and perhaps, said Mum, his lover too. Katya had also been a friend of Yuri Andropov from childhood. Andropov had led Russia briefly—although he was better known as one of the longest-serving and most feared KGB chairmen in its history. Katya still had impeccable political connections in Moscow, where she'd aligned herself with Yeltsin and had become good friends with his wife, Naina, and daughter Tanya.

Mum met her when Katya visited Australia in 1984 with a delegation of Russian poets and thought it quite possible that the poet had worked as a spy. My pragmatic mother advised me to meet both Izumov and Katya, as glasnost ("openness") was still in its early days and Russia might yet revert to Communism.

When Greg and I flew into Hong Kong, Ian was waiting for us at the airport. He looked quite suave in his jeans, white polo shirt, and dark sunglasses. He led us to his white Bentley and drove us to one of Hong Kong's oldest and finest hotels, the Shangri La, where we would stay. After we checked in, he invited us to a lunch he was giving the following day.

"All my people from around the world have gathered in Hong Kong to give me progress reports, so you'll meet everyone," he went on. "The address is 8 May Road, the Peak. Just catch a taxi up to the house." The Peak was Hong Kong's most desirable neighborhood and boasted a stunning view of Victoria Harbour. Our luxurious suite had panoramic views of both.

Ian left us to open the bottle of Moët sitting in a silver bucket atop a small table by the window. A note dangled from the bottle with the words "Welcome to Hong Kong—Ian."

I thought, *I could get used to this!*

Greg and I were the first guests to arrive for lunch the next day. Bobby, Ian's wife, opened the door. She was about forty with long blond hair, nice legs, and pretty eyes, although her face had seen too much sun. She was wearing a clingy, colorful miniskirt and a loose-fitting white shirt. She reminded me of an aging Barbie doll. Her stare seemed a little chilly as she looked me over.

I wore a new silky top and pants I'd bought just that morning. My hair was clipped at the back of my neck in a ponytail that I'd flipped over my shoulder so that it fell over my left breast to my waist.

"You must be Greg and Ludmila," she said in a very posh accent. "I'm Bobby."

"Nice to meet you. I hope Russia turns out well for all of us," I replied cheerfully.

"Yes. It's certainly taking up a lot of Ian's time."

I decided to ignore this comment and moved past Bobby into the living room. "Ludmila, could you please take off your shoes?" she called out after me.

"Sure thing," I replied without turning.

At the same moment, Ian appeared in the doorway in Speedos and a T-shirt. "I didn't think anyone was here yet," he said, grinning. I was surprised that he had such a good body at his age.

I learned later that Ian had met Bobby at a fashionable bar on the harbor in Sydney when she was working there as a bar manager. She didn't have a posh accent back then. Ian had walked into the bar for a drink with his best friend, Graeme Ellis. The two of them bet a bottle of Moët on who could get Bobby into bed first. Ian won.

At the time, Ian was still married to his first wife, Jan. But he left her soon after and eventually ended up living with Bobby in a rented terrace house in Sydney's eastern suburbs. Eight years later, Bobby gave Ian an ultimatum: "Marry me, or I'll leave." She got her wish. Their son, Angus, was born in 1982.

Chris—Ian's eldest son by his first wife, whom I would meet much later in Moscow—never forgave his father for leaving his mother for a "younger, blonder version" and never formed a close relationship with Angus. That was probably because of the twenty-three-year age gap as much as anything else.

When Angus was five, Ian moved the family to Hong Kong. Bobby loved entertaining their wealthy A-list friends in their stunning house at the Peak.

At the lunch that Greg and I attended, everyone sat around a dark-emerald marble table in a room decorated with priceless antique Chinese vases and sculptures. Ian's "people" took turns updating him on the various international mining and trading projects they were working on—mainly in Canada, Asia, and South America. I quietly vowed to myself that one day Ian would be praising me at this same table about my successes in Russia.

The following day, we all went out on Ian's boat, an old-fashioned Chinese houseboat fitted with a galley kitchen and a bar and capable of holding 200 people. We sipped Dom Pérignon and watched the canoe races on Hong Kong's harbor. In the evening, we went to a James Morrison concert at a local jazz club. James was a world-renowned trumpet maestro whom Ian had financed in the early days, and the talented musician was a close family friend.

The rest of the week was spent in the offices of Crusader Investments Ltd., Ian's company, which turned out to be a Hong Kong–listed offshoot of the Lee Ming Allied group. Lee's group was valued at US$129 million in 1990 and controlled five listed companies worth US$1.3 billion. Lee Ming himself was a Malaysian-born tycoon. However, as I would discover much later, he was a bit of a mystery figure. According to some news reports, nobody in Malaysia had heard of him before his tycoon days. A few years later, Lee would be jailed by Hong Kong authorities for undisclosed reasons.

Crusader eyes Brazilian gold

By ERIC ELLIS, in Hong Kong

Crusader Investments Ltd, a controversial Hong Kong-listed offshoot of the Lee Ming Tee group, has forecast it will be a "major world gold producer" of at least 1,800 kilograms (63,000 ounces) annually from June next year.

The upbeat forecast was made by Australian mining entrepreneur and Crusader director Mr Ian MacNee at a press conference yesterday after Crusader minority shareholders approved a proposal to acquire a $90 million collection of obscure Brazilian alluvial gold deposits.

Mr MacNee's forecast brings forward by two years a projection that was made on the deposit by independent mining consultants, Sydney-based Terence Willsteed and Associates.

Crusader, 38 per cent-owned by Mr Lee's Sunshine Pacific group, will issue shares and options to acquire the Chience group, owner of exploration rights to mine gold in the Amazonian jungle, for $US53.5 million ($A75 million). Chience is a Hong Kong incorporated company associated with Mr MacNee, a former chairman of Base Resources Ltd, Greaton Chemicals Ltd and a consortium of Hong Kong and Australian investors.

Mr Lee ... Crusader's major shareholder.

Under the deal Mr MacNee hopes to displace Mr Lee as the largest shareholder in Crusader, as Crusader exercises options held over the operation.

A similar deal had previously been held up by the Hong Kong Securities Commission last year on the grounds that the move into gold was out of step with Crusader's stated intention to invest in Hong Kong. While the reworked deal is little changed from the earlier proposal, the commission's moves were interpreted as a flexing of its muscles on deals that departed from stated intentions, serving as a warning to other entrepreneurs.

Mr MacNee said the Crusader had "put behind it the concerns of authorities" and looked forward to a bright future of "leading Brazil onto the world gold stage".

It was an impressive performance by Mr MacNee, well known to the Australian mining industry through his exploits with Base Resources and more recently with his association with the Lee group.

His also was a timely presentation in gold-crazy Hong Kong, coming as world bullion prices are skyrocketing. Hong Kong investors know little of the mining world and Mr MacNee's expansive references to a "gold rush" and Crusader's Brazilian acreage possibly rivalling Kalgoorlie and Coolgardie seemed to go over the collective heads of the Chinese business press.

Mr MacNee put costs of extraction from the Brazilian mine, situated some 4,500 kilometres from Rio de Janiero, at a maximum $US75 an ounce, scaling down to $US55 an ounce.

"We welcome the foresight, and of course the money, of Mr Lee in supporting this exciting venture," Mr MacNee said.

Ian was a director of the Lee Ming group and of Crusader, which was 38 percent owned by Mr. Lee and 62 percent by Ian and other Hong Kong investors, through a string of offshore companies. He told us that his partners were all rich Hong Kong businessmen. He said that Crusader had raised A$90 million for an alluvial operation in Brazil and had capability to fund the Russian project.

Greg and I met them all, including Mr. Lee, over lunch at an elite Chinese restaurant. I soon noticed that they didn't seem as enthusiastic about Russia as Ian was. They wanted a quick deal on the border, one of them said to me. Norilsk Nickel's mine tailings could be processed in a smelter in China. At the time, I saw nothing out of the ordinary about this suggestion, although I was concerned about the feasibility of doing a quick deal in Russia. Russia was still a Communist country, and it was imperative to develop strong connections before a deal could be done.

On May 29, 1990, I turned thirty. To celebrate, Ian took us to Peking Gardens, one of Hong Kong's most acclaimed restaurants, known for its world-famous Peking duck, my favorite Chinese dish. The Moët champagne and the dinner were delightful. The following day as I left Hong Kong for Moscow with Greg, I was more than a little infatuated with Ian.

Arbi, I knew, would be waiting for us at the Moscow airport. In all this time, he still hadn't produced the all-essential protocol of intent. However, he had sworn to me on a phone call that he would have the document in hand when we arrived.

True to his word, he was at the airport—but without the protocol. I demanded an explanation. "Don't worry, we will have a protocol! I swear on my mother's grave! We will have it!" he exclaimed.

"When do you think this will happen?" I asked.

"Tomorrow, I swear!"

Greg and I were staying at the Hotel Ukraina until we could find an apartment. The hotel was one of the "Seven Sisters," seven famous Stalinist skyscrapers also known as "wedding cakes" because of their tiered construction.

Most of Moscow's hotels were expensive and old-fashioned, with dingy foreign-currency bars and large, uninviting restaurants whose waiters only took bookings if you bribed them. The hotels were two-star at best, yet foreigners were charged five-star rates. The room charges were set in rubles, which was dirt cheap for Russians but extremely costly for foreigners because of an artificial exchange rate of 0.6 rubles per 1 US dollar.

Our room at the Hotel Ukraina was small. It contained two single beds covered with bright-orange bedspreads, a desk, and a very old black-and-white TV. The only saving grace was the stunning view of the Moscow River and the city skyline, including the Russian parliament house, known as "the White House." This beautiful art deco fortress clad in white marble is one of the most important buildings in Moscow. At that time, it was crowned by a tower with a large gold clock and the Soviet flag—a solid-red design with a golden hammer-and-sickle emblem in the upper left corner.

To either side, the wings boasted a row of tall, narrow windows standing like guardsmen at attention.

Of course, Yeltsin would soon dissolve the Soviet Union, and the flag would be replaced by the old imperial flag—a horizontal tricolor of white, blue, and red—and the clock by the Russian coat of arms (the two-headed eagle), representing the sovereignty of the Russian Federation.

We got changed and headed straight across the road to the Belgrade Hotel for dinner. The old Chechen gang was waiting for us. So was the champagne and black caviar.

Night after night, we partied with them while we waited for Arbi's protocol.

CHAPTER SEVEN

Katya to the Rescue

July came and Greg and I decided to rent a flat. Living out of my suitcase in a tiny hotel room with my husband had started to really depress me, and I was excited when we found a one-bedroom apartment with antique furniture, belonging to a popular children's author. The apartment had an open-plan dining and lounge room with a large, round mahogany table; a spacious bedroom; a small, narrow, old-style kitchen with lime-green walls; and a bathroom with large yellow tiles and a combined shower/bath. For security and to keep the cold out, it had a double-padded front door covered in black leather and silver studs, with two deadlocks and a door chain.

It cost US$200 per month. A rare find indeed in a city with a huge housing crisis. It also became Star's office. The address was

13/21 Smolenskaya Square, an area in the center of Moscow lined with trees and a five-minute walk from the White House.

One weekend, Arbi and Ica came over with a large suitcase. They asked if they could keep it in the apartment for a while.

"No problem. What's in there?" Greg and I inquired.

"Just money," they replied.

The next day, they returned. Ica opened the suitcase. It contained wads of greenbacks. My eyes almost fell out of my head.

"Is this your money?" I asked in disbelief.

"No, it's not. We must do a run to Grozny, capital of our country, and deliver it to our partners. We sold some four-wheel drives, and this is payment. Hey, why don't you come with us?"

"But what about visas?" I retorted.

"Forget visas. You will just have to crouch down on the floor of the car at border crossings. It will be okay," he assured me.

This great adventure was too exciting to resist, so we agreed.

The next morning, we took off in their brand-new Toyota four-wheel drive. As we approached the Chechnya border, Ica motioned for us to get down, and we obediently squatted on the floor of the back seat, holding our breath. Ica spoke to the guards in his native tongue and handed over a wad of green US dollars. They smiled and waved us through. We sat back up, relief dissolving my fear.

A few hours later, we reached Grozny, an old Muslim city full of majestic mosques intermingled with drab, ugly Soviet-style buildings. The streets were crowded with women shrouded in black from head to toe and men wearing bright "tea towels" around their heads.

We stayed at Arbi's home, a large, free-standing redbrick house, where we washed up and were invited to dinner with a hoard of Arbi's male relatives and Ica. Dressed in jeans and a jumper, I was the only woman at the massive oak dining table, smoking and drinking wine, which seemed to be accepted. All the wives and children were crowded around a tiny table in the kitchen, as they were not permitted to dine with the men. They were dressed in headgear and long black dresses that went to the ground, chatting, laughing, eating, and cooking, and looked perfectly happy.

The feast consisted of many Chechen dishes, including *kharcho*, a hot and spicy beef soup served with a cheesy flatbread; dumplings stuffed with meat, potatoes, and mushrooms; and lamb kebabs served with a fragrant dip made with peppers, tomatoes, carrots, apples, and garlic.

Two days later, we drove alongside the spectacular, gargantuan, snow-covered Caucasus Mountains reaching high into masses of wispy white clouds. Some had icy-cold lakes meandering at their feet. We stopped at a small fishing village on the Caspian Sea, and Arbi purchased a large fresh female sturgeon from one of the fishermen. He slit her belly open with a big knife and scooped the black caviar out, sliding this amazing delicacy into my mouth straight from the knife's blade.

The trip was extremely dangerous, especially in view of my imprisonment ten years before for visa violations, which was still etched in my memory. But luckily, our return journey was as successful as our outward one, and we safely reached Moscow in early October without being stopped, arrested, and jailed.

... All the while waiting for the elusive Norilsk Nickel protocol.

Finally, I ran out of patience and confronted Arbi. He confessed that the Moscow representative of Norilsk Nickel was demanding a payment of US$30,000. "I'm not paying that bastard!" he added.

Well, that certainly explained the holdup. I told Arbi to give me the phone number for this representative. It took several attempts to reach him, but finally he came to the phone.

"What do you want?" he barked.

"I have a deal with you and Arbi to mine your tailings, and I'm ringing to arrange a meeting with you to sign the protocol," I replied.

"I have already signed hundreds of protocols with foreign mining companies to mine the tailings. But we have decided to keep the tailings for ourselves. Goodbye."

The phone went dead. I was stunned. I'd convinced Ian to commit half a million dollars to the Norilsk Nickel project—claiming to have it under my belt—and it looked as if we'd been completely conned.

After an expressionless Arbi left, I rang my mother, who said that Arbi and Ica were clearly Chechen mafia and told me to go to Katya with the whole story. I immediately rang Katya, whom I still hadn't met, and she graciously invited Greg and me over to her place for tea that evening.

The woman who opened the door of her small, old-fashioned apartment a few hours later and shook our hands remains an enigma, just like her country—unfathomable, contradictory, entrancing, and mysterious.

Sixty-eight, short, and slim, with thinning hair dyed mahogany brown, and dark eyes that darted from side to side as she commented flirtatiously on my husband's good looks, Katya and I warmed to each other immediately. She became a big part of my life, although in all the time we spent together during the next few years, she never did tell me whether she had indeed spied for Russia. Nor did she ever reveal her true role in Yeltsin's government.

Katya's dining table, where we sat down, was laden with books and papers. In fact, her whole apartment resembled a small library. It soon became obvious that mentally, she was as sharp as a pencil; she related enthralling stories about the past, at one stage pulling out a photo of herself at the age of four, holding hands with five-year-old future KGB chairman Andropov. "My first boyfriend!" she declared.

After Andropov took over the KGB, he moved Katya into a huge ground-floor apartment in the Kremlin. "I helped him with his poetry there. He was a good man, and not the murdering animal the world portrayed him as," she said firmly, before adding, "I also accompanied Khrushchev on a trip to India once, as his personal translator. He got drunk before he addressed the people of India, and I had to change his speech in my translation. He scolded me later, but we ended up kissing."

Katya was a lot less kind about Gorbachev, whom she regarded as a spineless flake. She'd supported him originally but had decided he was two-faced. The country was in a state of acute crisis, she told us, and people were demoralized. "Gorbachev's forecasts for 1991 are totally unrealistic, and the government's budget is pure fiction," she said fiercely. "It will lead to sharp price increases, especially for food."

Gorbachev had initiated glasnost and perestroika—"openness" and "reconstruction," respectively—because he knew that the country needed radical economic reform and a new social and political system. But since he and his closest comrades were all Marxists, nothing had changed, continued Katya.

"Earlier this year he was forced into an alliance with Boris Yeltsin and his team of economists, who will finally make us ready for the nation's transition to a market economy. As far as I'm concerned, Gorbachev is finished. I'm sure he'll betray Yeltsin. I know Yeltsin well and am very close friends with both his wife and Tanya, his youngest daughter. I regularly have dinner with Tanya. We plot to overthrow Gorbachev! Yeltsin may be the present leader of the Russian parliament, but he is destined to become Russia's first democratic president."

Eventually we got on to the subject of Norilsk Nickel and the Chechens. That's when I mentioned the name of my new business partner, Ian MacNee. Katya's eyes started to gleam. She said she would find me a much better business deal and then suddenly announced, "Okay, this is what we will do. Get Ian to come to Moscow, and I'll take you both to see Yeltsin."

"You are my savior!" I exclaimed, hugging this remarkable woman.

Understandably, I felt euphoric. A meeting with Yeltsin! I couldn't wait to tell Ian.

However, I didn't ignore my mother's advice. The following day, I contacted Izumov, Mum's other Moscow contact. He spoke highly of my mother and invited me over for dinner that night. I went without Greg; Greg didn't speak Russian, and it slowed me down when I had to translate every word for him.

Izumov's apartment was three times as big as Katya's and opulent by comparison. Izumov himself was a tall man with a thick mane of white hair and warm, smiling eyes. He too regarded Gorbachev as a traitor, though not for the same reasons as Katya. Gorbachev, he said, was finished, and Gennady Zyuganov, leader of the Communist Party, would be Russia's next leader. He could introduce us if necessary. When I told Izumov what I was doing in Moscow, he said, "You should go to GlavGold, the head administration of gold mining in the Soviet Union. Talk to Vladimir; he's in charge of dealing with foreigners."

I duly put a call through to GlavGold, explaining that my good friend Izumov had instructed me to get in touch. A few minutes later, a man came on the line and introduced himself as Vladimir, the chief economist. He arranged to meet me the following day.

One of the major assets of Ian's company Crusader Investments was the ourocone, which consisted of large twin centrifuges that extracted fine gold from ore tailings with remarkable efficiency. Russian miners, using simple jigs (gravity concentrators) to recover gold, lost a whopping 60 percent as the gold was too fine. This fine gold was then unceremoniously dumped in huge piles as tailings on the mine sites. The average gold concentration of this "waste" was over three grams per ton, on par with many gold deposits in the world. Three ourocones attached to a sluice box (a long, narrow "box" with running water that separates gold ore from gravel) and a leach plant (a chemical plant that extracts gold from its ore) would increase the Russian gold recovery from 60 percent to 90 percent—a phenomenal result. The ourocone's inventor, Dr. John Thomas, was one of Ian's mining engineers, and Ian owned the rights to sell ourocones worldwide.

Vladimir was a typical Slav—tall, tanned, blond, and blue-eyed. Over the next week, the two of us thrashed out a deal between Star and GlavGold to mine gold tailings all over Russia, and the story was the same everywhere: Each mine had millions of tons of tailings with gold concentrations equal to or higher than most Western gold mines. The mines, called associations, were government owned but earmarked for privatization.

As part of the deal with Vladimir, I said that Star would provide funds and our ourocones to the project.

Vladimir liked the fact that I was Russian, and that Star was from Australia. "We dislike and distrust Americans," he said. "We like and trust you. Next, we would like to meet the president of your company."

A door had opened at last. My relief was enormous. Here was a legitimate offer to mine all the gold tailings in Russia—and to top that, I had the promise of a meeting with Yeltsin. Most importantly, I hadn't let Ian down.

On December 1, 1990, Ian flew into Moscow accompanied by Dr. Bryce Wood, an experienced, well-known geologist. The GlavGold meeting took place the next day, and the protocol to mine Russia's gold tailings with Star was signed and celebrated with vodka and cognac.

I then took Ian to Katya's house and introduced them. Katya instantly fell in love with Ian, and he was just as taken with her.

A few days later, she phoned me. "You have to meet Poltoranin before you meet with Yeltsin," she announced. "Poltoranin is the minister for information and mass media, and he's Yeltsin's best friend. He must approve of you first. If he likes you, he'll arrange a meeting with Yeltsin. We will take Poltoranin out to dinner."

The dinner Katya organized was held in the private room at the elite Writers' Club on Povarskaya Street. The club was a truly legendary place. In the 1960s, there was a famous à la carte buffet for writers with strict access, where only the most famous Soviet writers gathered, from Evtushenko to Solzhenitsyn, including Katya. Before the Communist revolution of 1917, it was a mansion belonging to a rich aristocratic Muscovite family, and its timber interior was later fully restored to its original style with stunningly embellished walls and doors, high ceilings, polished floors, and tall stained-glass windows. The rooms were fitted out with imperial-style furnishings, priceless paintings, chandeliers, Persian rugs, and three ornate fireplaces.

A thickset man with a large face covered in acne scars, Mikhail Poltoranin had small eyes and a mullet. He was dressed in an old-fashioned brown suit that looked as if it had been worn too many times. But he was jovial and had a wicked sense of humor. I could easily imagine him and Yeltsin enjoying many vodkas together.

The dinner was a huge success, and at the end of the night, Poltoranin promised to introduce us to Yeltsin. True to his word, a meeting was set up for Friday, December 5, at 9:30 a.m. at the White House.

We had dinner at Katya's place the night before this to prepare. After dinner, she called Yeltsin in front of us. Yeltsin tried apologetically to postpone the meeting to the following week because of an emergency parliamentary session that was going to spill over into Friday.

"If you don't see them tomorrow, I will take them to Gorbachev! Do you hear me?" yelled the formidable Katya.

To our amazement, we heard Yeltsin's voice booming out of the phone: "*Horosho, horosho.* [Okay, okay.] I will see them tomorrow."

When we walked into the White House with Katya at 9:20 sharp the next morning, I couldn't believe this was really happening. Ian looked like the multimillionaire he was, dressed in a black Armani suit with a white shirt and a maroon tie. Katya wore a black jacket and skirt with a light-blue shirt. I chose a brown woolen Chanel skirt ensemble with a silky orange blouse and high brown leather boots. My hair had been cut and permed in the fashionable style of the 1990s, hanging to my shoulders in a mass of frizzy blond curls. My eyes were accentuated by dark-brown eye shadow and my lips by my signature red lipstick.

We were greeted by one of Yeltsin's aides, whom we followed along a long, narrow parquet corridor leading to Yeltsin's office. We sat outside an enormous oak double door for ten minutes. Then the aide opened the door and ushered us inside.

Yeltsin stood in front of his desk, clad in a smart navy suit, starched white shirt, and striped navy tie. He was much taller than I had expected and had the charisma that goes with many powerful men. His distinctive white hair and broad smile made him seem very approachable, and I saw how easily such a man might conquer the hearts of the Russian people.

We introduced ourselves. Yeltsin nodded and waved us over to a long conference table. "How can I help you?" he asked in a rich, resonant voice once we were all seated.

Katya translated as Ian explained that we wanted to invest in Russia's mining industry, mainly in gold ore and tailings. So far, we'd only met with GlavGold, he added.

Yeltsin asked what Ian's yearly turnover was, to which Katya replied straight-faced that it was over one billion dollars.

Yeltsin narrowed his eyes. And then he made us a stunning offer.

"You are wasting your time with GlavGold," he told us. "I have a proposal for you. I need a line of credit for one to two billion American dollars. If you can provide this, I will guarantee the loan with gold deposits anywhere in Russia. GlavGold may control gold today, but soon, very soon, I will! All the gold in Russia will be in my hands!" he said, banging his fist on the table.

It was a breathtaking performance. Yeltsin was making it clear that both Gorbachev and Communism were dead in the water.

I realized that he took it for granted that Ian was a billionaire, like Bill Gates or George Soros. Ian certainly didn't give Yeltsin any reason to think otherwise. "Yes, I will try to organize the funds for you," Ian replied, adding that Star would like to introduce its own technology into Russia to mine the gold tailings.

Yeltsin nodded again and said that he wholeheartedly supported foreign investment. "Russia's mineral resources are so vast that they have the potential to impact on world commodity markets. But our whole mining industry is in ruins because of old equipment, and in addition, we can't commercialize the new technologies being developed in our brilliant research institutes. The only solution in the short term is the establishment of joint ventures with foreign companies.

"My advice to you is this," he went on. "Visit the gold mines of Siberia, and if you find someone out there who wants you, come back to me and I will support you!"

We ended this historic twenty-minute meeting by posing for a group photo with Yeltsin.

Consequently, I started planning a tour of Siberia with the blessing of the man who would become Russia's first president.

CHAPTER EIGHT

A Journey to Bodaibo

Yeltsin began opening the Russian gold mining landscape to foreigners in early 1991, allowing me to travel freely to Siberian gold mining areas. Yeltsin included the previously "secret" cities of Sverdlovsk (formerly Ekaterinburg, named after Katherine the Great and birthplace of my ancestors), Irkutsk, and Norilsk in this new mining landscape. All mining deals were to be approved by him before GlavGold approved them. As well, all proposals had to include an agreement to sell gold to the government for just below world prices. This was a huge relief, as previously the price paid to gold miners had been a fraction of the world price.

I went back to see Vladimir, the chief economist at GlavGold. He told me about a mining company called Lenzoloto Association. Lenzoloto was in the Irkutsk region, in the far east of Siberia, near the town of Bodaibo, northeast of Lake Baikal. It took its name from the Lena River, where alluvial gold had been mined for over a century. In fact, from 1906 to 1928 the alluvials had been mined by an Anglo-Russian joint company, Lena Goldfields Co. Ltd., listed on the London Stock Exchange, but Stalin threw all foreigners out of Russia four years after he became the Soviet leader. I hoped history wouldn't repeat itself.

Vladimir continued, "The gold there is finely dispersed, and there are already stockpiles of millions of tons of gold tailings. Varenikov, the director of Sunrise, one of the Lenzoloto mining artels, will be in Moscow in three weeks. We'll have a meeting with him."

"What are artels?" I asked.

"They're independent contractors, miners of alluvial gold who sell it to Lenzoloto for a fixed price," replied Vladimir.

On February 4, 1991, I received a fax from Ian. He was concerned about the political situation in Russia. Even though both Yeltsin and Gorbachev said they strongly supported foreign joint ventures and foreign investment, Gorbachev had started capitulating to the old hard-line Communists who were against the new reforms—just as Katya had predicted he would. Gorbachev was afraid of losing power.

Because of the increasingly murky and unpredictable political landscape, Ian explained in his fax, he hadn't been able to arrange the US$2 billion loan for Yeltsin. He ended with a question: "How is food supply?"

I wrote back: "Food supply is bad, even though more and more foreign supermarkets, shops, and hotels are being built."

Privately, I was very concerned that Ian's empty promise to Yeltsin was irresponsible and could backfire. I hadn't realized that our meeting with Yeltsin provided my first glimpse of how Ian operated. He overextended offers and promised people vast amounts of money, probably believing that he could deliver. This was his way of controlling those around him. He played on people's greed, and it worked in the short term. If I'd known how nasty things would get in the future, I would have been more fearful.

On February 27, Varenikov, the director of the Sunrise artel, came to our apartment. He was a rugged mining man, bronzed by the Siberian sun, with brooding eyes and a potbelly. He was also a self-confessed recovering alcoholic. He said that Lenzoloto had around five million tons of tailings stockpiled and that we should form a joint venture to mine them. "I will get samples and data," he promised. I told him about the ourocone, and he was immediately interested. He said he'd come back to Moscow on March 18 for another meeting.

More intriguingly, Varenikov mentioned a big gold deposit, which he said was a state secret but would soon be "opened" to foreign investment. He wasn't any more forthcoming than that—and he didn't mention the mysterious deposit when we next met. At the second meeting, he said simply that Lenzoloto's general director, Avlov, had approved our joint venture to mine Lenzoloto's tailings using the ourocone.

Ian started making plans to ship one of his ourocones from an alluvial gold mining venture in the Brazilian jungles. However, the inventor was concerned about patent protection. Dr. John Thomas faxed me, saying that the Russians and Chinese were notorious for ripping off Western technologies, and asked for more detailed information on Lenzoloto's deposits.

I told Ian that I could only get this information by traveling to Bodaibo to meet the Lenzoloto people myself. He agreed—and by April, GlavGold had organized the visit. Vladimir, who was now working undercover for Star, would come with me. We'd offered him employment, effectively becoming his sponsors for Australian residency. We now understood the machinations of quid pro quo when doing business in Russia.

On April 7, 1991, Vladimir and I flew to Siberia's Irkutsk region, leaving Greg behind in Moscow. I took lots of cognac and food since we were flying Aeroflot, not known for its in-flight service and infamous for crashing regularly due to poor maintenance, usually killing all on board. I tried to push this thought from my mind.

The flight took five hours. Irkutsk, the capital of the region, turned out to be a very clean city with beautiful white monuments, green parks, and a wide, sparkling river, still frozen. We stayed the night in Lenzoloto's hotel, a very modest one-star accommodation with tiny rooms, uncomfortable beds, and no hot water. However, it did have a small cafeteria on the ground floor, serving very basic food for breakfast, lunch, and dinner.

Early the next morning we boarded an old propeller plane to fly to Bodaibo, 1,438 kilometers northeast of Irkutsk. The noise of its engine gave me a migraine. I was grateful to land forty minutes later.

Bodaibo was a charming little village nestled between snowcapped mountains. It was beautiful but freezing—minus fifteen degrees Celsius. Varenikov greeted us at the plane. We hugged like old mates, and he drove us to a wooden guesthouse that had bunk beds, hot water (a rarity in Siberia), a lounge room with a fireplace, a kitchen, and, to my immense joy, a wonderful Russian *banya* (steam sauna).

Dinner that night was at Varenikov's headquarters. We sat at a long wooden table with the artel miners. They were a great bunch of Russian lads, and I thoroughly enjoyed their company. The whole evening reminded me of my mum's dinner parties at home with her Russian friends, sitting around the table all night, toasting, drinking, eating, smoking, laughing, and singing.

A couple of days later, I finally met Avlov, the general director and big boss of Lenzoloto, who ran Bodaibo as if he owned the town. He was a large, intimidating-looking man who bore an uncanny resemblance to Jack Nicholson, the famous Hollywood movie star. His oily brown hair was slicked back, revealing a large forehead and a widow's peak. His V-shaped eyebrows framed brown eyes, and his lips were heart-shaped but thin.

The two of us hit it off immediately. Avlov eventually told me that many years earlier, he'd fallen in love with a girl named Ludmila. But he was married, and their affair ended tragically when Ludmila committed suicide. I looked just like her, he added. It was as if his Ludmila had returned to him. I ignored his lustful look as he said this.

Vladimir and I spent a week in Bodaibo before the great moment finally came: Avlov and I signed a protocol to form a joint venture to mine Lenzoloto's gold tailings using the ourocone.

That night, we all celebrated at the artel headquarters—fifteen men and me! Outside, the temperature had dropped to minus forty degrees, and a snowstorm swirled through the darkness. At some point, Varenikov started talking again about the secret deposit he'd first mentioned in Moscow. It was a very big hard-rock deposit, he said. Right there, in Bodaibo. "We don't have the funds to mine it," he went on. "We'll have to get foreign investment when the law changes. Do you think Star would be interested?"

His voice had fallen to a whisper. I didn't understand why all the mystery, only that the deposit was listed in the Decree of Government Secrets. This meant, Vladimir later explained, that it was classified as a secret of national importance. Violating the secrecy attached to the decree was regarded as treason, punishable by life imprisonment or death.

I was fascinated.

The next morning, when we were both sober, I quizzed Vladimir about the secret deposit. He acknowledged its existence without, infuriatingly, adding anything more, although he promised to set up a meeting with GlavGold to discuss it. He then startled me by saying that GlavGold had the power to declassify the secrecy surrounding the deposit.

On our last morning in Bodaibo, we enjoyed leftover dinner for breakfast, washed down with cognac—a good Siberian tradition—before we left for the airport. The flight on an overcrowded plane, complete with a couple of chickens and a dog, shook the whole way to Irkutsk. I was relieved to finally land.

The next leg of the journey back to Moscow was over five hours long, so Vladimir and I again stocked up on cognac and food at the airport. Four and a half hours into the flight, with both of us in a mellow mood from the cognac, we started talking about love, sex, and marriage, and how Russian men were expected to keep a mistress. As Vladimir was gazing into my eyes, there was a loud explosion from the back of the plane.

"What was that?" I asked in a panic.

"It was a bomb!" shouted Vladimir, his face white. "Oh my God, we are all going to die!"

"Calm down," I ordered. After all, the plane wasn't plummeting to the ground. "We are not going to die."

I knew I sounded more certain about this than I felt. The other passengers were either screaming, crying, or praying. The hostesses were nowhere to be seen. There was a second, smaller explosion, and most of the passengers became hysterical. Vladimir was just as bad. He kept saying over and over that we were all going to die.

"Shut up and give me the bottle of cognac," I said furiously.

In all the commotion, we had lost our glasses and were forced to drink straight from the bottle. We both took turns swigging the cognac. I started to think that maybe Vladimir was right. Maybe we were about to crash and burn, which was why the crew was keeping silent. I suddenly felt very scared.

But a few minutes later the captain's voice came through the speakers: "My fellow passengers, the plane has experienced a minor problem. We have been cleared to land in Nizhny Novgorod, which is very close to our current position. I don't anticipate any problems in landing at this stage."

"There is something really wrong with the plane." Vladimir's voice shook as he spoke. "Nizhny Novgorod is a closed city. It makes MiGs and nuclear submarines and there are nuclear facilities at

Sarov, close by. Russians cannot enter without a special permit, and foreigners are forbidden. We are going to make a crash landing for sure."

Okay, I was now officially terrified. I started to think of all the people I would leave behind if I died. It was a ghastly feeling, anticipating your own death at any minute.

We spotted Nizhny Novgorod from the plane window. The plane circled the town a few times and finally began its descent. I noticed a bright-orange safety net at the end of the runway, and at that same moment, we were told to take our brace positions. The next few minutes seemed endless.

When the plane landed safely, the relief was immeasurable. All the passengers were taken to a holding deck inside the airport. There we found out that the "minor problem" had been the back engine, which had exploded.

Two hours later, we boarded another Aeroflot plane and eventually got safely back to Moscow. I've never been happier to disembark from a plane in my life.

CHAPTER NINE

Sukhoi Log Unveiled

The first thing I did when I walked back into the apartment was fax Ian a report about the mysterious gold deposit in the middle of Siberia. He called me immediately.

"It has been my lifelong quest to discover a gold deposit such as this," he said excitedly. "It's why I've spent millions exploring gold the world over. Big mining companies like Placer Dome, BHP, and American Barrick all started with just one big discovery. When can we have the data on it?"

"Well, it's still a government secret for now," I replied. "But Vladimir assures me they will open it up to foreigners as they don't have the funds to construct the mine, and Russia needs to produce more gold. We'll have to be patient and, for now, concentrate on the ourocone business."

On that front, things were moving. GlavGold had proposed that at the end of the mining season in Bodaibo, we hold an ourocone conference for all the major Russian mining companies. Star's destiny in Russia would depend on how successfully we demonstrated our technology at their conference.

Ian, who was still winding down his failed alluvial mining operation in Brazil, kept assuring me that an ourocone was on its way.

On April 20, 1991, Vladimir told me that GlavGold needed a copy of Star's annual return.

I knew that this was going to be a big problem, as most Russians believed that only companies with strong balance sheets, like Rio Tinto Zinc (RTZ), had money to invest. They didn't understand that a wealthy individual could raise hundreds of millions of dollars for a mining project through private investments or a public listing on the stock exchange. The Russians didn't have a stock exchange, and the concept of listing a company to raise funds from investors was completely alien to them. So, I stalled, telling Vladimir that Ian would bring all our financial documentation with him on his next trip to Russia.

Out of the blue, GlavGold summoned Avlov to Moscow for urgent talks on "the secret deposit." I heard more about this when Avlov and Vladimir showed up at the apartment the night after their meeting. As we sat around drinking, Avlov leaned over seductively and whispered in my ear, "Lenzoloto has a huge gold deposit called Sukhoi Log. It's the largest deposit in the world."

What he went on to tell me was extraordinary. Sukhoi Log had confirmed reserves of more than 1,100 tons of gold and probable reserves of another 2,000 tons. The estimated worth in American dollars, he said, was $21 billion. "We need foreign capital to construct the first stage of the mine—about thirty million American dollars—after which the profits can be used to construct the final stages. If Lenzoloto and Star form a joint venture to mine tailings, we might as well mine Sukhoi Log together too."

I wasn't sure what astounded me more: Avlov's revelation that the deposit was worth so much or the fact that we were being offered unthinkable riches because I resembled his long-lost dead love, Ludmila. Who would believe me?

The moment my visitors left, I called Ian and repeated the conversation.

"That's eighty-four million ounces of gold!" he exclaimed. "It's too big for Star. How much money does Avlov need?"

"He said about thirty million US to build the mine."

"Star would need to attract partners for this. Look, let's pursue it, and I'll see what I can do from my end. And, Ludmila—well done. You've certainly kicked a goal with this one!"

On the other front, however, we still didn't have the ourocone. Time was running out. The Russian mining season ended in September. After that, the ground would freeze over. I feared that if we didn't demonstrate our ourocone technology, we'd be out on our ear. The Russian miners would simply turn to the other Western mining companies who'd begun knocking on their doors.

In the middle of all this, the vigilant Katya delivered a fruit basket of mangoes and pawpaws to Yeltsin from Star. The note said: "Congratulations on your recent victories [in parliament] which have encouraged Star to continue pursuing business prospects in Russia. We hope the fruit assists your game."

The note was referring not only to Yeltsin's love of tennis but also to a far more serious game being played out in the political arena. Total economic collapse was now a real possibility in Russia. The Soviets had spent too much money on nuclear weapons to keep up with the Americans, and the Soviet Union was on the verge of bankruptcy. The shops were empty. Even the exclusive ones reserved for elite Communist leaders were bare. Miners were striking across the country. People were angry—and hungry. Gorbachev understood that many Russians believed Yeltsin was Russia's only hope.

I tried not to let the political tensions distract me. I'd begun discussing with Avlov the possibility of manufacturing the ourocone locally. He discussed this with GlavGold, and they endorsed a joint venture with Star to mine alluvials and tailings using locally manufactured ourocones. If this was successful, Star could build an open-pit mine at Sukhoi Log (a surface-mining technique that would extract the gold from a massive open pit in the ground).

At this point, John wrote to Ian to say that Star's credibility and future success was inextricably tied to the demonstration of the ourocone. I was on tenterhooks, waiting for Ian's answer. Because of this, I almost forgot that I was turning thirty-one on the 29th of May, but then Katya announced that she'd come up with a great birthday gift for me. She'd organized a meeting with the charismatic future Speaker of the Russian parliament, Ruslan Khasbulatov. He would be a useful ally in our quest to conquer Sukhoi Log, she said.

So once again, I found myself walking into the White House with the amazing Katya. We were taken into Khasbulatov's office to wait for him; a few minutes later, he appeared through heavy double doors leading from another room.

Khasbulatov had quite a reputation as a womanizer. I wondered whether he'd just come from the room where he did all his entertaining. He was a short man with the full ruby lips that give an impression of sensuality in some people and lasciviousness in others. In his case, it was the latter. He had thick black hair and dark-brown eyes. He sat next to me and held my hand tightly in his during the whole meeting. Though I can't deny that he was sexy, this felt awkward for me, but I dared not pull my hand away. A faint smell of cognac clung to him.

"What can I do for you, my lovely?" he asked. I replied that I was about to travel to Bodaibo to sign an agreement with Lenzoloto, which he knew about.

"Great!" exclaimed Khasbulatov. "Well, when you return to Moscow with the signed document, come straight back to me, and I will help you get it passed by all the appropriate authorities."

The meeting was over, so we stood and shook hands. Katya chose that moment to announce it was my birthday. Khasbulatov turned to me and gave me a wet, sloppy kiss on the cheek. As I turned to walk out of his office, he reached out and grabbed my bottom. I managed to maintain my composure and kept going, reminding myself that he was one of the most powerful men in the country.

Thanks to Katya, I now had the support of both Yeltsin and Khasbulatov. Not bad for a foreigner who'd been in the country for a relatively brief time! The omens were excellent—but suddenly, on June 3, a strange fax came from Ian. He wanted all faxes sent to his Aspen office in future, instead of Hong Kong.

It seemed that he was having huge problems with Crusader and his rich Chinese investors. They wanted out of Russia because no money had yet been made. I was mystified by their attitude, even though I knew that they'd always wanted a quick deal. Didn't they realize I was on the verge of striking a deal with Lenzoloto—to say nothing of my new friends in the White House? Didn't the significance of this mean anything to them? Or did they have a different agenda?

A few days later, Ian let me know that he'd decided to finance Russia himself. He also said he was hoping to float Star's interests on the Australian stock market through one of his companies, Central Mining NL, a shell company listed on the Australian Stock Exchange. I would soon have reason to wonder whether Ian had forgotten that he was only in Russia because of my mother—and me.

When Yeltsin won Russia's first presidential election on June 12, Ian sent him a telegram of congratulations. But just a week later, he sent me a harsh fax that was tremendously upsetting: "Do you have any comprehension of what the Russian project entails in terms of time and cost, and the required expertise?" he wrote. "Total planning and proper budgeting are necessary. My impression is, unless everything is coordinated, nothing will succeed. Don't forget also you need to consider how you will fund your share in the future. What provisions are you making?"

This could only mean, I thought in shock, that Ian didn't want to ship an ourocone to Russia. The Crusader funds had dried up, and he wasn't prepared to risk his personal money. But his words devastated me. I had no way to "fund my share." The original deal was that Greg and I would receive a 10 percent shareholding each in the company, and Ian would fund the Russian projects to a maximum of half a million dollars. Maybe this limit had been reached.

In my reply to him, I suggested that Greg and I simply pack our bags and go home. Ian then sent a conciliatory message confirming his commitment to fund Russia himself—and asked me to prepare a business plan on Lenzoloto.

This incident threw me. But I settled back down to work and spent July developing the business plan, getting Star registered in Russia, and structuring the Lenzoloto/Star joint venture. Avlov wanted to incorporate the whole of Lenzoloto in the joint venture, not just Sukhoi Log and the alluvials. This was much more complicated, because Lenzoloto owned factories, the railroad, the hydroelectric station, the shops, hotels, houses, cars, mining equipment, repair shops, schools, hospitals, and a lot more.

Avlov's dream was for one huge joint venture. He saw Star as the cash cow that would replace Gosplan, the old Communist central planning office that had previously bankrolled Lenzoloto.

Under the Communist regime, Gosplan would send money to Avlov every year, and if he spent all of it (constructing more roads, bridges, buildings, mines, railways, and hotels), he would get more money the following year. Avlov's only obligations were to meet the Gosplan gold quota and to continue construction. Stemming from

Lenin's indoctrination, Soviet mentality was that company profits were irrelevant, as everything was owned by the state and the state would provide.

But Ian didn't want Star to fund anything other than Sukhoi Log. He certainly didn't want to build roads and bridges and hydroelectric stations with Avlov.

Dr. John Thomas and his British girlfriend, Amie, arrived in Moscow in mid-July 1991 with the ourocone drawings. The three of us flew to Bodaibo for ten days. A gorgeous miner called Slava, who had big, azure-colored eyes framed by long black eyelashes, took us to Visochaishi, an alluvial gold mine being worked by Varenikov's Sunrise artel, a four-hour drive away.

It was stinking hot at thirty-five degrees Celsius. Amie and I had on shorts and sleeveless T-shirts. When Slava took us into the mess hall, the miners looked at us hard. They hadn't seen a woman in four months and had never met a foreign one. But even though they were rough and tough Siberians, they were polite and friendly. We quickly bonded and enjoyed many plates of Russian borsch (a tasty soap with stewed beef, potatoes, beetroot, carrots, cabbage, and onion) served in huge pots and washed down with cognac.

The living arrangements were basic. John, Amie, and I shared a cabin on stilts (to stop ferocious brown bears wandering in) and slept on bunks with smelly mattresses, no blankets, and lumpy pillows. There were no proper toilet facilities, so we had to trek into the forest to a small wooden shack with a large hole in the ground. The stench was unbearable. Luckily, our cabin was stocked with plenty of cognac.

On one occasion, walking home from the mines, we all got trapped in a sandstorm. Slava wrapped his arms around me, turning me around. We walked backward so the harsh sand wouldn't damage our eyes. At the edge of the forest, we turned to make a run for the cabin—and came face-to-face with two huge brown bears with a tiny cub at their feet. Slava and I froze, unable to take our eyes off the bears, but luckily the bears were also trying to flee the sandstorm and quickly disappeared.

Bears and sandstorms aside, John was impressed by what he found at Visochaishi. The minute we returned to Moscow, he wrote a glowing report to Ian. "The potential is tremendous," he said in a fax. "We could sell hundreds of ourocones to all the gold mining associations in Russia."

Ian replied, saying that the ourocone was scheduled to leave the jungle on August 6 and could be ready to freight from Salvador by the 18th.

Then, suddenly, he dropped out of sight. The funding dried up as well. For almost a fortnight, there was silence. We were bewildered. Where had Ian gone?

Just as abruptly, a fax arrived from him: "A number of changes have occurred since our start-up, and we have spent approximately US$250,000 on the project. As you know, Crusader has pulled out of Star, and a few other partners have also retired from my mining businesses, thus funding on my own is impossible. Is there another way we can approach the Russian projects?"

I'd really thought that Ian was over his mysterious financial difficulties. He was very secretive about his wealth and how much he was worth. Apparently, all his money was hidden in a discretionary trust in Switzerland and invested in various financial instruments by the trustees, earning a very high interest rate of 25 percent. But he never touched the principal; he just lived off the interest. For him, it was cheaper to borrow funds. My understanding, from the little I knew, was that he borrowed as much as possible for his mining ventures, with the intention of offering his creditors (usually friends and business associates) a share in these projects, once they were profitable. Unfortunately, ever since his one and only very successful oil venture in Malaysia years earlier, he'd had nothing but losses—in Vietnam, Bolivia, Brazil, and, so far, in Russia.

The real situation was slowly becoming clear to me: Ian was badly in debt.

But then, on August 12, funds miraculously started to flow again. Ian didn't tell me what had happened, or what had caused the turnaround. All I knew was that we were back in business.

CHAPTER TEN

Blood in the Streets

Shortly after being in the money again, on August 18, 1991, an attempted coup against Gorbachev threw everyone's lives into chaos, including ours. A group of hard-liners—the head of the KGB among them—put Gorbachev under house arrest at his dacha (holiday house) in Sochi on the Black Sea. Katya told me later that the plan had been to overthrow both Gorbachev and Yeltsin, and that Yeltsin had secretly flown to meet with Gorbachev in Sochi before the coup. However, on the way back to Moscow, Yeltsin's plane was fired upon, the missile narrowly missing the right wing, which would have been catastrophic. Katya claimed she had proof that Gorbachev gave in to the hard-liners and gave the order to shoot down Yeltsin's plane.

Early the next morning, pro-Communist tanks and armored carriers rumbled down Moscow's main boulevards toward

Smolenskaya Square, where Greg and I lived, which quickly filled with soldiers. Columns of tanks halted outside strategic buildings—including the Ministry of Foreign Affairs, which was diagonal from our apartment.

Yeltsin resisted from the White House. He broadcast a speech on the independent radio station Echo Moscow, urging all Russians to gather at the White House in support of democracy. Tens of thousands of pro-Yeltsin supporters promptly marched to the White House and streamed through the open gates into the courtyard.

Katya, Greg, and I joined the rally even though the Communist army was closing in on us. When we got to the White House, the courtyard was packed with pro-democracy demonstrators. A few soldiers had crossed over to Yeltsin's side, and their renegade tanks were stationed just across from us. My friend Khasbulatov and a few of Yeltsin's aides were leaning out of a window. I waved at them. Khasbulatov recognized me instantly and animatedly waved back, then blew me a flurry of kisses. I blew him one back. After that he kept staring at me.

A few hours later, Yeltsin emerged and climbed up on one of the tanks in a scene that was soon flashed around the world.

In a powerful and moving performance, he spoke to the people about a new Russia—a free and wonderful Russia—and about the end of Communism. He encouraged everyone to stand and fight for this. I was swept away by what he said, and proud to stand there with my fellow Russians, in defiance of our common enemy, and fight if it came to that. After all, my family had been robbed by the Communists and lost their home and country.

The crowd exploded with cries of "Rossiya! Rossiya! Rossiya!" (Russia! Russia! Russia!). Men and women of all ages rushed toward the tanks, screaming at the youngest soldiers to go home to their mothers.

We stayed at the White House until dusk and then returned to our apartment for an early night. Ian called a few times, worried about the latest events. I assured him the worst was over, as the Communists had not attacked the White House as predicted.

At exactly 11 p.m., Greg and I woke to the sound of gunfire ricocheting against the wall of our apartment building. We leaped out of bed as more gunfire lit up the Moscow sky. The Communists had decided to attack at night and barge into the White House from the south, not from the north as anticipated.

Greg and I rushed down into the street just as a stretched line of tanks and armored vehicles roared past with missiles and rockets. I was petrified. People started to attack the tanks and the soldiers. Outside the White House, Yeltsin's defenders had erected a barricade. Buses were pushed in front of the tanks, and Molotov cocktails soared into the buses to ignite them. One young man attempted to mount a tank but was dragged underneath, his body left dangling. Another young Russian was shot dead trying to help him. A third young man was standing in the road when a bullet took off half his head, his body falling into the gutter.

More and more people attacked the tanks, more buses were pushed across the roads, more fires were lit. The crowd grew savage, and the soldiers began to back off. Some of them got up on their tanks and yelled, "We refuse to kill fellow Russians! We will not proceed further with this madness!"

The soldiers started to join the people. Other tanks began to retreat. As the sun rose, I decided I needed a drink. I went back upstairs to our apartment, locked the door, threw back a vodka, and called Ian. He ordered us out of Russia immediately.

I again argued that the worst was now over, and it would be crazy to leave. Russia was on the verge of becoming a democracy, and Yeltsin was the undisputed leader. Gorbachev was almost certainly finished, as was the Communist Party, and we were on the verge of creating the first gold mining joint venture in post-Communist Russia. Ian kept insisting we leave, but I knew I could not. Greg felt the same.

Like everyone else in Moscow, we spent the next day taking stock of the damage from the fighting. There were numerous burned-out buses—some fires were still burning—and broken glass lay everywhere. Contrasting this were displays of flowers in memory of the three young men who'd been killed. The coup was proclaimed a failure. The offenders were arrested. Gorbachev flew into Moscow from Sochi. CNN showed him disembarking his plane. He looked pale, tired, and defeated—a shell of his former self.

Behind the scenes, Yeltsin was taking control of Russia. He didn't consult Gorbachev, who was still technically the leader of the USSR.

On August 22, 1991, Katya and I attended the historic session of Russian parliament that followed the failed coup. The hall was a massive auditorium where the deputies sat on seats covered in plush red velvet. Yeltsin, the new Russian president, and Khasbulatov, the new leader of the Russian parliament, replacing Yeltsin, proudly took center stage. Gorbachev stood beside them. Yeltsin had drafted numerous decrees, one of which gave him sweeping powers as president. Another decree proclaimed the end of the USSR and Communist Party rule and the birth of the Commonwealth of Independent States (CIS), headed by Russia. This meant that all the countries the Communists had controlled since 1922—Armenia, Azerbaijan, Belorussia, Estonia, Georgia, Kazakhstan, Kirgizia, Latvia, Lithuania, Moldavia, Russia, Tajikistan, Turkmenistan, Ukraine, and Uzbekistan—were now free countries again. Yeltsin pushed the decrees toward Gorbachev and roared, "Sign!"

Gorbachev signed.

Yeltsin then raised a billowing flag with white, blue, and red horizontal bands and boomed, "Long live Russia!" The applause was deafening. I was as elated as everyone else. The session ended with a minute's silence in memory of the three young men killed during the fighting.

On August 23, we came back to earth with a bang. Ian had stopped the ourocone delivery—supposedly because of the coup. Our only option now was to build one locally. John was keen, and Ian seemed happy to pay for this to happen.

We had a maximum of one month to build an ourocone and install it at the Visochaishi alluvial mine. We didn't know if it could be done that quickly. Eventually we chose a factory in Svirsk, a small, snowy town a three-hour drive north of Irkutsk that had all the necessary machinery. Once built, the ourocone could be easily transported to Bodaibo by rail. I set to work planning the trip, frantic to save our project.

John arrived in Moscow on September 7, and we flew to Irkutsk the next day. From there, a Lenzoloto representative drove us straight to Svirsk. We arrived at night to a huge banquet that had been prepared by the excited factory workers. Work on constructing the ourocone began early the next day. I watched—and translated. Once everything was going smoothly, I returned to Moscow.

Three weeks later, the first ourocone arrived at the Visochaishi mine in Bodaibo.

The ourocone conference, which ran for four days at the end of September, was a tremendous success. Ten companies representing all the main gold mining associations in Russia attended. Every single company signed protocols of intent to purchase ourocones.

When Avlov and I met in Moscow the day after the conference had ended, he told me that Lenzoloto and Star were the talk of the town. "Ludmila, listen carefully," he then went on. "I want to proceed full steam ahead with our joint venture, the Lenzoloto JSC, with Star as an equity partner."

It was fantastic news. I was on top of the world and even kissed Avlov on the cheek, which made him blush. John was just as thrilled when I relayed all this to him. Ian decided to give John the rights to the ourocone business, as he wanted to concentrate on Lenzoloto. And so, the Svirsk factory would become the manufacturing hub for ourocones, and John would sell hundreds of ourocones to Russian gold companies.

Avlov was now very keen to meet Ian. He let me know that he was about to turn fifty and invited both Ian and me to his birthday party in Bodaibo on November 10. I faxed Ian with the news, adding that he should use the opportunity to see Sukhoi Log, which was accessible by chopper. Ian agreed enthusiastically. The two of us met in Irkutsk a week later and flew to Bodaibo together.

Avlov was waiting at the Bodaibo airport to greet us when we arrived. We went straight to his office and, after the usual welcoming toast with cognac, got down to business and drafted a protocol of intent. Ian and Avlov signed it. It outlined our intention to transform the government-owned Lenzoloto Association into a private joint stock company, to be named Lenzoloto JSC.

Ian agreed that Star would get 31 percent of the JSC, as we knew the Russian government would never surrender control of its biggest deposit to a foreign company. Another 59 percent was earmarked for Lenzoloto management and employees, and the final 10 percent for the regional Irkutsk government.

During those few heady days in Bodaibo, something changed between Ian and me. We were growing closer. Ian was extremely well read, and I loved the conversations we had and was enthralled by his recollections of his life. He also obviously enjoyed the best things in life: first-class travel, good wine, good food, and five-star hotels.

The day before the party, Ian, Avlov, and I flew to the top of Sukhoi Log by helicopter. Even with the sun shining brightly, the cold wind froze our cheeks, noses, and hands. We had to shout to be heard over the rotating blades of the helicopter. Ian was very excited, but it just looked like a giant, barren, snow-covered mountain to me, and I couldn't wait to get off it!

We celebrated Avlov's birthday with twenty other guests in his big two-story house. We all sat around a huge oval table laden with culinary dishes and bottles of cognac and vodka. We drank toast after toast to Avlov, to Lenzoloto, and to Star and then danced the night away to Russian music, including songs by my favorite artist, Alexander Malinin. When I was in Moscow in the early 1980s, Malinin had just burst onto the music scene, and every female fell in love with him, including me. He was Russia's first rock god.

At 2 a.m., the party wound down, and Ian and I got ready to leave. The temperature outside was minus thirty. Avlov walked with us into the freezing-cold night, and as Ian was getting into the car, Avlov grabbed me, swung me around, and gave me a passionate tongue kiss. He then grinned like a little kid.

As we drove off, I said to Ian, "Avlov just kissed me!"

"Did he? How was it?" Ian asked curiously.

"Awful! What did you expect?" I retorted and gazed out the window the whole way back to the guesthouse without saying another word.

On our return to Moscow, we heard that Yeltsin had signed a decree allowing foreign companies to mine primary ore for the first time in Russia since 1927. This was a huge breakthrough for Star.

This was in the wind even before I left for the Bodaibo trip with Ian. Katya and I had been present at the inaugural parliamentary session of the Russian Federation. Yeltsin stood on the stage behind a podium. Above him soared the old Russian gold-crusted, double-headed eagle, replacing the Communist hammer and sickle, and beside him stood a flagpole with the old Russian flag, replacing the Communist flag of the Soviet Union. Many people, including myself, wept tears of joy.

Yeltsin made a speech promising to strengthen the ruble and make it convertible. He'd also pledged to continue privatization, the liberalization of prices, and land reforms—and to create attractive terms for foreign investment. He got overwhelming support, although many people were already wondering whether he'd overreached.

Before 1991 was out, Yeltsin would appoint Gaidar, a thirty-five-year-old economist, to be his first deputy prime minister. Although Gaidar impressed me initially, he would later prove spineless when it came to standing up for Star.

Ultimately Gaidar's free-market economics and massive privatization program would plunge the ruble into a free fall where inflation soared and the savings of ordinary people were wiped out. Overnight, a new class of powerful men called oligarchs seized possession of Russia's natural resources, banks, and media outlets for peanuts and become millionaires, and in some cases billionaires, overnight. These oligarchs were chiefly responsible for the "new" corrupt, chaotic, and violent Russia that emerged. Only a handful of Western companies could possibly succeed in such an environment. I was determined that Star would be one of them.

Yeltsin's speech in parliament that day was the starting point of all this. New Russian ministries were created, and this directly affected Star. GlavGold was to be dissolved and replaced by two departments—the Committee for Geology (Geolkom) and the Committee for Precious Metals (Komdragmet).

A mining guru named Boris Yatskevich was appointed first deputy chairman of Geolkom and ruled the roost. He had a long and pointy nose, small, narrow eyes, thin lips, and oily brown hair. A chain-smoker who constantly suffered from lung infections, he was known for his irrational behavior and outbursts.

A diamond guru named Bychkov was appointed the boss of Komdragmet. He had a round, balding head and a great smile and was extremely witty—and very rich, from smuggling the most sought-after Russian diamonds into Europe and the USA. He also enjoyed "premiums" from De Beers because of the lucrative exclusive contracts he signed with them. He liked to be wined and dined by rich Western partners and to travel abroad at their invitation. He regularly dined with Yeltsin and was a social snob.

Both men would influence Star's fate—one of them far more than the other.

CHAPTER ELEVEN

Falling in Love

The Lenzoloto protocol signed by Avlov and Ian had to be submitted to the Russian government for approval. Katya decided we should deliver it directly into the hands of Gaidar. By coincidence, she knew his father—Timor, a children's author—intimately! She duly took our documents to his house and made him promise to hand them to his son the very next day. Katya's powers of persuasion were amazing.

On November 25, 1991, Timor called me. He said that his son had read our document and had agreed to endorse the project and would meet us soon, but first we needed to draft a formal legal document in the form of a government order granting Lenzoloto permission to form a joint stock company with Star. This would then be signed by Gaidar. We needed a formal government order because our JSC would be the first joint foreign and Russian entity to mine gold in Russia since 1927.

Before that, though, I had to see Khasbulatov again, to hand him the Lenzoloto protocol, as he'd requested. Ian and John decided to come with me, which turned out to be a big mistake. Khasbulatov was furious when all three of us showed up.

He took the protocol from me and said coldly, "Fine. I promised to support you, and I will. If it ever ends up in parliament, I'll make sure that it's passed. Now go—and next time, Ludmila, come alone. Goodbye."

It wasn't exactly the reception I'd hoped for, but at least I knew we had Khasbulatov's support, which was important. The next day, Avlov called me, sounding jittery. He said that GlavGold had arranged a trip to a mining conference in Paris for the general directors of the Russian gold mining associations. He suspected that this was an attempt by GlavGold to hold on to power after privatization and get a slice of the gold mines, including the prized Sukhoi Log.

"You and Ian must meet me in Paris," he said. "Then we can finalize the ordinance for Gaidar and submit it as soon as we get back to Moscow. We must act quickly. The vultures have begun to circle Lenzoloto."

I spoke to Ian, who agreed with the plan. I flew to London to meet him and spent the night in his grand three-story Victorian townhouse, decorated in opulent vintage style and overlooking Hyde Park in Knightsbridge. Knightsbridge was a leafy suburb where wealthy international residents mingled in high-end restaurants, classy pubs, and designer shops, including the quintessential Harrods department store. Ian fit in perfectly.

Ian took me to a local pub before dinner. He ordered a glass of Pol Roger, and we sat at the bar sipping the delightful cold champagne. This was such a treat after experiencing pubs at home in Australia, where you couldn't buy champagne by the bottle, let alone by the glass. Ian was opening a whole new world for me, and I was absolutely loving it!

We had dinner at Motcombs, a fashionable restaurant that was famous for its Dickensian windows (as depicted in Charles Dickens's *A Christmas Carol*) and eclectic art on its walls telling stories of actors and politicians dining together. We ordered roast duck breast with orange pan sauce and mashed potatoes—both Ian's and my favorite dish—and a bottle of Dom Pérignon, also our favorite. The conversation flowed easily over dinner; there wasn't a single awkward moment. That night, lying awake in his guest bedroom, a part of me wished he would creep into my bed. I fell asleep feeling very much besotted by him.

We flew to Paris the next day and checked into Canopy by Hilton, where Avlov was staying. This vibrant hotel was steps from Jardins du Trocadéro, an open square in Paris bounded by the Seine River, with the Eiffel Tower on its opposite bank. The view from the rooftop bar was spectacular.

The three of us got straight to business and spent the next four days drafting the Lenzoloto ordinance, to be signed by Gaidar into Russian law. After that, we could submit our founding documents (the founders' agreement and company charter) to the Ministry of Finance for registration.

As well as building the Sukhoi Log mine, we promised to build a hydroelectric station, a road, and a railway station—all necessary infrastructure for the development of Sukhoi Log. Star would contribute US$30 million for all these projects, in return for a 31 percent share.

Ian decided to celebrate the birth of our joint venture with Avlov and a group of Ian's Parisian friends, including a real noble count, at one of Paris's most famous restaurants, the Grand Vefour, undoubtedly to impress Avlov. The Grand Vefour was a jewel of the lavish Rococo style and had been a gastronomic hot spot for politicians, artists, writers, and poets for more than 200 years.

I salivated over escargot followed by pan-fried duckling filet, served with *pommes fondantes*, carrot puree, caramelized onions, and a port jus. The table was crowded with bottles of Moët and French cognac. Ian made sure that everyone's glass was never empty, but I noticed that he himself hardly drank at all; he was there on business, not pleasure.

Afterward, back at the hotel, after we'd said goodnight to Avlov, Ian invited me to a bar on the top floor of the hotel for a nightcap. We sat sipping our glasses of Moët, staring at the sensational glittering view across the French capital. It was a magical moment, and I couldn't help being romantically drawn to him. Ian then admitted that he sometimes got very lonely as he spent most of his life traveling. When I asked if he missed Bobby, he said yes.

"Are you still in love with her?"

"Yes, madly, and she with me."

"That's wonderful," I said enviously, thinking, *Why is he here then with me, having a nightcap?* I did not want an affair with a married man; I wanted the whole package—the real deal.

Ian then asked about Greg and me, and I told him we had nothing in common and we'd drifted apart.

"You know, all the Russian men are in love with you," remarked Ian. "I go to these meetings and watch you operate. You are my secret weapon."

We finished our drinks, talked some more, and then Ian walked me to my room and kissed me goodnight—on the cheek—for the first time.

The next day, Ian left for Aspen, and Bobby. In the evening, I had dinner with Avlov at a little café near the hotel. It was to be my last evening in Paris, and I would rather have spent it with Ian. Over the whole of dinner, Avlov gazed at me with adoring eyes. He couldn't stop beaming. *Here we go again*, I thought. Avlov was a beefy, unsophisticated Siberian gold miner. Siberian women found him attractive—but not me, not even in Paris! I did, however, enjoy his company and respect him immensely.

After dinner, we walked along the Seine River arm in arm, back to the hotel. I said goodnight, hurried into the elevator, and raced to my room, locking the door behind me. I then got into my pajamas and climbed into bed with a book, feeling relaxed for the first time all week.

Tomorrow I was returning to Moscow to submit the ordinance to Gaidar. It was all about to happen: the first gold mining joint venture in Russia and the first foreign company to mine gold in post-Communist Russia. Not just any gold deposit, either. The largest gold deposit in the world!

Absorbed in these happy thoughts, I switched off the lights and closed my eyes.

The phone rang.

"Ludmila, I've found this fascinating article on Lenzoloto. Can I come up to your room to show it to you?" asked Avlov.

My heart started racing, and my voice was shaking when I said, "Oh, I'd love to see the article, but it's late, and I am already in bed. Is it really urgent, or can it wait until the morning?"

"Ah, I guess it can," Avlov replied sheepishly.

"Good," I said. "I'll meet you in the foyer for breakfast."

"Okay, goodnight then," he said abruptly and hung up the phone.

A wave of nausea hit me. What if the whole deal hinged on me sleeping with Avlov? What if it was all over? I could never sleep with him, under any circumstances—even if it meant losing the deal.

After a sleepless night, I showered, dressed, and nervously took the elevator to the ground floor. When the doors parted, Avlov was standing there in the new brown pinstriped Giorgio Armani suit Ian had bought him in Paris, holding the article in his hands.

"Good morning," I said with a smile.

"Good morning," he replied.

We had a buffet breakfast and read the article together. The late-night phone call wasn't mentioned. I was flying back to Moscow a day earlier than he was, so, an hour later, Avlov kissed me on the cheek and waved me off in a cab for the airport. I was incredibly relieved that everything between us was back to normal.

I got "home" to discover that a busy Yeltsin had signed yet another decree. This one liberalized prices. It set free the wholesale and retail prices of all goods and services, except for essential items such as sugar, salt, bread, vodka, milk, and petrol. Consequently, the cost of everything skyrocketed, including the cost to develop Sukhoi Log, which shot up to US$150 million.

Ian wasn't fazed when I rang him to discuss this. He said Star's return would still be very healthy. We reworked our figures and amended Star's contribution in the ordinance we'd drafted in Paris from US$30 million to US$150 million, ready for Katya and me to present to Gaidar.

Firstly, though, we had to meet Gaidar's first aide, Golovnin, for him to ascertain whether we were worthy to meet Gaidar. Katya had already booked dinner at Tremos, Russia's first American diner, and Ian flew in for the occasion. Tremos was painted in dark blue and decorated with American flags. It served steaks, ribs, burgers, chips, and apple pie. Golovnin was a short man with sandy-blond hair, small, bright-blue eyes, thin lips, and an alluring smile. He was dressed in an impeccable blue suit that enhanced his eyes. Ian got on well with Golovnin, who, after many cognac toasts, told us that he wholeheartedly supported the Lenzoloto JSC. After a few more, he became even more animated about our project and promised to set up a meeting with Gaidar in the next few days.

Ian was only in Moscow briefly before going back to Aspen on some mysterious urgent business, so he couldn't stay on to meet with Gaidar.

The next day, parliament was in session, and Katya and I went to the White House again. We took our usual seats in the front row of the press box on the right-hand side of the auditorium. It felt like being seated in a VIP box at the Bolshoi Theatre. Katya was sure Gaidar would be there. She was right. "Ludmila, look," she said, pointing. "He's the plump one with the balding head in the third row from the front."

Within seconds, she had taken out a notebook and pen from her handbag so I could write him a note introducing myself and telling him about Star's proposed venture. She then asked a young security guard to pass it to Gaidar—which he did, pointing in our direction as Gaidar opened the note. Gaidar looked up, and we both waved. He smiled.

"Success!" declared Katya.

She rang me that evening, very excited. "Golovnin just called to tell me Gaidar will meet the two of us, and Avlov, at ten tomorrow morning. Congratulations!"

I was elated!

The headquarters of the Russian government was in Staraya Ploshchad ("Old Square"), a historic building previously occupied by the Central Committee of the Communist Party of the Soviet Union. It was a large gray-and-cream structure topped by the Russian flag. In the Communist days, it had been impossible for a foreigner to enter this building, but when Katya and I arrived, we simply informed security that we had an appointment with Gaidar. The security man handed our passes to us, and we caught the lift to the third floor—unescorted—and wandered around "the corridors of power" until we found a large heavy door with "Gaidar" written on it.

Golovnin opened the door when we knocked. He greeted us warmly and asked us to take a seat and wait. Gaidar, he hoped, would be able to see us shortly.

But it wasn't to be. After three hours, Golovnin reappeared to explain that there was a crisis in parliament. Yeltsin had ordered Gaidar to come to the White House immediately. Come back at 9 a.m. in two days, Golovnin told us.

Two days later, Avlov and I went back, and this time, when we arrived in Gaidar's reception area, tea was made for us by his secretary, Looba. She was a plump middle-aged lady with bleached-blond hair and too much makeup, wearing a tight, pink, flowery dress with a knitted shawl draped around her wide shoulders. Thick brown stockings and flat black shoes completed her ensemble. It was a style typical of most middle-aged Russian women, who seemed to gain weight almost overnight once they turned forty.

Finally, at 3 p.m., Golovnin led us into Gaidar's office and introduced us to Russia's most talked-about economist. Gaidar was short and round with fat little hands, a round, puffy face, and narrow eyes that darted from side to side; his thinning black hair was slicked to one side. He wore a navy suit with a white shirt and spotted navy tie. "How can I help you?" he asked when we were all seated.

Avlov launched into a description of how he had transformed Bodaibo into a great gold mining town, spending every cent he'd received from Gosplan (the central government funding body) on construction of hospitals, schools, shops, and railway stations. Now, he went on, he wanted to transform Lenzoloto into a private company and use a foreign partner, Star Technology Ltd., to finance his projects. He then mentioned Sukhoi Log and our proposed joint venture and handed the ordinance we'd drafted to Gaidar.

But it was clear that Gaidar was impatient for Avlov to stop talking. Gaidar stood for capitalism. He wanted the old Soviet ways to be replaced with modern Western practices. What he actually wanted to hear was how we intended to sell the hospitals, schools, shops, railways, and all the rest of it—leaving Lenzoloto to do nothing else but mine gold and make a profit, which was exactly what Ian wanted.

"Tell me about Star," he said, turning to me.

"Star is an Australian consortium of very wealthy international investors who have been involved in mining for over twenty years," I replied. "We want to invest in Russia, and we've committed one hundred fifty million American dollars to Lenzoloto to develop Sukhoi Log. I believe it's the largest foreign investment to date."

"That it is," Gaidar agreed, rubbing his double chin with his fat little fingers. "I am familiar with your project, and I support it," he added. "I'll instruct the appropriate government people to work through the ordinance draft and report back to me."

He took a pen and scribbled the names of four ministers at the top of the draft. Then he thought for a moment: "Oh, I should include Rudakov, head of GlavGold, or he'll be offended," and in a chicken scrawl, he scribbled "Rudakov" at the bottom of the page. Gaidar didn't see my expression of absolute dread. It was a great pity that Rudakov was one of the five men we now had to lobby. He'd never forgiven Star for approaching Yeltsin at a time when GlavGold still controlled all the gold in the USSR. The best we could hope for was four out of five signatures.

Once Ian heard how well the meeting had gone, he decided it was now time to set up a proper office with a laser printer, a good computer, and office stationery—which would mean going to Finland to shop, since none of these things were available in Russia. Ian told me to put the purchases on my American Express credit card and said he'd reimburse me the following month.

Greg and I dutifully caught the train to Helsinki, the Finnish capital. We would spend Christmas there. We woke up in the morning with splitting headaches to find that both our wallets were missing, even though we had slept with them under our pillows and had locked the cabin door. Apparently, this was a regular occurrence on Russian trains. The conductor was usually in on it. Knock-out gas would be pumped into the cabin of unsuspecting foreigners. The conductor would then open the simple lock on the sliding door with his key, and the thieves would help themselves to whatever they wanted and then pay the conductor off. I was horrified that we had been drugged and robbed—especially considering I had fallen asleep on my bunk bed stark naked!

We arrived in Helsinki with no money and no credit cards. It was minus ten degrees and snowing heavily. Luckily the American Express office was a ten-minute walk from the station. We were instantly issued a replacement credit card and made our way to our hotel, still feeling groggy but very relieved.

We spent Christmas Eve shopping for office equipment, although my thoughts constantly returned to Ian.

On Christmas Day, Gorbachev officially resigned as the Russian Communist leader.

I should have been on top of the world. Instead, just before Christmas dinner, which we were having at the hotel, I went for a walk by myself, leaving Greg reading a book in front of the fireplace in the hotel lobby. All day I'd been feeling moody and restless. Lately, my sense of loneliness and discontent had been growing.

It started to snow again, and since no one else was around and the city felt like a morgue, I headed back to the hotel. I ran up to our room and rang my friend Fran in Australia to tell her that I'd fallen in love.

Fran had already worked this out for herself some time ago. She asked what I was going to do.

"Absolutely nothing," I replied. "Ian is a married man. He would never try anything."

On Boxing Day, Greg and I returned to Moscow. Volodya, our driver, was waiting on the railway platform when we arrived. He helped us carry everything to the car park.

"Guess what?" he said, pointing to a brand-new navy Volvo.

"Is that our new car?" I asked, surprised.

"Yes, Ian bought it for Star just before Christmas."

The new car on top of the new office equipment meant, to me, that Ian was really serious about Russia. This put me in a buoyant mood for New Year's Eve, which we celebrated with a group of friends from the Australian embassy in the brilliantly illuminated, famous Red Square. We gathered in front of the Kremlin, Yeltsin's new residence, surrounded by a massive redbrick fortress. To our left stood the glittering St. Basil's Cathedral, with its brightly painted, onion-shaped white, red, green, blue, and gold domes. Thousands of people had amassed there in the snow. When the huge clock on the main Kremlin tower struck midnight, fireworks exploded above us. Everyone cheered and threw confetti and paper streamers. Strangers kissed strangers. Music filled the square from a purpose-built stage with performers, and everyone danced, still hugging each other and jumping for joy! The champagne flowed on and on.

Around 1 a.m., with the temperature now twenty degrees below zero, ABC's Moscow correspondent, John Lombard, and his wife, Jean, invited all the expats back to their apartment, where we continued to party until the early hours of the morning. Like everyone else, I was full of optimism for Russia's future.

CHAPTER TWELVE

Ordinance #693-p

On January 2, 1992, Gaidar and his newly appointed team of young reformers went to work. Many of them, including a certain redhead called Anatoly Chubais, were his old university mates and best friends. They continued to implement Yeltsin's decree on the liberalization of prices, otherwise known as "shock therapy," freeing up prices on more and more goods that had been controlled by the state for seventy years.

I asked Katya what she thought.

"I've had long talks with Timor, Gaidar's dad," she replied. "Russia is bankrupt, as we know. Gaidar believes the only remedy is to replace Communism ruthlessly and rapidly with capitalism. But Communism is like a cancer, and even Gaidar and his team are going to find it extremely difficult to eradicate this cancer completely. His dad doubts his son realizes this."

"Is Gaidar as smart as they say?"

"He's a genius, the smartest economist in the country. That's why Yeltsin picked him."

"Well, I hope it works," I said doubtfully.

Ian and Avlov both arrived back in Moscow on January 10. Katya had made an appointment for us with Grigoriev, who was the most important of the five names Gaidar had scrawled on our draft—he was the *vedushi*, or "main one," in charge of our ordinance.

He turned out to be quite a character, with flaming-red hair and a large, elongated nose, coupled with a profound sense of humor and a very sharp mind.

"Well, Gaidar for some reason has dumped all gold on my head, and it's already given me a headache. Please sit down and tell me about Lenzoloto and your Star," he said.

Grigoriev liked what he heard and told us that he would help redraft the ordinance for Gaidar, which he did. We then circulated the document among the other four people on Gaidar's list. We decided to meet them in person—except for Rudakov. Katya successfully arranged all the meetings.

Two of them, the ministers of finance and foreign economic relations, were old schoolmates of Gaidar; they supported our project wholeheartedly. This left us with the head of Komdragmet, Bychkov, who was regarded as a shrewd crook. It was well known that his daughter walked around Moscow dripping in diamonds because her dad handled all of Russia's international diamond contracts, including with the diamond giant De Beers.

Our meeting with Bychkov was a disaster. He said rudely that he didn't support Star as it was a "nothing" company without assets. Ian tried to explain that Star had been formed by the world's leading experts and banks specifically to do work in Russia, which was why it wasn't well known.

"It sounds like a good idea, but I must end our meeting," replied Bychkov. "I'm due at the White House. Maybe we can meet again, later. Thank you for coming."

He got up and walked out of the room.

In the end, our ordinance wasn't ready to submit to Gaidar until February. All five signatures on it had comments. Three were positive and two negative. Luckily the positive ones carried much greater political clout than the negative ones from Rudakov and Bychkov.

I was hopeful that Gaidar would sign it by mid-February. But when Katya checked on its progress, she was told that the ordinance had disappeared into thin air; neither Golovnin nor Gaidar himself could find it! She had a tantrum and only calmed down after Golovnin promised her that he would drop everything to search for it.

On February 7, I received a phone call from a man called Borisov from the Department of Foreign Economic Relations in the president's administration. My heart sank when he told me that he had the ordinance.

"I won't release it to Gaidar," he said. "It won't be signed until you submit the following documents to me."

He needed a description of the company's international activities, plus a reference from the consortium's bank or financial institution stating that the Star consortium was in good standing and creditworthy for the sum of US$150 million.

"My dear, I strongly advise you to get these documents to me in the next few days," added Borisov. "I want you to bring them to me personally—then everything will go your way. Otherwise, the project will go to international tender."

Katya, mystified about how Borisov could simply hijack the document and make these demands, did some investigating and connected him to Star's bitter opponent Rudakov, who was, she claimed, a KGB general.

Katya then told me that she'd "somehow" found the transcript of a telephone conversation between the two men. I didn't press her for details. As far as I was concerned, Katya operated in mysterious ways. But she always got results.

The transcript, which I have translated below, was illuminating:

> BORISOV: I'm very suspicious of the Star Consortium. They claim they are a group of wealthy Hong Kong and Australian investors formed to conduct business in Russia, and claim they are willing to invest US$150 million into the Sukhoi Log mine. That's incredible. It's the largest investment into Russia to date. I'm afraid they may be con men, just out to make a killing on their stock exchange. Their shares will soar once the ordinance is signed. They are probably in cahoots with Gaidar and his damned "reformers."
>
> RUDAKOV: Yes, you may be right. I saw the document and wrote a negative response. I strongly feel there should be a tender for the right to mine Sukhoi Log. It's a twenty-one-billion-dollar project. It's Russia's pearl. Why should some small company of Gaidar's personal choice get Sukhoi Log? I will fight for a tender.
>
> BORISOV: Could you please carry out a full investigation of Star in Australia?
>
> RUDAKOV: No problem.

I was terrified of a tender, as Star would have no chance of winning. Tenders in Russia were covert vehicles for bribes; the company who was willing to pay the most money in entry fees won. The Lenzoloto JSC tender would attract every international gold mining company, and the entry fee would be tens of millions of dollars. Officials could then skim off the money. Both Borisov and Rudakov would almost certainly be on the Sukhoi Log tender committee—as would Bychkov and Yatskevich.

I faxed Ian, asking for a bank reference for the US$150 million. Obviously, the money would be invested over some years and would only be raised after the completion of a full feasibility study on Sukhoi Log, but the Russians wanted proof that Star had access to this kind of money, I said.

Katya and I decided to take Yeltsin's closest friend and minister for mass media Poltoranin to dinner again and quiz him over the Borisov situation. He wasn't at all surprised when we told him the story of the misplaced ordinance.

"There is Gaidar's administration—and the old administration of the president," he said. "The latter has no power and is gradually being wound down. To justify their existence, they're insisting on processing all presidential documents before Gaidar's staff does. I now take my documents personally to Gaidar and Yeltsin for signing, and I advise you to do the same."

He revealed that he'd already spoken to Gaidar, who had no problems with our joint venture and would sign the ordinance as soon as it was back on his desk.

"What about the two-billion-dollar line of credit for Yeltsin that Ian promised to arrange? Yeltsin would like to know this," Poltoranin added.

"Mr. Poltoranin, Ian is very hopeful," I replied. "Ian has become Russia's advocate in the West. He thinks these large funds for Yeltsin may come through soon."

"Tell Ian the timing is perfect," said Poltoranin dryly. "Yeltsin says that if the West does not provide more financial aid soon, his reforms, his government, and his democracy could perish."

By February 8, amazingly, our ordinance had been pulled from Borisov's grasp and returned safely to Golovnin. Borisov himself was suddenly posted to Mongolia for three years. I had to laugh—Mongolia of all places.

Now all I had to do was get the bank reference from Ian and take it straight to Gaidar.

A few days later, Ian asked me to get Lenzoloto's profit estimate for the next ten years. I sent him Avlov's table with all the forecasts from 1992 to 2002. The first stage of the Sukhoi Log mine would take four years to build. Production would start at ten tons of gold per year in 1996 and increase to sixty tons by 2002, its full capacity. The project was highly profitable; the net distributable Star profit by 2002 would be US$66.3 million per year!

But obstacles remained. We couldn't export the gold we produced. It had to be sold to the Russian government, who would only pay 508 rubles per gram, which was half the going world price, even though Yeltsin had promised just below world prices to gold miners.

Tax was a big problem too. Companies were required to pay so many taxes that nobody paid them at all, and thus the government was losing billions of dollars per year.

Many people had urged Gaidar to reduce taxes to encourage private industry. But he was more concerned with destroying the old Communist machine in one hit so that it could never resurrect itself. It was a suicide mission politically speaking, and Gaidar knew it. But his orders from Yeltsin were clear.

By February 18, 1992, it was obvious that Ian couldn't come up with a bank guarantee for US$150 million. None of his companies had this kind of money. He had an extraordinary ability to attract extremely wealthy investors to his projects, but of course most Russians found this way of operating hard to understand.

Ian was, however, talking with two reputable old British banks, Hambros and National Westminster (NatWest) in London, as well as Turnbull & Partners in Australia. Turnbull & Partners was a private investment house and a member of the elite "grandfathered" list of businesses in Australia. These grandfathered companies did not have to submit annual audited financial accounts, including tax contributions, to the Australian Securities and Investment Commission (ASIC), the tax-evasion watchdog.

All three banks, Ian said, were mesmerized by the allure of Sukhoi Log's unheard-of riches, even though the gold deposit was in the middle of Siberia.

Back in Russia, Gaidar was being pressured to reevaluate how much Star should pay for 31 percent of Lenzoloto JSC. The total cost of constructing the first stage of the Sukhoi Log mine and its auxiliary utilities was put at R$16 billion, equaling US$150 million, hence the original price. But some government officials voiced the opinion that the 31 percent share of Sukhoi Log should be auctioned off to determine its real value, which could be as high as US$300 million; while others doubted Star even had the money. Katya and Golovnin heard the whispers along the corridors and started to panic, as did I. But this project was my ticket to total independence and a great career, and I believed that no obstacle was impossible to overcome. I also truly believed that Star was good for Russia and that developing Sukhoi Log would propel Lenzoloto to become the largest gold mining company in the world.

On February 20, I met with Australian Ambassador Cavan Hogue, a friendly, tall man with large ears, a prominent nose, rosy cheeks, and a nice smile. I asked him for a letter of support, and he readily obliged, so I took a copy of the letter straight to Gaidar's office along with a performance letter signed by Ian, guaranteeing that Star would pay the US$150 million.

To this day, it amazes me how easy it was to simply wander the halls of Russian government, mingling with the ministers of the day. If I'd been a spy, I could have stolen any secret documents. On numerous occasions, I was left completely alone in Gaidar's office. I could have picked up a *vertushka* (the red direct phone to any minister or the Kremlin) and even spoken to Yeltsin.

Golovnin greeted me there with open arms. I handed him the two letters. He opened them and read them in front of me. "That's very impressive, Ludmila. I will hand these to Gaidar immediately," he said.

Four days later, Golovnin said that our ordinance was with Chubais, the new head of the Government Committee for Property (GKI)—in other words, the minister for privatization, who had to approve and sign the document as well.

Chubais was handsome and fiery, with a very sharp mind and a passionate desire to transform Russia into a great democracy. He was close to Yeltsin and had a crush on Tanya, Yeltsin's daughter. Later, he would be known as the man who sold Russia to the oligarchs.

The next day, Chubais's aide called to say that Chubais had signed the ordinance after making a few minor amendments. It was about to be delivered to Grigoriev, the man in charge of our ordinance, for final processing.

On March 6, Grigoriev stood outside Gaidar's office at 10 a.m. to report on our ordinance. I turned up too.

"Ludmila, please go away."

"What are you going to say to Gaidar?" I asked anxiously.

"Don't worry," replied Grigoriev, and he gave me a thumbs-up.

Gaidar poked his piglike face from behind his door and waved Grigoriev in.

Katya somehow knew only an hour after their meeting that everything had gone well. Grigoriev had given Gaidar a positive report on the Star/Lenzoloto project. I was so happy that I sent Grigoriev a bottle of fine cognac and a pack of cigars.

On March 9, Poltoranin asked Katya about the possibility of Ian returning to Moscow and meeting with Yeltsin again. Obviously, Yeltsin still thought Ian was good for the line of credit. I was really worried about this by now, as it was never going to happen. Ian was well practiced at manipulating people, but he was playing games with the president of Russia.

Katya and I met with Poltoranin that night. He said our ordinance was now with Yeltsin's lawyer, Orehov—the final step. Katya and I met Orehov, who greeted us a little coldly and quickly passed us on to his assistant, a lawyer named Azarova. She was tall with a good figure and always wore her brown hair pulled up into a bun and dressed conservatively.

After days of working on the amended ordinance with Azarova, and more frustration, we finally had a draft we were happy with. However, by midafternoon on March 26, we had fresh drama on our hands. Rudakov, the head of GlavGold, had ordered a KGB check on Star a few weeks earlier. Golovnin called to warn us that the check had come back negative. The Russian Embassy in Australia had found a tiny computer company under the name of Star Systems Ltd., owned by a husband-and-wife team. The company sold computers and had nothing to do with mining. Its phones had been disconnected, suggesting it had gone bankrupt.

In their report, the Russian embassy offered to find a real gold mining partner. The report had been forwarded to Gaidar, who was consequently in a panic.

I immediately went to see Cavan Hogue again, who instructed the Australian trade commissioner, Gerald Seeber, to write to Gaidar. Gerald wrote that Star was "a reputable Australian consortium, registered in the British Virgin Islands and consists of Australian and Hong Kong mining specialists and international finance companies. The president of the company is Mr. Ian MacNee." His letter emphasized that the company was not affiliated in any way with the one owned by the husband-and-wife team.

At 5 p.m. the same day, I had an appointment with Gaidar and handed him the letter. He skimmed it with his little eyes and smiled.

"Okay," he said. "This will fix it."

All bets were back on.

On April 3, Ian, Avlov, and I met the governor of Irkutsk, Yury Nozhikov, at the luxurious Radisson Hotel on the Moscow

River. Nozhikov, who was close to Yeltsin, was half Chinese and half Russian and was all smiles as we signed a protocol of intent confirming Irkutsk's 10 percent shareholding in Lenzoloto JSC. It was vital to include the local government as one of the founders to ensure their support.

Even so, it was said he was someone who wouldn't hesitate to stab you in the back. Accordingly, his nickname was "Nozh," an abbreviation of Nozhikov meaning "knife" in Russian.

A meeting of all ministers, chaired by Gaidar, then took place on April 4 to approve the final Lenzoloto ordinance. I waited all night for a confirming phone call. But it never came.

Katya called me early next morning. "I'm afraid I have grave news. The ministers rejected the ordinance and decided to tender your thirty-one percent of Sukhoi Log. Golovnin would like us to come to his dacha in the countryside tomorrow, Saturday, for *shashlik* [skewered, grilled cubes of juicy meat] to discuss the situation," she said.

I had to break the news to Ian. He was in Aspen. I braced myself when he picked up the phone. "Ian, I have very bad news. They decided to tender our thirty-one percent of Sukhoi Log."

There was a long silence.

"Can anything be done to save the deal?" he eventually asked.

"Maybe. Golovnin has invited Katya and me to his dacha tomorrow in the forest, for a private meeting. Business in Russia is often settled at dachas, as they are hard to bug," I added.

"Fine," said Ian. "I want to be at that meeting. I'll fly to Moscow immediately—on the Concorde if need be."

Ian flew into Moscow on the supersonic Concorde. We drove straight to Golovnin's dacha with Katya, which took two hours. The dacha was a charming white timber dwelling with a chimney, set among birch trees. It was surrounded by an array of vibrant spring forest wildflowers in all shades of red, yellow, orange, and violet. Golovnin and his wife, Masha, were grilling lamb shashliks over an open fire when we arrived at noon exactly. We all sat around a wooden picnic table, bathed in warm sunlight, and sipped on cold white wine while munching on the smoke-flavored lamb, as if we didn't have a care in the world. Then Golovnin explained what was happening. The problem, he said, was that powerful forces were now involved.

"Sukhoi Log is Russia's greatest gold deposit, and too many people want a slice of it. Most people in the government support the Lenzoloto/Star deal. We like the fact Star is private and small. We just needed to make sure you had the money."

"You know we have," interrupted Ian.

"Yes, we're now convinced. Otherwise, I wouldn't be talking to you here."

"So, what can be done?" asked Ian bluntly. Golovnin suggested that the two of them go for a walk. Katya would have to translate, he added.

I had to stay put and engage in small talk with Masha, which wasn't my forte at the best of times. The men returned thirty minutes later, but I was forced to wait until we'd left the dacha and were on our way back to Moscow before I could ask Ian straight out, "How much do they want?"

"Not in the car!" Katya screamed.

So I had to wait until we reached my apartment.

Ian and I went for a stroll down the street. "So?" I demanded again.

"They want us to contribute one million US into a fund set up by Chubais. He called it the 'protection of private property' fund. Gaidar will then sign the ordinance—and they'll guarantee that the deal goes through."

"How are we going to pay the money?"

"I can't discuss that, not even with you," replied Ian.

That same evening, he flew to Zurich. Much later Ian told me that he deposited the money into a secret Swiss bank account.

A frustrating waiting game ensued. On April 8, Katya and I sat outside Gaidar's office all day. Golovnin came out and told us to come back in the morning.

In the end, nothing happened until 3 p.m. the next day, when Golovnin ran out to us, shouting that Gaidar had signed after a small amendment, and that he was taking the Lenzoloto ordinance down to be typed up on government letterhead. "Then we will allocate a special number, and that's it!"

Unbeknown to us, Gaidar's "small amendment" would create major problems for us. Gaidar had deleted Star from the ordinance. He had changed "grant Lenzoloto and Star the right to form a joint stock company" to "grant Lenzoloto the right to attract an investor of its own choice," obviously being Star. He did this so no one could accuse him of being bribed by Star.

Ian arrived at 5 p.m. with a dozen bottles of Mumm champagne and lots of food, which we set out on Gaidar's table in his office. At 7 p.m., Golovnin ceremoniously entered the room with the official ordinance in his outstretched arms and handed it to Ian.

"Remember the number, Ian: 693-p. It's yours!"

A famous Australian journalist, Robert Haupt (the 1991 Australian Journalist of the Year for outstanding coverage of Soviet affairs), was also there. He interviewed Ian and took many photos before joining our celebrations. We toasted with champagne and partied until 9 p.m., when we were all unceremoniously thrown out of the building by security.

CHAPTER THIRTEEN

The Birth of Lenzoloto JSC

Less than a week later, Gaidar was forced to resign. This was a deliberate move to make it seem like he had been punished for introducing economic reforms that had caused ordinary Russians to suffer. But he and Yeltsin secretly agreed that Gaidar would make a political comeback soon.

We began work on implementing Gaidar's ordinance. The main task was to work out the initial charter-capital contribution of the Russian side in rubles. Star's had been preset at US$150 million in cash. The big problem was how to evaluate Lenzoloto's assets, as the gold deposits belonged to the Russian government; only the rights to mine them belonged to Lenzoloto. Apart from these rights, Lenzoloto owned mining equipment, housing, factories, buildings, hotels, etc.—most of which were old, run-down, and not worth much. Finally, it was agreed that Lenzoloto's assets amounted to RUB ₽2,016 million, so the Russian side's contribution to acquire 69 percent of Lenzoloto JSC would be 1,391 million, and Star's would be 625 million for its 31 percent. Of course, as Star's commitment was US$150 million in cash, we had to apply an artificial exchange rate in the founders' agreement.

A British journalist from London's *Financial Times*, Leyla Boulton, started trying to contact Ian. We would hear more from her soon enough.

On April 18, I had lunch at a trendy café in the Radisson Hotel with John Helmer, an Australian-born freelance journalist living in Moscow with a Russian wife, also a journalist. John was very tall and looked like a professor, with longish gray hair, a white beard and moustache, and round glasses. His news stories, a series titled "Dances with Bears," were published in the *Sydney Morning Herald*, a prominent Australian newspaper. He was a fascinating man, with a wealth of information on the Russian government. Katya would later make the startling claim that he was a CIA/KGB double agent.

John and I started to ring each other regularly to exchange information. He published positive articles on Star, and we eventually put him on the payroll.

Things were progressing well, and on April 28, the Regional Committee for Geology in Irkutsk issued the Lenzoloto Association with 106 new mining licenses, including one for Sukhoi Log, as per the new law on natural resources, and we rejoiced!

Enter Central Mining NL, a shell company listed on the Australian Stock Exchange in January 1986 and 80 percent owned by Ian through a string of offshore companies. It had opened at thirty-six cents on promises of gold and uranium discoveries but had plummeted to two cents in 1990.

Central Mining's directors were Ian; his best friend, Graeme Ellis; and a KPMG corporate adviser called Bill O'Neill, who was also Ian's personal financial adviser. The proposal was that Central Mining would acquire all the issued capital of Star Technology from its owners—Ian, Greg, and me—and then change its name to Star Mining NL to start raising capital for the Sukhoi Log project.

On May 1, Central Mining NL made an announcement to the market: Star would have 31 percent interest in the Sukhoi Log project with the remaining 69 percent shared by the local Irkutsk government and Lenzoloto management and workers. Its shares immediately jumped from two cents to six cents to twenty-eight cents and finally to thirty-two cents over the next few days, while its market capitalization increased sixteen times to A$16 million.

Three days later, a group of eight Star people, including mining experts, lawyers, and Ian's son Chris, who had moved from Brazil to Russia to work with Star, flew to Bodaibo to draft the Lenzoloto JSC's charter and founding documents. Chris was a couple of years older than me. He was a nice guy but not as sharp as his dad, though he had a great sense of humor.

In Bodaibo, we stayed in our usual cabin, which had four bedrooms, a small kitchen, a lounge room with a raging fireplace, and a Russian sauna.

Each morning we were picked up by Avlov's driver and taken to the main Lenzoloto office block, where we spent the entire day with Avlov and Kochetkov, his deputy, negotiating, drafting, and redrafting the founding documents of the Lenzoloto JSC in accordance with our ordinance. At night, we would go to Tanya's, the only public restaurant in Bodaibo, to eat, drink, and dance.

Tanya was a voluptuous middle-aged woman who'd obviously been a beauty in her younger days and was known around town as "the Madam." She had long legs, enormous breasts, and her long blond hair was always pinned in a high bun atop her head.

She had told me on previous visits about her great love affair with the former general director of Lenzoloto, who'd been found one day slumped half dead in his chair with a bloodied rifle lying on the floor next to him. There was also a suicide note carrying the simple message "I can't go on." He died on the way to hospital. But people were suspicious about what had happened since it's almost impossible to fire a long rifle through your own heart. It turned out that the dead man had been implicated in a scandal involving two tons of gold that had gone missing. After the "suicide," Avlov took over Lenzoloto. Tanya accused him of masterminding her lover's murder. It was a startling allegation.

Sometimes, when the rest of us staggered back from the restaurant to our cabin and hit the banya/sauna, Tanya and her two very attractive waiters would join us. They would bring vodka and cold appetizers from the restaurant, and we would spend all night drinking, snacking, and smoking in between the sauna sessions. In the banya, we threw water on the piping-hot coals and hit each other's bare flesh with a broom made of birch twigs before cooling off in an icy pool. The birch leaves invigorated our skin and got the blood pumping—the true essence of the banya experience!

I enjoyed Tanya's company and her never-ending stories about the locals immensely, although I was always careful about what I said to her, as I suspected Avlov had bugged our cabin.

Sure enough, one morning Avlov asked for a private meeting with me.

"I have heard you are very friendly with Tanya," he said. "This must stop. She is the town whore. I forbid you to go to her restaurant again. You can dine in the Lenzoloto cafeteria from now on. Do not invite her or her studs back to your cottage ever again."

"If you wish," I replied.

"Ludmila, we are building a great empire together. We need to work hard and behave correctly," Avlov went on. "There will be plenty of time for celebration later. Oh, and I'm building you a beautiful house by the Lena River. I will show you later. I am sure one day you will live in Bodaibo permanently."

That night, we ate at the Lenzoloto cafeteria. We were served tough, overcooked beefsteak, bland and soggy potatoes, and sweet apple juice. There was no alcohol. It was a dreadful meal. On our way home, we passed Tanya's, which was raging as usual. "Oh, fuck Avlov," said Chris. "Let's go in for a nightcap." Everybody agreed—so in we went.

The following evening, Ian developed a fever. Overnight his temperature rose to forty degrees Celsius. I called Avlov and told him to send a doctor. It turned out Ian had pneumonia, which could be fatal in Siberia. As the doctor injected an antibiotic into Ian's backside, I prayed the needle was sterile.

Ian got worse. His temperature crept up to forty-two degrees. The situation was now life-threatening. Since the antibiotics weren't working, we called in the American medical emergency plane from Moscow. I felt enormous relief when I learned the plane was on its way to Bodaibo with a handsome Canadian doctor, Miles, whom I'd met previously.

That night, the local caretaker dragged Ian into the sauna and gave him a massage. By morning, the fever had broken. The emergency plane arrived hours later. Miles examined Ian, confirmed he had severe pneumonia, and injected him with a massive dose of antibiotics. Since Ian was too sick to travel, Miles and the plane had to stay in Bodaibo overnight; the plan was to fly Ian back to Moscow first thing in the morning.

It was decided that the new arrivals should be taken to Tanya's for dinner. Tanya was ecstatic to have us back. She prepared a feast of piroshki (deep-fried meat pies), pelmeni (meat dumplings served with sour cream), *salo* (cured slabs of pork belly), smoked sausage, picked cucumbers, *holodets* (pork terrine), and lastly, a Russian potato salad (made with potatoes, peas, carrots, bologna, hard-boiled eggs, pickles, and a creamy dill mayonnaise dressing). Five-star quality Russian cuisine!

We toasted to Ian's health with much Armenian cognac and Russian vodka. It is Russian tradition, usually at weddings, to kiss the person at the table on your left and right after sculling vodka "to remove the bitterness of the vodka with the sweetness of a kiss," and Tanya enforced this tradition upon us that very night. I couldn't believe my luck, as I was sitting next to Miles!

Over dinner, my secretary, Masha, told me she'd noticed that Ian hated that he was ill while the rest of us continued to work and party. He kept asking after me, she added. "You're off with Avlov all day and with Tanya's boys all night. I think you should spend some time with Ian instead," she suggested.

It's funny the way things can develop between two people. Up to now, I'd tried to hide from myself that I'd fallen in love with Ian because he was married; but in Bodaibo, I dared to wonder if Ian was falling in love with me. The fact that he was nearly twice my age didn't matter at all, but the fact that he was married *did*. He wasn't in a loveless marriage like I was. I wondered whether he would ever leave his wife—probably not. I also doubted that Ian would ever make a move, as he seemed too much of a prude.

The next morning, Ian felt much better. His temperature was almost normal. Against advice, he refused to go back to Moscow, so Miles departed on the plane, leaving plenty of antibiotics for the Russian doctor to continue the injections.

On May 7, after numerous amendments, Avlov and his 9,600 workers formally approved the founding documents of the Lenzoloto JSC with Star as the foreign partner.

Everything was starting to fall into place when Leyla Boulton, the journalist from the *Financial Times*, sprang to print with an article on Star and the Lenzoloto JSC.

> Russia's largest gold deposit goes to Australia's smallest mining company
>
> Star Mining is a small Australian company, delisted from the Australian Stock Exchange in 1987, 1988, and 1991 for not submitting its tax return. It had a tiny capitalisation of A$1,000,000; each Star share worth two cents. Acting Prime

Minister, Gaidar, on 9th April 1992 approved the joint venture between Star and Lenzoloto, to mine 106 gold deposits, including the world's largest known hard rock deposit called Sukhoi Log. The burning questions being asked by many Russian Government officials and Rudakov, head of GlavGold, is why Sukhoi Log did not go to international tender? Why was it given to such a small, unknown company like Star? How could Star possibly fund the development of the Sukhoi Log billion-dollar project? Apparently, Star is to get a 31 percent stake in Lenzoloto for US$150 million. But, according to Bychkov, Head of the Committee for Precious Metals of the Russian Federation, the gold reserves of Lenzoloto are worth US$21 billion. This means after ten years of production, Lenzoloto JSC could be worth over 20 billion dollars. Bychkov said, "I totally oppose Star. Sukhoi Log is Russia's pearl. A major mining company like Rio Tinto Zinc (RTZ) should be involved. A tender process should decide how much money the 31 percent stake is really worth. I am on my way to Irkutsk to urgently meet with Nozhikov. Also, Gaidar's Ordinance contravenes the new Antimonopoly Law and must be annulled."[3]

I was stunned. The bitch! RTZ had evidently decided they wanted Sukhoi Log—and then attacked. They'd also quite obviously spent time with Boulton, while Ian never bothered to call her back. For this to happen on the eve of signing the founding documents was devastating.

---

3   Leyla Boulton, "Russia's largest gold deposit goes to Australia's smallest mining company," *Financial Times*, May 7, 1992.

That afternoon, Avlov got a phone call from Nozhikov. RTZ certainly hadn't wasted any time. Its company representatives had hired a plane in Moscow and, with Bychkov and Boulton on board, were already in Irkutsk. They'd gone straight to Nozhikov and tried to convince him to drop Star.

RTZ brazenly offered US$300 million for a 51 percent stake in Sukhoi Log. It turned out that the company's representatives had been in Moscow all week, conspiring with Bychkov and, surprisingly, Grigoriev (former head of our ordinance) to oust Star.

The story with Bychkov was simple: It seemed probable to me that RTZ had paid him off with a lucrative job offer after his retirement from politics. It was difficult for large publicly listed companies to skim money off for cash bribes, but job offers were doable.

But what happened with Grigoriev was almost unbelievable. We'd spent days working with him in early 1992. He was totally sold on our joint venture. But after reading Leyla Boulton's article, he ran to Gaidar and told him he'd made a dreadful mistake. Later we found out that Grigoriev had thought that Star was short for Golden Star Resources, a large international company operating gold mines on the prolific Ashanti Gold Belt in Ghana, West Africa, as well as in South America. During our meetings, he had referred to Star as the "gold star" in Russian, but I thought that was a play on words. Apparently, he only realized his mistake after reading Boulton's article. This was reflective of the naivety and lack of business acumen of the new young Russian government reformers!

Luckily, Avlov stood defiant. He said he backed Star all the way. But Nozhikov was swayed by RTZ's propaganda. He ordered Avlov to let them land in Bodaibo the next day and meet with them to consider their proposals. "Don't worry," Avlov told me. "I'll protect you from the wolves. We must finish our founding documents and sign them tomorrow." He ordered his secretaries to start typing, and to type all night if necessary.

We all assembled in Avlov's office the next morning at nine. Avlov told us he was meeting with RTZ at noon. "My girls have been typing all night. I want the documents signed before I meet RTZ," he added.

Shortly before noon, five copies of the founding documents were laid out on the table. Avlov signed.

"Done," he said, with a huge smile at me. "While I talk to the wolves next door, you'd better sign. Tomorrow we'll have our first board meeting in the hall, which will be followed by a banquet to celebrate the inauguration of Lenzoloto JSC." Everyone signed—and then we waited.

CHAPTER FOURTEEN

Drug Money?

One and a half hours later, Avlov strode back in. "It's over. They're gone. I listened to the offer and rejected it."

It was great news, even if Varenikov, who'd invited me to Bodaibo before anyone else and had introduced me to Avlov, was now our mortal enemy. As head of his own artel, he'd long argued that the artels were much more productive than the Lenzoloto miners and hence were entitled to the licenses for the alluvials they worked. But all the alluvial and hard-rock deposits in Bodaibo now belonged to Lenzoloto JSC. So the artels, led by Varenikov, formed the Siberian Gold Association to fight against Avlov and Star and eventually joined with Nozhikov, who would play a double game till the end. His deputy, Suitkin, a short, fat man with beady eyes, would become Nozhikov's mouthpiece in the local parliament and local press.

June 3 was our last night in Bodaibo. We had a farewell dinner at Tanya's. Even Avlov and his deputy turned up for a brief time.

The next day, we flew out of Bodaibo at 6 a.m. for Irkutsk. I felt exhilarated. I had five copies of the founding documents with me to take back to Moscow for registration, and the only missing signature was Nozhikov's. My mission was to secure it, but Nozhikov wouldn't even return my calls. I waited for five hours—then caught my flight to Moscow. Nozhikov had clearly decided to distance himself from the Lenzoloto JSC.

Upon my return to Moscow, Katya once again had grave news to deliver. Shokhin, the newly appointed deputy prime minister for foreign economic relations, had held a secret meeting on Lenzoloto. The attendees included Gaidar and some KGB people.

"Everybody voted in favor to tender the shareholding in Lenzoloto JSC," she said. I felt sick.

"You mean not just Sukhoi Log but Star's whole thirty-one-percent share?"

"Yes. Rudakov was waving around the old telegram from the Russian embassy—the four-page report on the other Australian company called Star Systems."

"Oh, Katya, not that again!" I exclaimed. "They have the wrong company. Gaidar should know this by now!"

"Yes," she agreed. "But it swayed everybody. However, the decision is not yet official. Golovnin says Gaidar is hesitating."

"So, there's still time to overturn the decision?"

"Yes. Now I must tell you something else."

"Go on," I said grimly.

"During the meeting, Shokhin asked where Star was getting all this money from. He concluded it was probably drug money. It seems that our enemies convinced him that Star must be a front for someone else, as nobody has ever heard of Star. Shokhin then asked if Star was a front for a drug syndicate."

"It's a silly remark. I think we should just ignore it."

"No," said Katya sharply. "Golovnin thinks we should clear Star's name."

"What do we do?"

"We send Shokhin a telegram through special channels, stating that Star's money comes from reputable international investment houses that are willing to invest in Russia through Star. Then we demand an apology."

"Fine. Send the letter," I replied.

At this point, Katya gestured that we should go into the bathroom. There, she turned on the shower. And everything took a more sinister turn. For years afterward, I would think—wrongly—that we escaped repercussions from the solution Katya had come up with.

The shower muffling her words, she told me about "the shadows." These were the people who were going to choose and control the next Russian government, she claimed. The main shadow was "M," short for Michael. Katya knew him well. Michael's assistant was Andrei. There was also a woman called Dasha. Katya then astonished me further by alleging that it was Gaidar who suggested we meet Michael to get help.

"Ian must meet with them," she repeated. "Gaidar will break. He's made of jelly. We need protection."

"Katya, who are these people? Where do they operate from?" I asked.

"From the elite central hospital. It's where Yeltsin is treated. It's where I go for any treatment I need. Michael runs the hospital. When politicians are admitted there for any reason, deals are made."

The hospital Katya was talking about was on the outskirts of Moscow and known as "the little Kremlin." I'd heard about it. Everyone had. Everyone was also aware that it was not accessible to ordinary Russians. What Katya was saying was amazing.

"I presume this will cost money," I said pointedly.

"Of course, my dear. But not as much as you gave Gaidar."

I faxed Ian, who'd already left Moscow, to tell him there was still time to stop a tender and asked him to get something in writing from one of our banks. Then I told him about Katya's "shadows," which probably wasn't the wisest thing to put in a fax. Then again, I doubted that the "shadows" could operate without the KGB's knowledge.

Ian replied that the future of investment in Russia would depend on the West's perception of Russian credibility when it came to keeping its word, and on remaining corruption-free. He must have forgotten that we'd paid Gaidar US$1 million to sign the ordinance.

On June 10, Ian flew back to Moscow to meet the mysterious Michael. However, I wouldn't be meeting Michael, Katya told me. "This is for your own protection, as meeting him could endanger your life," she said, then added that I would be going with them to the central hospital all the same, since M's assistant, Andrei, had a few questions for me.

Ian was staying at the Radisson, only ten minutes from my apartment. I walked to the hotel, and then Katya and her driver picked us up.

From there, we drove directly to the hospital. It was hidden behind a tall electronic gate. Katya showed the security people some kind of permit, and the gate opened. We then followed a road to a large blue building. All the other buildings set among the beautiful gardens, lakes, and fountains were white.

So, this is where the Communist elite are taken care of, I thought, gazing around curiously. Brezhnev had spent most of his last days here while they pumped him full of painkillers and other drugs to keep him alive.

Dasha, the woman Katya had mentioned, greeted us at the entrance of the building. She was extremely thin, tall, and pale, with brown hair cropped short and no makeup.

"Welcome," she said, smiling. "Katya, you take Mr. MacNee straight to Michael. Ludmila, you come with me. We have much to do."

I followed her down a corridor to a very large office, where she left me. Five minutes later, M's assistant walked in. I gasped. Andrei was the sexiest man I'd ever met. He had jet-black hair cut short at the sides; the biggest, blackest eyes I'd ever seen; thick, soft lips; and freckles on his cheeks. He bore an uncanny resemblance to my long-lost love, Artyr, the wonderful boy I'd met at Moscow University in 1979 who had mysteriously disappeared.

Andrei took my hand and kissed it.

"I'm charmed to meet you, Ludmila."

"Yes" was all I managed to say in reply.

Andrei and I started talking. I told him how Gaidar had signed an ordinance approving the Lenzoloto JSC but was being pressured to take Sukhoi Log to tender.

"Did you pay Gaidar any money?" asked Andrei.

Katya had told me not to hold back information. So I said that Ian had put US$1 million into a Swiss bank account, which we were told was for Chubais's fund, although I was sure that Gaidar had dipped his fat little fingers into the honeypot for his share.

"Yes, that's the way it works," Andrei said with a nod before asking me for the names of the people who were holding up the registration. "I need as much information as you can give me."

I named Rudakov and Bychkov, adding that Bychkov was close to the large Anglo-Australian multinational mining company RTZ. "They're our main enemy. They tried to gazump our deal and turned Nozhikov against us."

"Well, I can't touch RTZ, but let's concentrate on Rudakov and Bychkov. I need photographs and addresses—where they work and where they live," said Andrei.

"Photographs?" I asked, growing uneasy.

"Yes, I'll need to go and talk to them."

"I don't have any, but I could try to get some," I said tentatively as I tried to work out where all this was going.

"Okay. If you can't, give me a detailed description of what they look like. For now, I'll take the founding documents and start the registration process at GKI by getting the documents signed. I must go," Andrei added. "See you soon." He took my hand again and kissed it. "Ludmila, it has been an absolute delight to meet you."

I returned to the reception area. Ian and Katya were still with Michael, and Dasha had disappeared. I had no idea who these people really were. All I knew was that Katya was in favor of their involvement and that they ran the country's best, most elite hospital, which housed some of the world's most brilliant doctors and surgeons and most advanced medical equipment.

An hour later, Ian and Katya appeared, and we went out to where our driver was waiting. We got into the car. Katya signaled me to keep quiet, so we drove back into Moscow in silence. Ian and I got out at the Radisson Hotel and went inside.

"What did you think of Michael?" I asked after he'd ordered a bottle of Dom Pérignon.

"Interesting. I think they can help us," he replied without going into details. "You know, Michael has this cane. It's always with him," he added.

"Do you think it's a gun? Or maybe a long sword!" I suggested.

"Who knows?"

Ian's son Chris joined us a few hours later, and the three of us had dinner together, followed by a nightcap.

Chris had spent his life following his father around the world and, at the age of thirty-three, was still working for him, although he was also a brilliant chef and talented at languages. He spoke Spanish and Portuguese and was rapidly learning Russian. He'd accepted his transfer from Rio to Moscow because, like all of us, he thought he was going to make a fortune from Star. His main job was to assist his dad when Ian stayed in Moscow.

At midnight, our driver, Volodya, drove me home. Most visiting foreigners had drivers in Moscow. The roads were terrible and hazardous in winter, and no one observed the road rules, as cops could be easily paid off with bribes. It was also becoming unsafe to simply hail any car in the street, which was the custom in Communist days. Even in taxis now, you could be unsafe.

An Australian journalist vividly described Russia as it was at this time in an article for the *Sydney Morning Herald* in 2000—many years after the collapse of Communism and on the eve of Putin's inauguration as president:

> Foreign visitors to Moscow are immediately aware of the corrupt lawlessness the moment they step into Russia at Sheremetyevo international airport and are confronted by a gauntlet of unscrupulous taxi touters.... This is the bottom-end reality of Russian corruption, the community-level version of the lawlessness which at its most spectacular level spawned the "oligarchs," the former apparatchiks of the Communist Party who "insider traded" their privileged positions to take control of Russia's wealthiest state-owned businesses when they were privatized and amass vast personal fortunes. Can Putin bring an end to this corruption?[4]

This was the environment in Russia when I started working there. Most foreign companies, especially publicly listed ones, simply weren't able to operate. How could they explain the millions of dollars in bribes or working with mafia groups to get results? Most of those companies left Russia and never returned.

---

4   Author unknown, article title unknown; *Sydney Morning Herald*, WORLD section, May 6, 2000.

Ian, though, with his mysterious source of money in Switzerland, could personally fund the bribes. It was worth it for him, because if Star shares increased to a dollar a share, he stood to make US$250 million. As for me, I was in the "whatever it takes" category. This was my ticket to a spectacular career in the country of my ancestors, and to great wealth and the freedom that came with it. I did not want to live my life any other way.

But I hadn't factored in dealing with "the shadows" if we wanted to succeed in Russia.

CHAPTER FIFTEEN

Among the Shadows

The day after our visit to the central hospital, Katya told me that a second meeting with Michael was already arranged for the following week. I would be seeing Andrei again, she said, adding that he'd described me as "a great beauty" to his boss. Despite my disquiet, I was thrilled to hear this. Part of me wanted Andrei so badly that it hurt.
This time when we arrived at the hospital, Ian went straight into M's office with Katya. Dasha asked me to wait in the foyer as Andrei was running late.

His navy Mercedes pulled up in front of the entrance an hour later. He rushed in, took my hand, and kissed it.

"Please forgive me, Ludmila, but I've been trying to get your documents registered. No one will take them. No one even wants to touch them. Let's go outside for a walk in the gardens."

I understood immediately. Even here, the walls had ears.

"There's only one solution to your problem," he went on, once we were standing on a little bridge crossing a creek in the gardens. "Certain government officials backed by their own mafia groups have blacklisted the project. Michael has asked Ian to bring in one hundred thousand US cash in a suitcase, as a goodwill gesture. Ian has agreed to this. But, Ludmila, does Ian realize that when the killing starts, Ian will be a target himself? It will be one for one."

I froze. I looked into Andrei's dark, pitiless eyes. At that moment, all I saw was a hit man with a blackened soul.

"Andrei, I don't know what Ian and Michael have discussed. But I'll tell Ian so he understands," I replied, adding, "I guess I could be in danger too."

"I will protect you, my darling. You have nothing to fear. Did you know it's my birthday today?"

Hit man or not, Andrei had still managed to disarm me. And he was undeniably the most desirable man I'd ever seen. I kissed him on the cheek.

"Happy birthday," I murmured.

I still had a question for him, though, and asked it tentatively. "When will you start carrying out the plan?"

"When Ian delivers the cash."

We returned to the main building. I desperately needed to talk to Ian. But Dasha told me that he and Katya had already left.

Andrei drove me back to my apartment in his Mercedes—thankfully, without further mention of what we'd discussed on the bridge. He said he would see me soon and drove off.

I got inside and poured myself a large glass of cold chardonnay. Ian had apparently embraced the idea of working with the shadows, as if this were a completely normal thing for him to do. It seemed clear to me that Katya had introduced us to a special arm of the Russian mafia working for the Russian government. What did this say about Katya, or Gaidar, who, according to Katya, had recommended we engage these people?

The following day, I met Ian at the Radisson Hotel and, in true Russian style, asked him to walk around the block with me.

"Ian, what did you agree to with Michael?"

"Oh, just that he would join up with Star and help," Ian answered vaguely.

He was often vague, and it really irritated me. I'm the sort of person who likes clarity and detail.

"Are you going to bring in the money?" I asked pointedly.

"Yes, if you think we need their help. I hear you are fond of Andrei. If you want to be with him, I'll continue the association and bring in the cash. Then you can work together."

"Don't be ridiculous," I said tersely. "Do you understand who these people are? Their plan is to get rid of our opponents, which could also put your life in jeopardy."

"Oh, I'm not worried about myself," replied Ian easily. "What do you think? Should we continue with them?"

"No. In fact, I think we should get our original founding documents back from Andrei."

"Well, all right, you do that. I'll see Michael and make sure it ends nicely, so no one loses face." I was so relieved that I didn't even question the casual way Ian had backtracked. I was more astounded by his naivety, a naivety combined with recklessness. Perhaps that was what made him so charismatic to both men and women. Even so, I couldn't help wondering whether it was a facade. Something did not add up, and at some level, I knew this. But at the time I told myself, *It's just my overactive imagination. Moscow is getting to me.*

I rang Katya and told her I wanted to get the original founding documents back from Andrei. "I'll take them to GKI myself," I said.

Katya rang back ten minutes later and said we were expected at the hospital at 10 a.m. the next day. Andrei would return the documents to me.

When Katya and I turned up the next day as agreed, there was no sign of Andrei. Dasha took both of us straight to an office.

A few minutes later, a man of about forty-five walked in. He had thinning black hair and wore a dark-blue striped Armani suit. I noticed immediately that he was carrying a polished wooden walking stick with a gold handle—the same one Ian had described—but did not have a limp. This was the mysterious Michael.

"So, Ludmila, how is our Ian?" he asked.

"He's fine," I answered. I felt like getting up and running as far away as possible.

"I just want to tell you that without our help, you will fail. There are forces in the government who will never allow Lenzoloto JSC to proceed."

"Why?"

"They have different agendas."

"We can't bribe everybody!" I exclaimed. "We had to make a choice, and we chose Yeltsin."

"My dear, now that Yeltsin is president, even I find it difficult to get to see him," replied Michael. "There are certain people in the government who will fight you all the way. You need a network of people to protect you. I am that network. Ian understood this, and he needs to give me the cash to distribute as I see fit. You will not even know when and how I do it. But you will see the results of my work. You won't encounter any more problems, as I will clear the path before you go down it. It's the only way."

"That's for you and Ian to discuss. I just want to get my founding documents back from Andrei," I responded.

"Don't worry about that. He doesn't need them anymore. Ludmila, apart from the cash, Ian needs to invest in a couple of Mercedes-Benz cars. Image is very important."

"Fine," I said. I just wanted to get out of there. Was this really the only way to do business in Yeltsin's Russia? To employ mafia to bribe or kill your enemies—and to ride around in a Mercedes and dress in designer clothes, looking like a mafia mole?

"I assure you it's the only way," Michael repeated, as if reading my thoughts.

Dasha walked in with coffee for everyone. The smell was delicious. I took my cup and sipped slowly.

"Ludmila, Andrei did a lot of investigating. We know who your enemies are," repeated Michael. "But to start, Ian must bring in the cash. I have told him this. Time is short."

Michael went on lecturing me until I was fed up. After two hours, there was still no sign of Andrei. I told Michael I couldn't wait any longer. He suggested I come back the following afternoon; he guaranteed that Andrei would have my documents.

"I thought I wasn't supposed to meet Michael for my own protection," I said disdainfully to Katya as soon as we were out of the hospital grounds.

"He obviously thought it necessary, as Ian is procrastinating with the money," she replied equably.

I saw Katya in a whole new light now, but I said nothing about her apparent mafia connections.

The following afternoon, she and I returned to the hospital, where Michael greeted us and said that Andrei should be there any minute.

"Coffee?" he asked.

I nodded, frustrated.

"So, did you get a chance to talk to Ian?"

"No, he left for Aspen yesterday, and it's not a conversation that one has over the phone," I said.

"When will he be back in Moscow?"

"Next week."

"Good. I'll start putting the people together for our network. Now, I have some good news and some bad. Which would you like to hear first?"

"The bad," I replied.

"A group called Goldman Sachs has been in Gaidar's ear. They've talked him into a tender for Sukhoi Log and have offered to oversee the tender process."

"Yes, I know. I also know that Gaidar listens to every word they say. What's the good news?"

Michael smiled. "Yeltsin has checked into my hospital," he said. "He will be here for a week, and I'll discuss Lenzoloto and Star with him personally."

"Really? That would be great," I said, and meant it.

"Yes. I sit by his bed when he's here, and we discuss many things."

"When will Andrei be here? I'm getting sick of waiting for him."

"Patience is a virtue, my dear."

"It's not one of my virtues, I'm afraid."

Michael smiled again. He said he had to go to another meeting but that Andrei had rung to say he was on his way.

One hour later, Andrei finally appeared with the documents in his hands. They were crumpled and dirty—but at least he had them.

"Here are your documents, Ludmila. I'm sorry I couldn't do anything with them. Michael has taken over your project. I need to leave urgently for St. Petersburg."

"Will I ever see you again?" I asked.

"Of course you will. Bye, my lovely." He leaned down, gently kissed me on the cheek, and disappeared out the door.

I looked at Katya. "I don't have a good feeling about any of this."

"Neither do I," she said worriedly. "Let's go."

I was at a total loss to know what to do. Katya and I ended up seeing Golovnin, Gaidar's chief aide, again. He suggested we meet with Petr Aven, the minister for foreign economic relations, who was close to Gaidar and could possibly help.

Naturally, Katya knew Aven. She called his secretary and organized a meeting for the following afternoon.

The Ministry of Foreign Economic Relations stood diagonal to my apartment and was within easy walking distance along the underground tunnel crossing Smolenskaya Square. This monumental building was another one of the "wedding cake" skyscrapers, like the Hotel Ukraina. The main building was tiered, had two massive wings, and was topped by a tall metal spire, its facade covered in sandstone-colored ceramic blocks and decorated with merlons and obelisks.

Katya and I walked through a massive revolving door and into a colossal foyer. The high ceiling was lined in white marble, contrasting the polished black granite of the walls, floor, and columns. Aven's chief aide, a chubby young man called Kuzmin, awaited us by the elevators, wearing an ill-fitting brown striped suit. He led us into a huge room with thick red carpet and decorated with magnificent antiques from the monarchy era, as well as Van Gogh originals on the walls. This was Aven's office.

Aven himself was a thin, tall man with black hair and dark eyes and was dressed in an immaculate navy suit. He wasn't attractive, but he had class. He shook hands with us, his expression neutral.

"What can I do for you?"

I explained the problem. Star had spent a great deal of money, and Yeltsin backed our joint venture. But Gaidar was being pressured to hold an international tender.

"Why are you so afraid of a tender?" asked Aven.

"Because we both know that the outcome of the tender will be decided before it begins," I replied.

Aven then revealed that he had already spoken to Gaidar about Star. "I want you to work with Kuzmin, who will investigate the whole deal and report back to me," he went on. "After that, we will send our recommendations to Shokhin. Goodbye and good luck."

Shokhin was the deputy minister for foreign economic relations who had accused Star of being a front for drug money. One day in the distant future, I would realize the irony of my indignation over this.

The meeting was over. Kuzmin escorted us back to the ground floor of the ministry and told me to come back on Monday at 9 a.m. with all the relevant documents.

I returned to the ministry on Monday, July 6, 1992, bright and early. Kuzmin took me to a conference room and started peppering me with questions about Star—and about Ian's background. I told him that Ian owned mines all over the world, including in Malaysia, Vietnam, Brazil, Bolivia, and the United States.

"Can you name some of these?" asked Kuzmin.

"Yes. His first project was an oil field in Malaysia. His company there, Base Resources Ltd., made forty million US dollars. In 1984, he set up a company with his son Chris in Brazil. The company explored alluvial gold and platinum in the state of Goias. Ian also went to Bolivia in 1988, after the world tin market collapsed. He received an exploration permit to work on a gold deposit called the Lost Spanish Gold Mine, at La Riviera in Western Cordillera. His latest project involves gold and platinum exploration in Nevada."

"Sounds fascinating, but he doesn't do this by himself. Who is he involved with?"

"Ian has a knack for identifying good projects. He attracts the world's best geologists, bankers, accountants, and so on." I didn't mention that Ian had lost US$20 million in Brazil and had to pull out.

"So, tell me about your company, Star."

"Star has a consortium of bankers and investors behind it who have guaranteed to provide one hundred fifty million US in capital and a further seven hundred fifty million in debt financing," I went on.

Kuzmin was obviously impressed.

"I have a letter from one of Ian's Hong Kong bankers, guaranteeing to provide the capital," I added, passing over the letter signed by S. Y. Hui, Ian's accountant.

"Who are these Hong Kong bankers?"

"Ian lived and worked in Hong Kong for many years. He formed a company called Crusader. His partners are a consortium of very rich Chinese businessmen who are interested in Russian gold."

"Yes, but we don't want yellow faces in Russia. You know thousands of illegals cross the border into Siberia every day. They must be stopped."

"Well, these are rich Hong Kong Chinese businessmen who have no desire to live in Russia," I retorted.

The conversation switched to Sukhoi Log and then to Katya. Kuzmin knew almost nothing about her. I told him she was close to Yeltsin and described how she'd shouted at Yeltsin over the phone in front of me. I also said that Yeltsin had asked Ian for a US$2 billion line of credit.

"Can MacNee get such money?" asked Kuzmin with some excitement.

"He says he can organize it from New York." I might have been uneasy about what was probably a false promise from Ian, but I needed to present Ian as a business magnate.

"Does Yeltsin still support you?"

"Katya assures me he does."

Kuzmin finished the interrogation at 4 p.m. He told me he would discuss everything with Aven and asked me to come back the following morning.

Back I went.

Kuzmin presented what he and Aven believed was a solution. Other mining companies were willing to invest as much as US$300 million in Sukhoi Log, and as a result, many people now believed that Star's offer of US$150 million was too paltry, he said. They felt that Lenzoloto JSC was worth US$1 billion—and that 31 percent of Star should be worth around US$300 million.

"Yes, but RTZ offered three hundred million for fifty-one percent, and they'd never settle for less than a controlling interest," I argued.

"True. So, how much money does Star have? Can you match three hundred million or, say, even two hundred and fifty million?" asked Kuzmin.

"I have no idea. It may not be economically viable."

Kuzmin then brought up the subject of the telegram on file at the Embassy of Russia in Canberra.

"Oh, for God's sake! Don't tell me that stupid telegram is still causing trouble!" I couldn't conceal my frustration. "Rudakov had them search the wrong company on purpose, to undermine Star. He became our enemy when we went to Yeltsin and not to him. Obviously we made the right choice!"

Kuzmin evidently already knew this. He said he'd asked Nesterov, the Russian trade commissioner in Canberra, to forward a telegram to Moscow confirming the company investigated in March 1992 was not our company, Star Technology. He now had to wait until he received Nesterov's response.

"Fine," I said, disappointed.

"Smile," countered Kuzmin. "This is the last hurdle."

Sure, I thought.

I faxed Ian, asking him to contact Nesterov and push for a retraction. I emphasized the urgency of the situation. Big mining companies, including Australia's BHP, were in Moscow and circling Gaidar like sharks. Ian responded instantly and said he'd asked Tess, his personal accountant, to handle the matter. Tess was an efficient, astute Filipina who didn't miss a trick.

Tess spoke to Nesterov, who told her he'd never said Star was connected to the bankrupt Australian company. On the contrary, he'd called Star "a solid company."

So Rudakov had independently used an unknown, bankrupt company to slander us. Bastard!

Later that day, Ian faxed, saying that both NatWest and Hambros would provide letters to Gaidar. By July 18, the letters confirming a guarantee of US$150 million from each bank had arrived.

Kuzmin was now ready to see me again.

When I turned up at the ministry, he was in a very good mood. He'd received a telegram from Nesterov, clearing Star's reputation. Better still, he and Aven had come up with a compromise.

"There are several conditions," Kuzmin added. "The most important one is that Star must increase its investment from one hundred fifty to two hundred fifty million for its thirty-one-percent share. If you agree to this, you will be mining Sukhoi Log. If you don't, you won't. It's that simple."

"Star and the banks think we have a deal," I countered. "To change the terms of the deal at this late stage—"

Kuzmin waved his hand, shutting me down.

"Ludmila, go now and talk to MacNee. The message is clear. If you want to mine Sukhoi Log, you must pay two hundred fifty million. If you agree to this, I guarantee your success in Russia."

I walked home with a sinking heart, imagining Ian's response, and rang him as soon as I walked through the door of my apartment.

"You can't be serious? The deal is done!" he said furiously. "The banks have agreed. No one will pay more. The rate of return will be too low. They can't change the deal now. It's too late!"

"Ian, they will simply tender thirty-one percent of Lenzoloto JSC and probably get three hundred million."

"Don't be ridiculous."

"Well, that's the opinion of everybody in the government and even our supporters, including Gaidar. I don't think we have a choice."

Ian finally agreed to rework the figures with Jeff Pollack, the banker from Hambros, and Graeme Newing from NatWest; he said he would call me back the next day.

Ultimately, the three of them decided that we should proceed. But Ian emphasized when he rang me that it hadn't been easy to convince the two bankers: "The word in London is that the Russians see foreigners as gullible outsiders fit for milking, and deals are not worth the paper they are written on. You are to express my great annoyance to Kuzmin," he said. "To change the deal at this late stage is very poor form. Accordingly, we have a few conditions of our own. Firstly, we agree to invest two hundred fifty million—but over five years, not one. This is the condition of our investment banks, as Russia is seen as too risky. Secondly, guarantees of payment for the gold in dollars at world prices. And lastly, and most importantly, full control of the finances and management of the hard-rock mines. Try for tax relief too, at least during construction of the Sukhoi Log mine."

"All right. I'll try my best. What is our rate of return now?" I asked.

"It's seventeen percent, which is the absolute minimum the banks would agree to," he replied. "This is based on world gold prices. It's no longer a good deal but an average one, which will make fundraising more difficult, considering the political uncertainty in Russia.

"Ludmila, you must get them to agree to these extra conditions. They're nonnegotiable. It's up to you."

CHAPTER SIXTEEN

Argy-Bargy

I called the ministry the next morning and made an appointment with Kuzmin for two o'clock that afternoon.

"Well, what does MacNee have to say?" he asked as soon as I turned up.

I told him, exactly. Kuzmin didn't demur about anything until I got to Ian's final ask: tax relief.

"Now, that I can't promise," Kuzmin said instantly. "You know that the government is desperately trying to collect taxes. Their attitude will be 'Star stands to make so much money out of this it should pay its taxes.'"

"Ian said our conditions are not negotiable."

"Well, then you'd better go back to him for a rethink," retorted Kuzmin. He added that certain Russian companies had emerged who indicated they could invest US$300 million in Sukhoi Log right away for a 31 percent share.

"My dear Kuzmin," I interrupted. "These post-Communist businessmen have grabbed Russia's best assets and shunted the cash into Cyprus. I very much doubt they're willing to bring three hundred million back into the country and risk losing it—or worse, be imprisoned."

"Yes, I'm aware of this," said Kuzmin without blinking.

"They have their millions stashed in Cyprus and Switzerland, and they're sitting pretty. Did you know that just about every beachfront mansion in Cyprus now is owned by a Russian?" I told him that Ian had an office in Cyprus (for tax purposes) and had described to me the Russian mansions and their lavish super cruisers, and how they partied day and night.

"I get the picture. But there are a few serious Russian businessmen living in Moscow who want to mine Sukhoi Log, like Chugaevsky, whom I've met," replied Kuzmin.

"And you are convinced this guy has the money?"

"He can raise it from London banks, just like you are doing."

"I doubt it, but let me talk to Ian again."

I called Ian once I got back to the apartment and filled him in.

"Look, we've come this far," he said finally. "Later down the track, we'll tackle the taxes. Tell Kuzmin we have a deal, but that's it. No more surprises."

The temperature in Moscow the next day was a hot thirty-eight degrees. I put on a sleeveless silk dress in azure blue to wear to Friday-night drinks at the Australian embassy, a peach building surrounded by a courtyard with lovely tall balsam poplar trees. Meeting at this bar was a ritual for foreigners living in Moscow, and both Greg and I needed to unwind. The bar was below ground level, dimly lit, and crowded with expats, celebrities, businesspeople, politicians, tourists, and embassy folk from all over the world. I thoroughly enjoyed mingling with them and listening to their colorful tales.

On July 26, Katya burst into my apartment with awesome news: Shokhin had chaired a secret meeting, and it was decided that the joint venture with Lenzoloto and Star should go ahead, should include Sukhoi Log, and should be registered immediately, with Star investing the higher amount of US$250 million over three years.

"Ian wanted five," I said.

"We can discuss it with Gaidar."

"Okay, what else?"

"The KGB voted against Star but was overruled. I couldn't find out why."

"Will this be a problem?"

"Maybe, but we'll fix it when the time comes. They probably just want a bribe," she remarked, and laughed.

"So, what happens next?" I asked.

Shokhin had appointed Mostovoy, the first deputy minister of the Government Committee for Property (GKI), to take charge of our case, continued Katya—though Shokhin himself would write a secret report to Gaidar with all his recommendations.

"Some of these are so secret that Golovnin wouldn't talk about them to me. They aim to register the Lenzoloto JSC in the shortest possible time frame, hopefully by August 12," Katya added.

I called Ian immediately to tell him the good news. He was in Aspen and was so excited that he didn't complain about the three-year timeline. I suggested he fly to Moscow urgently, since we were due to start work with Mostovoy almost immediately.

Ian arrived on the Concorde on July 29. I picked him up at the airport and told him we were meeting Mostovoy at 7 p.m.

Ian looked tanned and rested in faded blue jeans and a purple Aspen ski jacket and dark sunglasses, but the glasses were to hide his bloodshot eyes from too much partying on the Concorde, he said.

We arrived at GKI on time with all our documents and waited patiently in Mostovoy's reception room. His secretary, Lena, was young and pretty and not wearing the ugly knee-high stockings I hated so much. I'd brought her a small gift, a stuffed koala (the national animal of Australia) holding a box of chocolates. A gift could save hours of waiting.

"How wonderful!" she said, beaming. "My son will just love it."

Ten minutes later, we walked into Mostovoy's office, a small, dark room with a large desk, three armchairs, and three tall bookshelves full of legal publications. The deputy minister was sitting behind his desk but jumped up immediately, shook Ian's hand, and kissed mine. He was a short, balding, thirty-five-year-old man with a bit of a belly but also a certain vibrant energy about him and intelligent eyes. I knew that he too had studied at university with Gaidar and was a lawyer.

"Okay, this morning I received a top-secret document from Shokhin," he said. "It contains very specific instructions on how to set up the Lenzoloto JSC. Most of the terms you already know. The main one is that you're investing two hundred fifty million over three years for a thirty-one-percent shareholding of Lenzoloto JSC."

As he spoke, he took a pipe from his top drawer, stuffed it with tobacco from a tin on his desk labeled "Autumn Evening, Virginia, USA," and lit up. The room instantly filled with a sweet scent, like freshly made pancakes. Mostovoy then told us he wanted us to work with Olga, GKI's lawyer, to redraft the Lenzoloto JSC founding documents in accordance with Shokhin's document. Hopefully, the work would take no more than one week. The meeting ended. He kissed my hand again, shook Ian's, and opened his office doors. "Until next time."

Olga, whom we met the next day, turned out to be a striking woman with stunning green eyes and cropped blond hair. In her opinion, Gaidar's ordinance was unclear, ambiguous, and in parts contradicted Russian law. The biggest surprise in Shokhin's secret instructions was the elimination of Avlov and his workers and the Irkutsk government as founders, which Mostovoy had not mentioned to us. The only founders were to be Star and GKI. However, after the registration of the newly formed Lenzoloto closed the joint stock company, GKI would transfer a portion of its shares to Avlov and the workers. This was in accordance with the new law on privatization.

It seemed that Shokhin, acting upon direct instructions from Yeltsin, wanted control of Sukhoi Log. As Nozhikov was already our enemy, I presumed it didn't matter that his 10 percent had been axed. As for Avlov, he was used to taking orders from Moscow without questioning them.

Olga told us to open a bank account for Star in Moscow, as our bank account number had to be included in the founders' agreement, along with our registered addresses in Moscow and in Australia.

The only private bank in Moscow with a corresponding American bank was the Dialogue Bank, with offices in the Radisson Hotel, which was very convenient. We set up a USD bank account that day.

That weekend, at Ian's request, Azarova—"the lady lawyer," as he called her (she was, of course, one of the top presidential lawyers and worked for Orehov, Yeltsin's chief lawyer)—came over to discuss the problem.

"Before we start, we need to go for a walk," she said to me. It was routine, by now, to go for walks, or to talk in bathrooms with the water running.

We caught the elevator to the ground floor. Outside, it was a beautiful, hot summer day.

"Did you know every word you say is recorded and listened to?" asked Azarova once we were safely in the street. "Just recently, I picked up the phone in my office and dialed your number. It didn't ring, but I could hear your voice, as if on loudspeaker." She'd heard me enter the apartment and swear about Bychkov (head of the

Committee for Precious Metals). Then she heard everything I said and did.

Even though I already knew from Katya that I was being bugged, I still felt a chill. It seemed the KGB was listening around the clock and heard everything I did. This monumental invasion of privacy was unsettling.

"You must be very careful with what you say," she went on. "Don't swear about Bychkov anymore. And be careful what you write in your faxes. Now, let me tell you what the big picture is. You are all pieces in a chess game. Yeltsin is the king and wants control of Sukhoi Log. Mostovoy is just a pawn in this chess game. Gaidar is the bishop, willing to be sacrificed for the cause; and Star is the brave knight fighting for their cause. You must play the game or walk away. This is no ordinary business deal."

"Okay, it all makes sense. I will inform Ian of this."

We walked back to the apartment, where Ian was waiting for us. I grabbed a piece of paper and wrote, "KGB is listening, so be careful of what you say." Ian didn't look surprised and simply nodded.

Azarova set to work and immediately spotted that there was no protection for Star if the Russian government failed to lift the secrecy from the Sukhoi Log. Star would default if it failed to invest the US$250 million irrespective of whether the secrecy had been lifted.

She'd go through everything with Mostovoy, she went on, and strongly recommended that we insert a "safety net" clause to protect Star from default if the Russian government failed to secure the rights to mine all Lenzoloto's deposits, including Sukhoi Log, and to release all the geological data. "As you know, Sukhoi Log is on the list of government secrets and can only be declassified by government decree," she added.

I turned to Ian. "We have to play the game, Ian, or walk away today."

"Let's play," he replied. He seemed excited by the challenge.

The next morning, I woke up feeling really sick; my lungs were so congested that I had difficulty breathing. Greg panicked and called Katya. She immediately booked me into M's central hospital for a lung X-ray. As I smoked two packets of cigarettes a day, I was extremely worried about the possibility of lung cancer.

The X-ray was clear of cancer but revealed a large infection, which was confirmed as pneumonia. Katya immediately arranged a bed for me in the hospital, where the nurses injected large volumes of penicillin into my bottom twice daily. I was both anxious and excited by the possibility of seeing Andrei again, but Greg was terribly concerned that Michael would somehow "get to me."

As it turned out, I never saw either of them, though I strolled through the gardens once I recovered, hoping to bump into Andrei. When I questioned Katya about him, she played dumb, saying that he was still in St. Petersburg as far as she knew. I later heard that St. Petersburg was the hub of the president's mafia and hit men—in my time, Yeltsin's, and then his successor's, Putin.

CHAPTER SEVENTEEN

Start of an Affair and a New Enemy

Fully recovered, it was back to the drawing board.

One evening, Ian and I went to the bar at the Radisson Hotel, which had become our hangout by now. Chris arrived and broke the good news that he'd found us an office—in the same building as my apartment, but on the ninth floor. The Star team of secretaries and translators could move in almost immediately. From now on, my apartment would only be used for private meetings. Thank goodness.

We had one final meeting with Mostovoy, to go through the documents. The default clause that Azarova had requested, protecting Star in case the Russian government failed to lift the secrecy from the geological data on Sukhoi Log, was missing.

"Ian, this has all been approved at the highest levels," Mostovoy protested when Ian raised the subject. "The secrecy lifting has been approved. I will issue an ordinance ordering the Geolkom to disclose the data. There is absolutely nothing to fear. I guarantee this."

Ian reluctantly agreed. And Star's fate was sealed with a stroke of the pen.

On August 27, 1992, the night of the official signing (in Mostovoy's office), there was a raging storm in Moscow. Russians believe rain is a good omen. We held our first founders' meeting as gale-force winds buffeted the building. We elected Mostovoy and Ian as directors of the board, and they both signed the founding documents, which were very different from the now obsolete ones we'd signed in Bodaibo with Avlov.

Afterward, we toasted Lenzoloto with five-star Armenian cognac, sculling our drinks. Mostovoy toasted Ian, who toasted Mostovoy. We all sculled and kissed.

Then my turn came to be toasted. "To Ludmila. My dear, without you this wouldn't have happened!" cried Mostovoy. This time, his lips interlocked with mine.

With every cognac, his kisses became more passionate. Outside, the rain beat down.

On the home front, I was desperate to end my marriage. Greg and I had been leading separate lives for some time. My husband's role had become that of a PA. He spent the rest of his time playing tennis and lying on our bed, reading books and magazines, while I continued to work twelve-plus-hour days. We were worlds apart in every way.

Greg went on a shopping trip to Poland, and when he returned, I told him the marriage was over.

Chris had moved into a two-bedroom apartment in the building next to mine. When Ian arrived back in Moscow shortly after, Chris cooked spaghetti bolognaise for the three of us, a longtime favorite dish of mine. During the meal, I announced that Greg and I were getting divorced. Nobody seemed surprised.

The following day, Ian told me that he would like to take me to a special dinner that night to celebrate our success. Wear a nice dress, he said. The only dress I had in my wardrobe in Moscow was a backless snakeskin affair. Luckily Moscow was experiencing a late summer.

We started the evening at the Radisson bar as usual and then went to the Hotel Metropol. The Metropol, a historic luxury hotel, is one of the finest in Russia, located in the center of Moscow, opposite the Bolshoi Theatre. The building's incredible exterior is in the Art Nouveau style. The interior is decorated in pastel colors, opulent antique furniture, and priceless, magnificent paintings, sculptures, vase-shaped floor lamps, chandeliers, and gold-framed mirrors. At the time it also happened to house one of Russia's most beautiful restaurants, the Balalaika, where Ian and I dined.

After we finished dinner, Ian took my hand.

"I really want to fuck you," he said.

To say I was shocked is an understatement. It wasn't just that the whole thing was so unexpected. Ian's language was totally out of character. I had never heard him swear before.

"Ludmila, I have wanted you from the moment I first saw you," he went on. "The only problem is, how would you cope if we started fucking, and Bobby came to Moscow?"

This was too much for me.

"Ian, I think we should go home and just see what happens," I said.

He seemed happy with this. In the taxi, he held my hand, but I felt awkward and couldn't wait to escape. Back at the building, he walked me to the door and kissed me good night on the cheek. "See you tomorrow," he said and winked.

Lying in bed that night, I had to admit that Ian had become my whole world, and maybe, just maybe, something could happen between us. But should it?

We had a quiet dinner together at the Radisson Hotel a couple of nights later. After dinner, Ian asked me if I wanted a nightcap. "Yes, I would," I answered. I started heading toward the bar when he said he had a couple of bottles of Mumm in his room. "We could have a glass or two before Volodya drives you home."

I agreed reluctantly, and we took the lift up to his room. Ian opened the champagne and poured two glasses.

"To us," he said.

He sat next to me, and as we sipped our drinks, he told me that his life with Bobby was totally over. Then, without warning, he pulled me to him and kissed me passionately.

And there it was. The line had been crossed. We kissed and talked and kissed again.

Finally, at 2 a.m., I decided I should go home. Poor Volodya had been waiting for me in his car all this time. Usually an extra ten greenbacks made up for the late hour.

The next day, I ended up in Ian's room again. This time we went further. But at precisely the wrong moment, the phone rang, and the call was transferred to the answering machine. Bobby's posh voice broke the stillness: "Hello, darling, just calling to see how you are. Call me back when you can. Bye."

Ian, seeing the expression on my face, insisted that everything was over with Bobby and that they were putting up a facade for Angus's sake. Bobby had probably made the phone call in front of Angus.

She had someone in Aspen, Ian added—a guy who'd been divorced five times. "She asked me if we could stay married until Angus finishes primary school. After that, Angus will go to boarding school and will be less affected by the divorce. I agreed."

I accepted the explanation but had mixed emotions about starting an affair with Ian, as thrilling as it was. The fact remained that he was a married man many years my senior. And I wasn't interested in just an affair. I wanted marriage, kids, a beautiful family home, first-class travel, and a dazzling social life, all of which Ian could give me.

At least I was a free woman now. Greg had decided to return permanently to Australia. He still had his 10 percent in Star, which he would eventually sell for three million dollars. He would do very well on his free ride.

Ian left Moscow and returned to Aspen. He next called me in early October to talk about the investor who most excited him: Malcolm Turnbull.

"He's the genius behind the bank Turnbull and Partners. He's very dynamic."

"I have never heard of Malcolm Turnbull."

"He's running the campaign for Australia to become a republic," Ian continued. "I think he wants the first presidency."

"Now, *that* I could sell to the Russians," I said immediately. "You know what terrible snobs the Russian politicians are. It's either fame or fortune, preferably both, when it comes to the people they want to deal with."

I was due to go home for a break in a couple of weeks. Ian mentioned that the confidentiality agreement was ready for Mr. Turnbull to sign and asked me to deliver it to him.

An auspicious signing of a different kind took place on October 4. The Lenzoloto JSC was finally registered by the Ministry of Finance. Central Mining announced this to the market, and its shares skyrocketed to forty-six cents—a record high since its listing in 1986.

That night, Chris and I went to Moscow's first and only Irish bar, the Shamrock, to celebrate. I told him a story about how I'd once almost lost my Bronte Beach apartment, which was mortgaged, because Ian hadn't paid my wages, and how he'd failed to deliver the ourocone and at one stage had threatened to pull out of Russia due to lack of funds. I asked Chris about his father's financial situation.

"Dad has a nest egg in Switzerland, but he would never touch it," replied Chris, but he wouldn't elaborate and was more interested in discussing the registration party we were throwing before I left for Sydney the following week.

The party, which took place that Saturday, October 10, in Chris's apartment, was packed with expats and people from the Australian embassy. Chris knew how to throw a party! The Moët flowed like there was no tomorrow. We danced and partied well into the night, indulging in a few ecstasy tablets. Even the Australian ambassador, Cavan Hogue, made a short appearance and gave a celebratory speech in Star's honor.

Then I departed for Sydney. I was staying at Fran's house because my Bronte Beach apartment was leased out. Ian was due to arrive back the same week.

I dropped off the confidentiality agreement at Turnbull's bank as I'd promised I would and met one of the partners, Christian, but there was no sign of Malcolm.

Ian was staying at the Intercontinental Hotel, and I joined him there for the following two nights. By the time he left for Lambruk, his Victorian estate, I was deeply in love and extremely happy. Only later did something he said about Bobby—"She said she had a dreadful feeling that I was with another woman"—register. A "dreadful feeling"?

I decided to call him and quiz him about this. I wanted to know where he slept when he was at Lambruk; he said that he stayed in a stone cottage on the property.

"Who actually owns Lambruk?" I asked.

"Lambruk is owned by Lambruk Holdings P/L," Ian replied. "Bobby is the sole beneficiary shareholder. However, one of my companies owns the cars on the property. I own the original stone cottage on the hill."

"How much is Lambruk worth?"

"The last estimate was four million Australian. My car collection is worth around five million. They're my only assets in Australia."

"Why did you move from Hong Kong to Aspen?"

"I love it there. Hong Kong wasn't going to last forever, and I always wanted to live in America. It's a great country. America is where all the money is."

He added that Bobby hated leaving Hong Kong and her life there and had been very unhappy in Aspen.

"What about Angus?"

"Angus is ten and attends an excellent private school, Aspen Day School. I bought a ski lodge right at the foot of the mountains for one million US, which is easy to lock up and leave. I'll take you skiing there one day."

"Where does Angus prefer to be?"

"Oh, Angus loves Lambruk. He regards it as his home. He'll eventually end up boarding at Geelong Grammar, which is close to Lambruk." Geelong Grammar was an elite private school for rich kids in Victoria.

"Were your parents rich?"

"No. My father was a dentist. My mother was a housewife and raised my sister and me. I went to boarding school and then started an economics degree at Melbourne University."

"Did you finish it?"

"No. I met the patriarch of the Bushells family—as in Bushells Tea. He offered me a job going all around the world, promoting his teas. I always had a knack for numbers, and I figured why spend the next four years at university to end up with the same kind of job four years later? So I accepted the job and traveled to England, Europe, Asia, and South America. It was the best education for an ambitious seventeen-year-old."

"What happened next?"

"I met Jan, my first wife. I was twenty. I knew on my wedding day that marrying her was a big mistake. Soon afterwards, Chris was born, and then Cathy. Cathy was an accident. I was really angry, as I didn't want to have two children straightaway. The crunch came when I broke my leg playing First Grade AFL [Australian Football

League] for Footscray. I loved football. I spent all my time traveling on business or playing football. After I broke my leg, I was forced to stay at home. Chris and Cathy screamed all the time. They were four and two years old. It drove me mad. I couldn't handle it, so I left. My best friend, Graeme, had divorced his wife, so we moved in together into a waterfront apartment in Kirribilli. It was one of the best times of my life."

"How did you make all your money?"

"Graeme and I started a business importing shoes from Hong Kong. It did really well. Then the Australian government prohibited all future shoe imports into Australia, to encourage the development of a local shoe industry. Graeme and I sold our import license in 1960 for two million Australian."

"That's the year I was born," I commented.

Ian then told me that soon after meeting Bobby, he went back to Jan, who'd been diagnosed with cancer. The two of them embarked on a first-class trip around the world to see if the marriage might still work. They both realized very quickly it wouldn't and decided to divorce. He and Bobby then got back together, and a few years later, Angus was born.

"And business-wise?" I asked.

"I invested the money from the shoe business into the financial markets. I shorted gold in the 1980s and made five million US. Then I shorted the market in 1987 and made a lot more money. I remember when I made a million in just one night. I'd also started a company called Base Resources Ltd., which had oil wells in Malaysia. I've been lucky with oil. We sold the company for ten million. But I have always wanted to strike it lucky with gold."

I'd fallen in love with a thrilling man. He was eccentric and a real highflier. I was on top of the world and believed every promise Ian made to me, including a life together. I was also euphoric about owning shares in potentially the largest gold mine on the planet! But I came crashing back down to earth the very next day when Ian told me I had to return to Moscow immediately. He'd just received a panicked call from Katya.

"Yatskevich has raised all hell and has teamed up with Nozhikov. The Irkutsk government has started court proceedings to annul the Lenzoloto JSC. They claim everything Gaidar and Mostovoy have done is illegal because we bribed him. The claim is signed by Nozhikov."

I knew it. Yatskevich, as deputy chairman of Geolkom, was going to cause problems because we hadn't included him in the joint venture and hadn't bribed him.

The following day, I boarded a plane to Moscow; Ian would join me there the following week. I no longer had to slum it on Aeroflot. Ian even let me fly business class.

Katya picked me up from Sheremetyevo Airport and briefed me as we drove.

"Yatskevich is acting like a hysterical fishwife," she said. "He is trolling around the government shouting that Sukhoi Log should be taken to tender. He claims Lenzoloto's shares are worth five billion US and the Star deal is harmful to Russia, as Star should be paying thirty percent of five billion. He has been in to see Gaidar and Golovnin."

"This is unbelievable. The prime minister issues an ordinance ruling that the license must be reissued to Lenzoloto JSC, and some buffoon from the Committee for Geology chooses to ignore it without any consequences!" I exclaimed. "What does this guy want? Oh, stupid question, I guess! And he's going to make it as hard as possible for us, until we bribe him—just like Gaidar and Chubais. What about Nozhikov?" I added.

"Same," replied Katya.

Katya dropped me at the apartment, and I collapsed on the bed. Greg had already packed up and left, so I had the place all to myself.

I rang Gerald Seeber, the trade commissioner at the Australian embassy, to see if he knew Yatskevich. He did. "You can meet him yourself tomorrow night," he added. "The embassy is having a function for Russian government officials, and he's invited."

I felt a little nervous walking into the embassy the following evening. My plan was to charm the pants off Yatskevich and then ask for a formal meeting. I made my way over to Gerald, a very tall man with thick black eyebrows and dark, deep-set eyes.

"So, where's the prick?" I asked undiplomatically.

"Over there," replied Gerald, pointing to a thin man with greasy brown hair, a very prominent nose, narrow eyes, and a pointy chin; he looked like a rat in his scungy brown suit.

I went straight to him. "Good evening. My name is Ludmila. I'm from Star."

Yatskevich eyed me up and down and smiled. "Good evening, my dear. Your reputation precedes you."

"As does yours," I said flirtatiously. "So. You're trying to steal my Sukhoi Log."

"No, I have already stolen it!" he replied with a deadly look.

"I'm only joking. I just wanted to know why you are so against Star."

"Because it's a small, unknown company," Yatskevich said bluntly. "It doesn't deserve to have Sukhoi Log. The pearl of Russia should go to the pearl of the international mining world like RTZ."

"Shouldn't the pearl of Russia go to Russians?" I retorted.

"What, Avlov and his mob? They're fat, lazy, and useless! I'd rather see Sukhoi Log go to Varenikov," added Yatskevich. "At least the artels know how to mine gold!"

"But the artels are shareholders of Lenzoloto JSC."

"Oh yes, you gave them a few crumbs. Varenikov will tell you himself what you can do with his shares."

"I know him quite well. He was the first person who told me about Sukhoi Log."

"Then you betrayed him and went off to Avlov."

"I hate to point out the obvious, but Avlov and Lenzoloto hold the license to mine Sukhoi Log."

Yatskevich looked triumphant. "No, my dear, they do not," he said. "You're wrong. The old Lenzoloto Association had mining rights to Sukhoi Log, but not the Lenzoloto JSC. If I have it my way, Sukhoi Log will go to tender, and the alluvials will go to the artels."

"That's unacceptable," I told him, and asked if we could meet the next day at his office to discuss it further.

Yatskevich agreed to this. "I like contrary women," he added. "How does 11 a.m. sound?"

He then walked off. As he did so, his wife, who'd been standing there with him, grabbed my arm. "Don't worry, dear. My husband likes to roar like a lion, but he's very kind and very fair. If your company is good for the project, he will see this and support you," she said.

"Thank you for your kind words," I replied.

The next day, I walked into Geolkom at 10:50 a.m. Yatskevich's secretary, Marina, came down to greet me. She was plump and round-faced with a bird's nest hairstyle, and of course she was wearing those knee-high stockings with flat black shoes! She approached me with a wide smile and asked me to follow her. I suddenly lost my confidence and felt butterflies in my stomach.

When we finally sat down to talk, Yatskevich was friendly enough; but early on in my pitch, as I was emphasizing that our banks had US$50 billion in assets, I realized he was ignoring what I was saying.

"Does Star have two hundred fifty million in its bank account?" he asked.

"Of course not. Star's banks will provide this money."

"Do you have a guarantee from the banks for the amount of two hundred fifty million US dollars?"

"If you need this, I can get you that guarantee, even though it's difficult without a feasibility study," I replied.

"My dear, you will never get that far!" he said confidently. "Come over here. Let me show you something."

He led me over to a collection of ore samples displayed in a glass cabinet and took out a large piece of rock covered in silvery specks. I thought that maybe he was coming around. "See this? It's a sample from Sukhoi Log. You will only mine this over my dead body."

I stepped backward in dismay. "Yeltsin says we will."

"I don't give a rat's arse about that alcoholic," said Yatskevich. "I'm the only person who can give you the license, and that will never happen. Sukhoi Log is going to tender. I'm already preparing it."

When I remonstrated that the regional Irkutsk Committee for Geology had already issued Lenzoloto with the license to mine Sukhoi Log, he replied that for deposits containing over 100 tons gold, the license had to be issued jointly between the regional and federal committees, so our license was invalid.

"Even if that is the case," I countered, "the Lenzoloto Association has had the mining rights to Sukhoi Log since 1977, when the deposit was extensively explored. This makes a tender illegal."

"No, no, my dear. The Lenzoloto Association stopped existing when you formed the Lenzoloto JSC, so you lost all your mining rights."

"Are you saying the Lenzoloto JSC has no mining rights to any deposits?"

"Look, you can have the alluvials," said Yatskevich at this point. "The potential of the alluvials is much greater than you think. But Sukhoi Log will go to tender. Lenzoloto JSC can participate if you want. All the local people will be given a chance too—not just Avlov and his cronies. This is the new justice system in the new Russia."

"I don't want to participate in a tender," I replied.

"What are you afraid of?"

"Tenders are just another form of corruption. Everyone knows that."

"Not my tenders."

"Why do you hate Star so much?"

"I have my reasons." He didn't explain this cryptic remark.

"What can we do to change this?"

"Nothing."

"Well, can I ring you in the future?"

"If you wish, of course you can call me. I am happy to talk to you anytime."

And that was that. I was devastated. I'd hit a brick wall. I needed to speak to Katya urgently.

When I got back to the office, she was already there. Ian was paying her US$1,000 per month, and she was now officially Star's consultant.

When I told her what had occurred with Yatskevich, Katya said that she had a friend called Alexei. "He's a legal expert in mining. He's also a good friend of Yatskevich's. They often drink together at Yatskevich's home. I'll get him to call you."

Alexei called me the following day, October 24, just a few hours before I was due to go to Sheremetyevo to pick up Ian. As it happened, Alexei was on his way to Finland. We arranged to meet in the cafeteria section of a petrol station not far from the airport.

Ian, after we'd met at the airport, asked whether Alexei was KGB. Katya thought he was a KGB informant, I replied.

The cafeteria was empty when we arrived, except for a tall, skinny, debonair figure with a generous moustache. Alexei. "Look, I have about thirty minutes, so please let me get straight to the point," he said. He was well spoken and direct. "You're in a mess because you followed Shokhin's instructions and liquidated the old Lenzoloto Association when you formed the Lenzoloto JSC—so you inherit nothing, and this allows a tender for Sukhoi Log."

"Well, we don't know that it *is* correct," Ian cut in. "Shokhin's instructions stipulate that we did inherit all Lenzoloto's mining licenses."

"My dear Mr. MacNee, you have been tricked. The instructions contradict the law. Once a government entity is liquidated, all its assets pass back to the government. You should have transformed it into the JSC in accordance with the law on privatization."

When I pointed out that Mostovoy had said that if we didn't agree to follow Shokhin's instructions, there wouldn't be a Lenzoloto JSC, Alexei replied that he was sure Mostovoy had been instructed to keep the government's share of Lenzoloto or let the deal fall through. "They have obviously planned to give ownership of the shares to someone, sometime in the future," he added.

"How?" I asked.

"Oh, for a nominal price through a closed, rigged auction."

I was stunned. "Are you kidding?"

"No, I'm deadly serious. Yeltsin and his young reformers know they can't last in the government, so they're paving the way for their retirement," Alexei went on. "But you now have a huge problem. Yatskevich has told me he will never reissue the Sukhoi Log license to Lenzoloto irrespective of Gaidar's ordinance instructing him to do so. He's telling everyone he will take it to tender, in the best interests of Russia, and I'm afraid he has the power to do it."

"So, how do we get to this man?" asked Ian bluntly. "We satisfied Chubais, and now we just have to find a way to satisfy this man."

"Correct. But he's just one of many enemies you have. Basically, anyone who has missed out on a slice of Sukhoi Log is your enemy. What we must do first is fix up the founding documents, to disarm your enemies. I have worked out a possible solution. I need to know whether the Lenzoloto Association has actually been struck off the government registry."

"I don't think it has," I exclaimed. "I spoke to Avlov only two days ago, and he said he was getting ready to strike it off."

"You must stop him. Call him now and tell him to do nothing. It means the Lenzoloto Association still exists and still owns the licenses. All we need to do is legally merge the two entities—the Lenzoloto Association and the Lenzoloto JSC—and amend the founding documents to reflect this. This way the Lenzoloto JSC inherits all the mining rights of the Lenzoloto Association."

I thought this a brilliant solution.

Alexei looked at his watch. "I must leave. Let's plan to meet after I get back from Finland. If you like what you hear, we can discuss a fee and go from there."

"Fine," said Ian and shook Alexei's hand. Our new friend then jumped up and hurried away.

CHAPTER EIGHTEEN

A Pregnancy and a Betrayal

On November 28, 1992, two weeks after Ian once again left Moscow for London, I faxed Fran: "If one thinks one might be pregnant, how many glasses of wine is one allowed to drink per night?"
She wrote back, "None!"

Two days later, I went to the foreign clinic for a pregnancy test and afterward sat in the waiting room feeling nervous, but also blissful at the thought of having Ian's child, and of the three of us becoming a family. I was sure he would divorce Bobby and marry me.

Twenty minutes later, the American nurse who'd taken my blood reappeared, beaming. "Congratulations! You're six weeks pregnant," she said, to my joy.

However, after I left the clinic and the news sank in, I panicked. I had so much work to do in Russia. And what the hell was I going to say to Ian? He was rather old to be a father again. I had no idea if he would be thrilled or angry. But I knew I had to tell him immediately. It was just as well he was due in Moscow again.

Katya called me about a week later, hysterical and sobbing. Gaidar had caved in under enormous pressure and signed a decree announcing an international tender for Sukhoi Log.

I was in tears. I simply couldn't believe it was going to end like this.

"Listen, don't do anything just yet," said Katya through her sobs. "Don't tell Ian. I'm on my way over to see Golovnin to get all the details of why Gaidar betrayed us. Afterwards, I'll come to you."

I couldn't stop crying.

Katya arrived two hours later. She looked tired and shell-shocked. "Okay, listen. Gaidar is a yellow-bellied snake. The only good news is that he's really in trouble. The parliament is refusing to confirm his candidacy as prime minister. I think he is on his way out."

"Shit! What did Golovnin say?"

"He said the pressure on Gaidar was just too great. Ludmila, I've been thinking. There's only one thing left to do in this desperate moment."

"What?"

"Go to Yeltsin. Tell him Gaidar is a traitor. I'll go and see him tomorrow."

I woke with a knot in my stomach, and it wasn't just the baby. I threw up repeatedly in the bathroom. When I'd stopped vomiting, I paced the apartment. Would Katya really be able to see Yeltsin, who was busy fighting his own battles? Just the day before, he'd accused the parliament of being "a fortress of conservative and reactionary forces which needs to be replaced." The hostile parliament had responded by voting to take control of the Russian army.

At 2 p.m., Katya finally rang. "It's me. I'm on my way over to you. Relax, it's going to be fine."

Thirty minutes later, she arrived at the apartment, grinning from ear to ear. "It's all done! Yeltsin will make the decree disappear!" she cried.

I demanded to hear everything in detail, starting from the moment Katya got to the White House. Predictably, Katya suggested we go for a walk around the block.

"I arrived at 10 a.m. and waited for almost three hours," she began. "Yeltsin was in an emergency cabinet meeting. Suddenly he came out of one of the rooms. I charged toward him and stood there, shaking and crying.

"'Ekaterina, what's wrong?' he asked, surprised.

"'President Yeltsin, something awful has happened,' I replied. 'Gaidar has acted against your wishes. He signed an illegal decree in direct violation of your orders. Here it is.' I then handed it to him."

Yeltsin, she went on, was furious. He said that if this was true, he would overturn Gaidar's illegal decree immediately. "Ekaterina, dry your tears," he told her. "I will fix this."

"Katya, you are my hero!" I cried. "Are you sure he will do it?"

"One hundred percent."

"How did Yeltsin look?"

"Like Zeus with all the heavens crashing around him."

A few days later we heard that when Yatskevich discovered Gaidar's tender decree had vanished into thin air, he exploded with rage—which we had a good laugh about.

The day after, Yeltsin and Khasbulatov (the leader of parliament and one of my suitors) reached a compromise with the estranged parliament. If Yeltsin withdrew his nomination for Gaidar's premiership, the parliament would endorse a national referendum on the new Russian constitution to be held in April, with most of Yeltsin's temporary extraordinary powers extended until then—including power to appoint the prime minister and the military leadership without parliamentary approval, as well as to appoint the new members of the powerful Security Council, which he headed. If a vote of no confidence against the government were passed, the president could keep office for three months and dissolve the parliament if it cast the same vote again. Lastly, the president couldn't be impeached for contravening the Constitution.

So, Gaidar was effectively sacked.

Two days later, Yeltsin nominated Chernomyrdin for the role of prime minister. The parliament supported Chernomyrdin as he was an old Communist baron in charge of Gazprom—the state gas and oil enterprise—but still a supporter of privatization and reform, albeit at a slower pace. Chernomyrdin was a heavily built man with thinning gray hair and frameless glasses. He possessed an endearing demeanor, unlike Gaidar.

Ian returned to Moscow that same day. He was shocked when I told him how Gaidar had betrayed us.

"Are you sure the decree has been destroyed?" he asked.

"Yes. Gaidar is gone, so his decree was never registered. In Russia, if it's not entered into the registry, it doesn't exist."

I decided to wait to tell Ian about my pregnancy. We'd been invited that evening to the home of Dr. Boris Lebedev, one of Russia's leading nuclear research scientists, who worked at the Ministry of Atomic Energy (MinAtom). Lebedev had been born in Astana, the capital of Kazakhstan (a former Soviet Union republic rich in gold deposits), but now lived in Moscow.

According to Ian, Lebedev was also involved in a big gold deal in Kazakhstan. Ian had been introduced to Lebedev by a woman called Nadya. Not long ago, when Ian was escorting me to the airport, hers was the black stretch limousine with blacked-out windows that intercepted our car; she accepted a large yellow envelope from Ian before speeding off, and Ian casually explained that her name was Nadya, and she was a Ukrainian scientist who had introduced him to an interesting gold deal in Kazakhstan. At the time, I was focused on Lenzoloto and dismissed the encounter. Years later, when more pieces of the Ian MacNee puzzle fell into place and the real reason for his interest in Kazakhstan emerged, I would look at Lebedev with new eyes too.

Lebedev was a short, stocky man with a nice smile. Getting through dinner with him and his family was a strain. By this stage of my pregnancy, constant nausea and tiredness had kicked in. Lebedev did not mention the gold deposit in Kazakhstan and only discussed Lenzoloto at the table. He stressed how important it was for MinAtom to be a player in Sukhoi Log and how important it was to win the support of the minister, Viktor Mikhaylov.

Finally, the evening came to an end. We arrived back at the apartment just as it started to snow. Ian, Chris, and I stood on the pavement for a magical moment, watching the snowflakes fall in the soft glow of the streetlights. It was surreal, and a rare moment when we took time out, albeit briefly, to appreciate Moscow's more enchanting qualities.

Then we went inside and up to Chris's apartment for a nightcap. Ian opened a bottle of Mumm champagne. He was in a party mood, but all I wanted to do was return to my apartment and tell him the news. Eventually I made an excuse to leave. Ian said he'd walk me home. My apartment was in the same block as Chris's but had a different entrance, which meant that I had to walk back along the street. Moscow at night was no longer safe.

We got inside the apartment, and Ian started to kiss me. I kissed him back and then wriggled out of his embrace. "Let's sit down. I have something to tell you."

He sat next to me and held my hands.

"I'm pregnant."

Ian's face broke into the widest smile I'd ever seen.

"That's wonderful!" he exclaimed.

I then told him how scared I'd been that he might be angry.

"Never! Never! To have another Angus all over again is fantastic." He was actually shouting.

We discussed the future and our child. Ian said that he loved me and I wasn't to worry about Russia. By the time I needed to return home to have the baby, everything would be sewn up.

On December 17, I met with Mikhaylov as Lebedev had suggested. Mikhaylov traded Russia's uranium and oversaw the nuclear program. He was a big, strong man in his fifties who thought he was God. He reminded me of Avlov.

At the end of the meeting, he gave me a signed copy of his autobiography, *I Am a Hawk*, and said he would test me on its contents at our second meeting. If I passed, he would support Star. I spent all night reading the damned book, which was egocentric and rather boring.

Mikhaylov called the next day. "Did you enjoy my book?"

"Very much, especially the part when you were awarded the prize for excellence by Gorbachev."

"Ahhh, I see you read it. Good girl. I'll be in touch."

Ian was preparing to leave Russia to spend Christmas with Bobby and Angus in Aspen. For the first time since we'd met, this hurt. Before his departure, he revealed that Malcolm Turnbull was keen to join Star. "He can raise the money needed for Lenzoloto. He makes his own decisions and can act fast, which is a refreshing change from dealing with the NatWest and Hambros banks. I think we'll go with him. The others can invest funds when Malcolm floats Star, i.e., offers Star shares in a public offering through the Australian Stock Exchange."

Ian then switched the subject to my own shareholding in Star.

"As you know, my eighty percent in Star is held through several overseas companies registered in the British Virgin Islands, mainly for tax purposes," he said. "You'll be better off if you hide your Star shares in one of these overseas companies. I suggest Pan Pacific Sulphur. It will work a lot better, tax-wise. In a few years, we'll sell Pan Pacific for one hundred million and reap the profit, tax-free. You stand to end up with twenty million."

"Ian, I really don't know anything about offshore accounts and international tax matters, but it sounds good."

"Think about it and let me know."

"What about Greg?"

Ian replied that he'd proposed the same arrangement to Greg and hoped he would agree. "The last thing we want is Greg selling shares on the open market—or worse, to someone like RTZ. He could do it."

I was very impressed with how Ian conducted his business. Only millionaires had offshore companies, and I wanted to be part of this world. I was pregnant, in love, and, naively, trusted him implicitly. The next day, I faxed Tess, his accountant, instructing her to set up the Pan Pacific shares for me.

She faxed me back the forms transferring my Star shares to Pan Pacific. I ended up with 20 percent of Pan Pacific, which was equivalent to my 10 percent of Star.

Greg called to discuss his shares. He was reluctant to give them over to Ian. I told him I was going to agree to it. In the end, he agreed to have his shareholding in Star annulled in return for 20 percent of Pan Pacific. So, I owned 20 percent of Pan Pacific Ltd., as did Greg. Ian had 60 percent—the controlling interest.

CHAPTER NINETEEN

Australia's First President?

I flew home for Christmas and was back in Moscow on January 10, 1993. Even though we were still a long way from securing Sukhoi Log, I felt that the big pot of gold (literally) at the end of the rainbow was in sight. I planned to work in Russia for as long as I could, then return home to have the baby. I would hire a live-in nanny and travel back and forth.

In February, Ian and I made another trip to Bodaibo to see Avlov, who was spending money left, right, and center. He was also borrowing money and spending that too. This was a real worry as it was critical to present Lenzoloto as a profitable company when we asked the stock market for funds.

Avlov invited us to the company dacha for a big lunch on the shores of Lake Baikal, the deepest lake in the world. As it was winter, the river was frozen solid. The only way to get to the dacha was to drive across the ice. Avlov assured us it was perfectly safe.

We got into a black Volga car with Avlov and Peter, the head of the only artel who'd remained faithful to Avlov. Normally I would have been enthusiastic about the trip across the lake, but since I was four months pregnant by now, I wasn't sure I wanted to go. Ian, however, was very excited, and my consolation was that he was right there next to me.

As the car sped along the ice, Ian grabbed my hand and squeezed it, and gradually, I started to enjoy the ride. The ice glistened before us as far as the eye could see and then exploded into a blinding haze of light. It felt eerie, as if we were on another planet. Three hours later, we arrived.

The dacha was stunning. The snow had melted, revealing a gorgeous two-story timber cabin painted in white and light blue. At the back stood a timber sauna, smoke pouring from its chimney. Later Ian and I watched as a group of Lenzoloto miners emerged from the sauna naked and laughing and jumped into an ice-cold plunge hole in the snow to cool off before reentering the sauna. We settled on the balcony overlooking the lake. It was simply enchanting.

Ian grabbed my hand. "I love you, little girl," he whispered.

"I love you too," I replied.

Lunch, once it started, lasted almost until sunset. Everyone except for the driver and me was drunk in the car on the way back. Avlov sat in the front passenger seat, and Ian, Peter, and I sat in the back. We were merrily singing Russian songs when suddenly Peter lunged at Avlov from behind and locked his strong miner's hands around Avlov's neck.

"You bastard," Peter cried, "I hate you! You have Lenzoloto. You have wealth and respect. And now you have Ludmila too. I am going to kill you!"

As Avlov struggled to escape Peter's grasp, the driver grabbed Peter's arm, trying to push Peter backward, causing the car to swerve and then slide all over the ice.

"Stop the car!" I yelled hysterically.

The driver managed to regain control of the car, and we ground to a halt on the ice. Avlov reached for his pocket and pulled out a gun, pointing it in Peter's direction.

Ian pulled open my car door and yelled, "Get out!"

As we scrambled from the car, we watched Avlov struggle with Peter. Finally, Peter let go of Avlov's neck, and Avlov lowered the gun.

When we got back into the car, Peter was sobbing. A few minutes later he'd fallen asleep. Avlov held my hand from the front seat. I held Ian's hand in the back seat.

"Sorry about this," said Avlov.

"Do you always carry a gun?" I asked.

"Lately, yes. I've had so many death threats. There are many people who would love to kill me and wouldn't hesitate to do so. They all want Sukhoi Log—but they're not going to get it. It belongs to us. I will never give it up. So, for now, I carry a gun."

I was relieved to get into bed that night with Ian's arms firmly around me.

Back in Moscow, our new friend Alexei had become Star's newly appointed corporate lawyer and part of our team. Ian was paying him US$5,000 per month to solve our legal problems. Earlier, Alexei had come up with a brilliant and simple solution to our legal problems: merging the Lenzoloto Association with the Lenzoloto JSC so that Lenzoloto JSC would end up with the mining rights.

We presented the scheme and the amendments to Mostovoy. Since he was a lawyer and a very smart man, he immediately accepted everything we proposed.

I decided to take advantage of the situation. "Mr. Mostovoy, can I also suggest that we include in the amendments transferring ten percent of Lenzoloto to Irkutsk and ten percent to MinAtom? I'm friends with Mikhaylov, the minister—"

"Stop right there!" he said, cutting me off. "I have spoken to the powers above about this question, and I can't do anything at present. Please don't raise this issue again. My hands are tied."

"But I thought you had agreed in principle to—"

"The decision is from above. End of conversation."

"Fine," I said shortly, feeling incredibly frustrated at the greed, ignorance, and misplaced self-belief of these young government reformers.

On March 23, Mostovoy issued a new ordinance on the merger of the Lenzoloto Association and the Lenzoloto JSC. That same day, as per Ian's original plan, Central Mining made a joyous announcement to the market: "We are on track to acquire the whole of Star Technology."

At this point, the journalist Leyla Boulton resurfaced with an article on April 1 in the *Financial Times*. She wrote that according to Yatskevich, Lenzoloto JSC did not own the Sukhoi Log license and the deposit was earmarked for a tender—and the KGB also wanted a tender, which was why they hadn't declassified the data on the deposit.

As if we didn't have enough problems without Ms. Boulton's poison pen!

Ian panicked and asked Alexei to prepare a legal brief on the lawfulness of the Lenzoloto JSC and an opinion on the political risks of investing in Lenzoloto JSC. This was for our three banks—NatWest, Hambros, and Turnbull & Partners; after all, he was asking these people for the US$250 million charter capital, plus a further US$750 million in loans to build the Sukhoi Log mine.

After Ian read Alexei's very positive formal advice, I asked if he felt better about things. "Yes, I do," he replied. "I just wish we'd listened to Azarova and insisted on the clause she drafted protecting Star from any default by the Russian government if it failed to lift the secrecy on time."

"We tried, but Mostovoy flatly refused. If you remember, he guaranteed the secrecy would be lifted on time."

"Yes, but it hasn't happened, and time is ticking on. We're at risk of defaulting on our obligations under the founding documents. Our deadline to come up with one hundred twenty-five million is March 1994. The KGB isn't budging. Nobody will give me money if the secrecy isn't lifted. We need the geological data the Russians put together. Only then can we prepare a bankable feasibility study."

"Katya is on it," I replied. "She's trying to find out exactly who in the KGB is blocking us and what can be done to make them go away."

I added that I'd talk to Alexei again. He seemed very creative and could hopefully solve this problem for us too.

"Oh, my love, what would I ever do without you?" he asked.

"Oh, you'd fail," I laughed.

Later, we talked about the baby. "You know, I would love to call the baby Hamish if it's a boy. But people would know straightaway it's mine," said Ian at one point.

It was another major slip. At the time, considering everything else that was going on, it glided over me.

On April 10, Alexei let Ian know that the minister of security (KGB), whose signature could lift the secrecy on Sukhoi Log, had told him that Star needed to show the color of its money before he'd do anything.

Ian speculated that Malcolm Turnbull might agree to raise the money without the secrecy lifting.

"Well, I'd make him a priority then," I replied. "We can suggest that he transfer the money on a guarantee from the KGB to lift the secrecy. We have to blow apart this stalemate ASAP."

Ian was talking all the time now about Malcolm Turnbull—about how successful and fearless he was. I was more cautious. No matter how gutsy he might be, Malcolm was still a lawyer. He would examine the founding documents with a microscope and find holes.

Privately, I wondered: Did Malcolm really know what he was in for? Of course, the upside was that Star held a 31 percent stake in the world's richest goldfield. Millions could be made on the stock exchange once we listed.

Avlov came to Moscow with a full financial report on Lenzoloto. I faxed the main pages to Ian in Aspen. The report was mostly incomprehensible, but the bottom line was that Lenzoloto was operating at a loss. This was a shock. When we first looked at Lenzoloto in April 1991, it was making a yearly profit of US$14.6 million.

The problem was that Ian had already provided Malcolm Turnbull with figures showing a profit. "What are you going to do?" I asked him over the phone.

"Oh, nothing. I can't change the story now," he replied. "The project is still highly profitable. Sukhoi Log alone holds at least eleven hundred tons of gold, which is worth about twenty-one billion. It's a jackpot for Malcolm."

"Fine, but what are we going to do about Avlov?"

"He must be stopped, or he could bankrupt the company. Between you and me, I'd much rather set up a new company specifically to mine Sukhoi Log, with a similar shareholding. Star could then contribute its money directly into this new company."

"Ian, that's like starting all over again!" I said, exasperated.

I was becoming seriously concerned with the way Ian constantly came up with ideas and new projects, only to abandon them a few months later. It sometimes seemed he was incapable of seeing any one project through to the end. Perhaps this was why he hadn't really succeeded at anything since we'd met. And yet he was extremely wealthy. It was paradoxical.

My belly was growing rapidly. I was lucky the nausea had subsided, but I felt tired and washed out all the time, and I was also very lonely when Ian was out of town. I avoided all social life in Moscow, as I hadn't told anyone I was pregnant. The girls in the office suspected, for sure. But the guys, including Chris, were clueless.

I worked from my apartment during the day and into the evening before going to bed early and watching CNN (an American news channel) until I fell asleep. I kept telling myself that everything would turn out well. Ian had suggested we find a nice apartment to rent in an upmarket suburb called Kirribilli on the edge of Sydney Harbour. He said he was also considering sending Angus to Geelong Grammar in July, which would mean Bobby moving to Lambruk. He continued to talk of taking me to Aspen.

It all sounded wonderful. But in Moscow, I was living on a knife's edge. One moment we were in control of what was happening with Star, and the next moment, we weren't. It was a roller coaster ride in a corrupt land of smoke and mirrors.

At least Yeltsin was having better luck. On April 25, the national referendum was held, and remarkably, the Russian people supported the president and his young reformers. Katya and I rejoiced. Saved once again!

On April 29, Ian finally came through with the long-awaited funds. He sent a letter addressed to Mostovoy and Avlov from our banks, NatWest in London and Turnbull's in Sydney, confirming they were in the process of raising A$50 million, US$20 million of which would be deposited into Star's Dialogue Bank account in Moscow on May 31 and then transferred into Lenzoloto's account.

The only real competitor we had now was that Russian businessman Chugaevsky, the same guy Kuzmin had mentioned to me, who was claiming he had the capital from several London banks to mine Sukhoi Log. I asked Katya to investigate. Katya rang him. Like magic, Chugaevsky agreed to see her.

She had lunch with him at his dacha in the forest and reported back that he could be a real threat to us. He had hundreds of files on Sukhoi Log in his library, as well as the official reserve document, which he showed Katya. "It's dated December 30, 1967, and states that you can mine twenty million ounces per year for twenty years," she said.

"Katya, that's four hundred million ounces of ore!" I did some quick calculations and came up with a reserve figure of 4,200 tons of gold, four times the reserve figure Avlov gave us. "Katya, I'd love a copy of that protocol!"

"Impossible. We need permission first."

"Well, how the hell did Chugaevsky get it?" I demanded.

"He's a patriot and feels that Russian assets should be in Russian hands," said Katya. "He has met with Yeltsin and is also Gaidar's close friend. He thinks our main mistake was not keeping up relations with Gaidar, who still decides everything to this day. He's close to the minister of finance too, and he's best buddies with Yatskevich."

"Of course he is," I said sarcastically. "I'm sure Yatskevich gave him the secret protocol."

"Probably. He has met with Mikhaylov three times too."

"What, my Mikhaylov, the minister of atomic energy?" I said incredulously.

"Yes, and he says he has opened the minister's eyes regarding a tender for Sukhoi Log. But he respects Star and regards us as a serious competitor even though he intends to fight for a tender with only Russian companies. He hinted he may meet with you in the future."

"Did you tell him Lenzoloto already has the license to mine Sukhoi Log?"

"Yes, but Yatskevich told him the old license is invalid, and only he can issue a new license, which he never will."

"I'm so sick of Yatskevich!" I cried. "Something really must be done to stop him."

"I think we should meet with Yeltsin's new aide, Sukhanov, and expose Yatskevich."

"How much will it cost?"

"Oh, nothing. I'm a good friend of Sukhanov," said Katya. "I think we should also take Chugaevsky's advice and see Golovnin to reopen our relationship with Gaidar," she continued.

"Yes, when?"

"Last week of May."

"The twenty million should be in Moscow by then, which will change the status quo in our favor," I said.

"I will arrange it immediately."

I let Ian know the latest. He was now working closely with Malcolm. My news about Chugaevsky possessing the official reserve document spurred them on. I also sent them a detailed report with as much ammunition and information as I could dig up. Ian faxed, praising what I'd done. I now felt confident that Malcolm Turnbull would come to the party.

Then Leyla Boulton spoiled everything again. She was like a dog with a bone. On May 7, she wrote another article in the British *Financial Times* on Lenzoloto and Star. She'd interviewed Alexei and twisted his words. Alexei had explained to her that Star was legally entitled to the data on Sukhoi Log. The only problem was that the deposit was listed in the decree of government secrets and would need another government decree to declassify it. "So how," wrote Ms. Boulton, "could Star invest USD250 million without seeing the data?"

I've often wondered why Leyla was so negative toward Star. Financial journalists were regularly wined and dined by Russian politicians and the big foreign corporations. The only explanation for her bias was that we hadn't pampered her when she first contacted us. The best way to counteract her was to pamper Australian journalist John Helmer, her rival, who would publish the true facts about Star in the *Australian Financial Review*, the *Sydney Morning Herald*, the *Business Review Weekly*, and in the major international mining publications.

Ian was working with Malcolm Turnbull in Sydney, and things were moving fast. He wanted me back in Sydney too, as soon as possible, especially since I'd been told that I couldn't fly once my pregnancy passed seven months.

Regardless, I felt that I needed to stay in Moscow for another week, to see Golovnin and visit the Kremlin and make sure Malcolm had all the information he needed. Once I left, it would be like a blackout for a few months.

Chris came down to the apartment for a rare visit and asked when the baby was due. It was the first time he'd asked about the baby. I told him the father was a guy from home. Jokingly, I asked if Chris wanted to take over from me. He laughed and said, "No way! I wish I was pregnant and on my way home." His ambivalence about his father's project had never been more evident.

Just as I'd predicted, questions from Malcolm started pouring in for me to answer, which I did, meticulously. Ian then faxed to say that Central Mining had completed its A$6 million fundraising for working capital. We were cashed up!

On May 14, Central Mining Corporation NL (CMC) made an announcement to the market that an agreement had been reached with Malcolm Turnbull to do the fundraising for CMC to take over Star.

The following day, Chris, Katya, and I drove out to Golovnin's dacha, where we'd been invited for shashlik before I left Moscow. We were in the middle of the Russian forest, with the sun setting slowly through the pine trees. It was a lovely setting for my farewell.

"So, Ludmila, will we ever see you again?" asked Golovnin.

"Yes, of course. I intend to travel back and forth after the baby is born. How is Gaidar?" I asked, changing the subject. Baby talk bored me to tears.

"He has been following your progress with interest."

"Is he still supporting a tender?"

"No, no, he actually never was. He was just pushed into signing the decree by the KGB and certain political factions. In the end, he had no choice."

I commented that I'd been devastated by Gaidar's actions, but that it was history and we should move on.

Golovnin chose this point to reveal that Gaidar would be returning to government as the first deputy prime minister soon—and that he, Golovnin, would be Gaidar's aide once more. And then, at the end of the evening, just as we were leaving, he told us the rest. "I have a message from Gaidar. You must put in some money, even just ten or twenty million. You must do it now, to show you have money. You will see how fast the situation will change in your favor once this is done. It's worth the risk," he added.

Fine. Now it was my turn. I said that a very powerful investment banker had just joined Star. "In fact, he's poised to be Australia's first president," I added.

Then I told Golovnin his name.

CHAPTER TWENTY

The Miracle of Conversion

On May 16 in Irkutsk, Nozhikov got wind that Star planned to contribute US$20 million by May 31. He promptly sent a message to Moscow, threatening Irkutsk's secession from Russia if a tender wasn't announced immediately.

In response, Yatskevich declared he was ready to tender Sukhoi Log. I called Katya and asked her to organize an urgent meeting with Sukhanov, Yeltsin's first aide.

She called back ten minutes later. "Tomorrow at 10 a.m. He knows about the message from Nozhikov. He asked if the money will be in Moscow by the end of this month."

"Great. I'll discuss it all with him tomorrow."

The next morning, Katya and I drove into the Kremlin. We walked up the marble steps and into the Grand Kremlin Palace, a grandiose, golden-yellow building with carved white-stone windows and a sage-green roof topped by a golden dome and four gilded clocks. This was Yeltsin's residence and was closed to the public. We were met by a friendly young man who escorted us to a marble bench inside the entrance hall and asked us to wait. An hour passed.

"Katya, I have to go to the toilet."

"Cross your legs, girl. I will have to find out where one is."

Luckily, the same young man was able to show me where the toilet was—just in time. Ten minutes after I returned, Sukhanov appeared and led us into a lavish office decorated with marble and gold statues and exquisite oil paintings.

He sat us down on a plush brown leather couch and took an armchair opposite us. It made for quite a scene: a little old lady and a very pregnant woman sitting with the president's aide in the Kremlin, discussing how to get a US$21 billion project back on track.

"Tell me your woes," said Sukhanov.

I did—including the fact that Nozhikov wanted 10 percent of Lenzoloto JSC.

"Of course he does," replied Sukhanov. "Yeltsin feels Irkutsk should have ten percent."

"We agree, but Mostovoy is being difficult."

"I'll give Mostovoy a call. You said there were a couple of people trying to stop you," Sukhanov added.

"Yes. The main problem is Yatskevich," I replied. "He feels a pearl like Sukhoi Log should go to a famous international company like RTZ."

"Sukhoi Log will never fall into foreign hands," said Sukhanov reassuringly. "Star is a minority shareholder supplying the capital Russia needs. This is an acceptable scenario. I think your main problem is that a lot of people doubt whether you have the capital."

"Yes, I know, but we're about to make our first contribution of twenty million US. This has been arranged by a very prominent banker called Malcolm Turnbull, who stands to be the first president."

"You can't mean Russia's, as we already have one—so you must mean Australia's?" said Sukhanov with a grin.

"Yes, Australia's," I replied, smiling back at him. "We are finally becoming a republic, and Malcolm is spearheading the Republic Movement."

"What does Queen Elizabeth think about that? You know, Yeltsin entertained her in this very palace. He found her amusing, but they had very little in common."

"As do we. If Australia votes to become a republic, she will have to accept it. She is just a figurehead, and Malcolm will become Australia's first president."

"All this is very solid indeed. Very impressive." Sukhanov seemed to mean what he was saying. "I will see what I can do about Yatskevich, but frankly, he's not that important. Once your money is in, he'll have no choice but to follow orders."

It was the perfect opportunity to introduce the problem of the secrecy ruling on Sukhoi Log's data, which I did. "It's a real hindrance to us contributing the funds on time," I added.

"It's a complicated problem," acknowledged Sukhanov. "Again, once you have made your first contribution, we'll see what can be done. Thank you for coming, and good luck."

It was a sobering meeting, but at least Yeltsin still seemed to be supporting us. I now felt we were under the protective eye of the Kremlin. Everything, though, hinged on Star delivering the money. I hoped Malcolm Turnbull was as good as he sounded.

I had no idea what Ian said to convince him, but from what I understood, Malcolm had committed to raising AU$50 million without the secrecy being lifted—and without the new licenses being issued.

Malcolm's main condition was that the Lenzoloto founding agreement (including the secrecy lifting and the issuing of new licenses) had to be ratified by a reputable law firm. On cue, I received a fax from Turnbull's bank asking Baker & McKenzie, which had opened an office in Moscow in 1989, to ratify the Lenzoloto founding agreement and charter. This was a concern, because Baker & McKenzie might very well take the document apart, as lawyers liked to do. But at least they'd had experience with Russian peculiarities.

The problem in the document was the clause forcing Star to contribute US$125 million (50 percent of its charter capital) by March 26, 1994, whether the Russian side carried out its obligations or not, including the secrecy lifting. It was one thing to commit US$20 million blindly—but another US$105 million? No way! Even Sukhanov had no immediate solution. Someone in the KGB was blocking it.

Alexei was laboring over a legal solution to this. I decided to work with him over the next few days. I knew I had to resolve it before I flew home to be interrogated by Mr. Turnbull.

May 29 was my birthday. I was thirty-three, single, and seven months pregnant. Ian rang to wish me a happy birthday: "I love you and I will see you soon. When are you leaving?"

"June 3."

"The ticket is on its way."

A first-class ticket on Lufthansa arrived. First class! I'd never flown first class before. I was still exulting over this when Alexei paid me a surprise visit to say that he'd solved the problem of the US$125 million contribution. Better still, he had already run it past Mostovoy—who agreed.

"Well, don't keep me in suspense!" I exclaimed.

"In a nutshell, with the Russian side's sixty-nine-percent share valued at 1,391 million in rubles, Star's thirty-one percent, in rubles, equals 625 million—"

"Which means," I said excitedly, interrupting him, "that to satisfy the law on foreign investment, Star can contribute fifty percent of 625 million rubles, which converted into dollars is only—"

"892,857 dollars US!" interjected Alexei.

"Oh, Alexei, you are brilliant! And you say Mostovoy has approved this?"

"Yes. Mostovoy still wants Star to pay a total of one hundred twenty-five million by the end of 1994 and a total of two hundred fifty by March 26, 1996, but he's thrilled with my idea. I am drafting up the amendments."

I was so happy I kissed him on the cheek. Then, after he'd gone, I called Ian and summed up the state of play.

We had the license to mine Sukhoi Log; it just needed to be reregistered with Geolkom, which Sukhanov, Yeltsin's aide, said Yatskevich would be ordered to do. The secrecy would be lifted once the Russians had received our US$20 million. Then we had until the end of 1994 to contribute the balance of US$125 million, which was plenty of time. Malcolm Turnbull's bank could now proceed with the job of raising the A$50 million. Just as good, Baker & McKenzie had signed off on our founding documents.

Moreover, I was going home to have Ian's baby!

CHAPTER TWENTY-ONE

A Baby Is Born

My plane landed in Sydney bright and early. Ian was waiting at the airport. He'd arranged for us to stay at the Park Hyatt in the Rocks on the harbor before I moved into my Bronte Beach apartment. This modern, luxurious five-star hotel was reminiscent of an exclusive harborside residence, boasting unparalleled views of the iconic Opera House and Sydney Harbour Bridge. We caught a taxi there and, after checking into our penthouse suite, went downstairs for lunch.

The rest of the weekend was a blissful orgy of sex, food, and a little champagne. I was deliriously happy. Over dinner, I questioned Ian about Angus. So much seemed to depend on this kid.

"The decision has been made. He and his mother arrive in three weeks," said Ian.

"Oh, great, just in time for the birth!" I exclaimed sarcastically. A mistake. Ian's face screwed up with displeasure. "So, Angus will be starting boarding school immediately?" I went on.

"Yes. Once he's at high school, Bobby and I will go our separate ways. Don't worry, little girl, everything will be fine," he added, and kissed me on the forehead.

On Monday, I moved back into my apartment in Bronte Beach. It felt wonderful to be home. The apartment was in an older block of four, with spectacular ocean views. There were two levels, with the lower one opening onto a pretty, country-style garden. I had also installed a huge balcony with sliding glass doors off the lounge room, to capture the stunning views of the Pacific Ocean.

I unpacked and made a cup of tea, since I'd completely gone off my beloved coffee during my pregnancy. The beauty of the shimmering bright-blue sea was mesmerizing. I adored the ocean—the smell of the salty spray and the sound of the waves. I actually preferred the ocean to the harbor. Even so, my dream was to own a mansion on Sydney Harbour, with a little beach house somewhere up the coast.

A couple of days later, I finally visited an obstetrician and learned that I'd developed gestational diabetes. Too many hamburgers and Caramello chocolate bears in Moscow! Everything else, though, was fine. We calculated that the baby was due around July 26. The doctor said that if I didn't have the baby by then, we'd have to induce the birth using a gel. The baby was getting too much glucose from me and could go into shock after birth due to a sharp drop in blood sugar levels. At worst, my child could become too fat and die in the womb. So, it was important to get the baby out exactly on the due date.

The doctor put me on a very strict diet and sent me to the Diabetes Centre in the highly reputable Royal North Shore Hospital, where they equipped me with a kit containing a needle to prick my finger half an hour after every meal to measure my sugar level. If it reached a certain level, I had to call the obstetrician immediately, presumably for an urgent Caesarean. So, I started a sugarless diet and pricked myself religiously.

Ian's desire was the give the baby a Scottish name, and we finally settled on the name Lachlan for a boy and Bonny if it was a girl.

To be safe, my doctor booked the Mater Hospital in North Sydney for the night of July 26, when I would be induced and hopefully give birth the next day. I couldn't wait; I was over being pregnant.

July 1 was Ian's birthday—only, he was in Moscow, about to travel to Irkutsk with Mostovoy, who insisted he come. Mostovoy also insisted that at least US$5 million be deposited into an escrow account in the name of Lenzoloto JSC, to be released upon the secrecy lifting. After much discussion, Ian and Malcolm—whom I still hadn't met—decided to oblige. Central Mining transferred the money into an escrow account in the name of Lenzoloto JSC with the Dialogue Bank in Moscow before Ian left for Moscow.

He and Mostovoy spent seven days in Irkutsk, flying Lenzoloto's flag in an attempt to win over the Irkutsk government. To Ian's face, everyone was positive and polite. Ian, being the eternal optimist, declared the visit a triumph.

But it wasn't so. And by mid-July, it became apparent that the situation in Irkutsk had grown worse. The local press was full of negative articles about the visit. One article even printed a photo of Ian with a little figure of Mostovoy in his suit pocket. The title read, "Australian con man bribes deputy minister of GKI." It suggested that Ian was simply out to make a quick killing on the stock market and was paying Mostovoy off.

Shortly after, Mostovoy forwarded me a copy of the long and at times emotional letter he had written to Yeltsin, essentially asking Yeltsin to help clean up the Lenzoloto mess.

What he said was eye-opening and on the mark. In one stunning revelation, he wrote:

> In mid-1992, the new tender process for major deposits... created the illusion of attracting foreign investors in a *civilised* and fair way. However, problems arose on how to safeguard certain deposits of national significance, including gold. It became imperative for the government to retain control of these deposits, and attempts to negotiate terms acceptable to both the foreign investor and the Government so far have not produced positive results. This is partly due to the lack of understanding on the Russian side of Western business practices, partly due to the egotism of regional governments and partly to the corrupt and personal interests of the organizers of the tender.

In the meantime, I had more urgent, personal problems. By July 26, the baby still hadn't come. That evening, I was to be induced. I met Ian at Fran's place at 7 p.m. He arrived with three bottles of Moët, which he consumed with Fran, so I had to drive myself and them to the hospital. Upon my being checked into a room in the birth ward, the doctor came in and applied a thick, warm gel inside the birth canal. The gel would work overnight, he explained, and I should go into labor the next day.

The nurse came in, looked at Ian, and exclaimed, "You must be the grandfather!" Ian laughed it off nervously. He stayed a little longer, then escaped.

When I woke up the next morning, I felt much the same, but by the time Fran arrived at 11 a.m., I had started to experience mild cramps every ten minutes or so. We walked around the hospital, and the pain intensified.

"You know, I hate this already," I confided to her. "I would be much more comfortable in a suit in a boardroom!"

"Of course you would!"

By lunchtime, I was in excruciating pain, and at 6 p.m., I finally agreed to laughing gas. It didn't help. I then agreed to pethidine. It didn't help. The room started to spin, and I grabbed onto the bed to stop from fainting. Though my threshold for pain had always been high, I found the pain of childbirth unbearable.

"I want an epidural now!" I yelled.

The nurse ran off to catch the anesthetist, who was about to leave the hospital. He came to my room and injected the drug into my spine. Ten minutes later, like magic, the pain was gone, and feeling euphoric, I completely relaxed. The nurse examined me shortly afterward and declared that I was ten centimeters dilated, which meant I was ready to give birth. She rushed to the phone and called my obstetrician, who was in the middle of his dinner. She returned with a large round mirror so I could witness the birth and told me to keep my legs closed till my doctor arrived. Fifteen minutes later, he arrived and instructed me to open my legs and push when told. A few minutes later, at 8:36 p.m., I gave birth to a beautiful, healthy baby boy.

"Would you like to cut the umbilical cord?" asked the doctor.

"No, thank you" was my reply. I'd had enough of all the gore of childbirth.

My child was a different matter. I fell in love with him instantly. He was perfect, with jet-black hair and big brown eyes. The nurse eased him onto my nipple, and he happily suckled away. Suddenly, I remembered Ian.

Fran ran out to fetch him. Ian's face was purple with stress when he walked in. I gave him Lachlan and staggered to the shower. The cool water running all over my body was delicious. While I was in the shower, Ian tried to talk Fran into going to the pub. Fran said she thought it best to stay with me.

Lachlan's glucose had to be monitored overnight. A nurse took him away, and another nurse showed me to a new private room. Fran and I shared a pot of tea. Ian had already gone—to the pub.

"Too old! Couldn't hack it!" said Fran, laughing. I was rather shell-shocked myself.

Ian returned a day later, looking anxious. At the time, I thought he was still in shock. After all, he was married, and at his age, becoming a father again possibly wasn't a dream come true. Yet all I could see was a blissful little family living together happily ever after.

I asked him if he was all right, and he broke the news that Bobby was in town.

"Why is she here?" I demanded. This wasn't what I needed at all.

"Oh, to attend her friend's fiftieth. It's just bad timing," replied Ian.

"Yes, it certainly is," I said, not the least bit happy. "Just get rid of her."

"I'm trying."

I changed the subject by saying I thought we should hire a nanny as soon as possible. He agreed and suggested I sell my Bronte Beach apartment and stay temporarily with Fran while looking for an apartment on the harbor in Kirribilli. Ian regarded Bronte as a low-class area, which offended me greatly, but I kept that to myself. Ian was incorrect, as Bronte later would become one of the most expensive and exclusive suburbs of Sydney!

"And I want to return to work immediately," I went on. "Any news regarding Russia?"

"Malcolm Turnbull is totally committed to us. He has convinced NatWest in London to join him in the fundraising, so the money is practically a done deal. I've told Mostovoy we will release the five million dollars US as soon as the secrecy is lifted. He's trying his best to get this done."

After Ian left, more flowers were brought into my room. I'd already had flowers from my family and friends. The new flowers were a striking arrangement of two dozen long-stemmed roses in shades of pink, red, and yellow. I opened the card. It read, "To dear Ludmila, Congratulations on a baby boy. Love from Bobby and Ian."

I ran into the bathroom to throw up and stayed in there for an hour, crying my eyes out. It felt like the end of the world. I cursed Bobby and, when I finally emerged, ripped the roses apart and threw them in the bin.

July 31 was checkout day from the hospital. I would've preferred to stay longer, surrounded by the lovely nurses who took such good care of Lachie and me, but they said it was time to leave the nest and face the real world, which scared me. I had no idea what to do with a baby.

Both Fran and Ian were there. I didn't mention the offensive card to Ian. He paid the bill and then, to my surprise, said he had to race to a meeting. Before I could argue, he was in a taxi and gone.

I stared at Fran in disbelief. "He's gone!" My bottom lip was quivering.

"Don't worry," she replied. "He gave me two bottles of Moët. Let's go home and drink them." Fran had brought something called a capsule. She strapped Lachlan into it, adjusted the seat belts around him, and we drove to her place. Lachlan was asleep when we got there, so we left him in the capsule on the floor.

As we sat back and drank the champagne, I kept staring at the baby. "Hon, what am I supposed to do now?" I asked in despair.

"You'll learn," replied Fran.

I did.

The next period of my life was a blur. It was a time of never getting out of my flannelette pajamas and of desperately trying to put Lachie to sleep. I would anxiously await Fran's arrival home from work so I could hand Lachie over to her and have a shower. At one stage, I craved adult company so much that I stood waiting for her at the front gate—but at the same time, I loved my baby dearly.

One night, Ian took me to dinner at La Grillade, a local French restaurant. As I still had a "mummy tummy," I'd just managed to squeeze into a black jersey dress, which was stretched to its limits. But Ian couldn't take his eyes off me.

"You look absolutely radiant!" he exclaimed. "Motherhood really suits you. I bet you have taken to it like a fish to water!"

I could never tell him I was more like a fish out of water. Ian was old-fashioned. He thought that women were born knowing how to cook, clean, and rear children—and that men were not. He leaned over and kissed me passionately on the cheek. He had lust in his eyes. Unfortunately, sex was the furthest thing from my mind.

As we ate dinner, he asked when I was going to have Lachie circumcised.

"I'm not. No one does that anymore," I replied.

"Oh, you must," said Ian instantly. "I want him to look like his dad, so when we piddle together, we look the same." We argued about this briefly, but it seemed so important to Ian that eventually, reluctantly, I agreed.

We returned to Fran's place, and Ian pushed me into the bedroom. Fran and David, her husband, didn't even realize we were home.

On August 9, an article by John Helmer appeared in the *Sydney Morning Herald*, on Russia's new law on mineral wealth, which was about to be signed by Yeltsin. John wrote that this was great news for Ian MacNee's Central Mining NL and Star Technology, as it endorsed foreign entities mining precious metals, including gold ore and not just gold tailings.[5]

The article said that by acquiring Star Technology, Central Mining would instantly become the largest gold producer in the

---

5   John Helmer, "Russia's New Law on Mineral Wealth," *Sydney Morning Herald*, August 9, 1993.

Asia–Pacific region and would also increase its capitalization from 78.2 million shares to 381.3 million shares—all underwritten by Malcolm Turnbull's bank, acting for Star, which had been formed by a group of international investors wanting to invest in Russia's gold industry.

Malcolm was busily investigating Lenzoloto himself. He asked for independent opinions from both Gavrilov, the trade commissioner at the Russian Embassy in Canberra, and a conservative legal firm in London, Frere Cholmeley Bischoff, on Lenzoloto JSC and the Russian legal system.

I held my breath. Because of all the controversy, I was worried the reports could come back negative. But with a week-old son to look after, there was nothing I could do.

On August 25, 1993, Mostovoy issued an ordinance naming the directors of Lenzoloto JSC on the Russian side. Kuranov, first adviser to the minister of atomic energy, was on the list, which meant we still had the minister's support. The other directors were Mostovoy and Avlov; Kotliar, Bychkov's first deputy, as Bychkov refused to be a director; Andrey Nechayev, the minister for economics; and Yevgeny Fedorov, minister for finance. A rather prestigious board.

As word got around town about Malcolm joining Central Mining, its shares hit a record high of sixty-six cents. At that price, I calculated my shareholding to be worth close to A$8 million after the acquisition of Star.

Gavrilov's legal opinion came in. Surprisingly, it was good. Malcolm then wrote to Gavrilov, confirming that the US$20 million commitment should be provided to Lenzoloto before the end of the month.

He had no idea that a spiteful man called Yatskevich (we had nicknamed him "Yat the Rat") was sitting in Moscow, vowing that Star would never get the Sukhoi Log license unless it was over his dead body and refusing to take any orders from Yeltsin.

One evening at around seven o'clock, I was lying in bed, exhausted, as Lachlan had been circumcised that day, and both he and I were traumatized. Lachlan had just finally fallen asleep on my lap when the phone rang. An unfamiliar voice boomed down the line.

"Can I speak to Ludmila, please?"

"Speaking," I replied.

"This is Malcolm Turnbull."

"Oh, yes, I know about you," I replied, struggling blearily up on an elbow, trying not to wake Lachie and thinking, *What an inopportune time to ring me.*

"Ludmila, I'm trying very hard to get the fundraising underway. But I have a lot of questions, and no one seems to be able to answer them. I'm told you put the whole deal together and you are the only one who can help me."

"Well, yes, I am sure I can answer all your queries. But did you know that I've just had a baby?"

"Yes, I've been told. When do you expect to come back to work?"

"Soon. I know there are pressing issues."

He pounced. "Like what?"

"Like the licenses and secrecy lifting."

"Yes, and I would really love to discuss all that with you," said Malcolm. "We're aiming to sign the deal shortly. Will you be able to attend a meeting in my offices in a couple of weeks?"

"Yes, of course."

"Great. Nice to finally talk with you, Ludmila. I've heard a lot about you."

"Likewise, Malcolm. I'm really glad you have joined us."

"Thanks. Bye."

He hung up.

CHAPTER TWENTY-TWO

Meeting Malcolm

At home with Lachie, I spent hours reading and watching TV, monitoring what was happening in Russia. On September 18, Yeltsin announced he was bringing Gaidar back as first deputy prime minister. An enraged parliament rejected Gaidar's nomination. Nonetheless, Gaidar returned to government as acting first deputy prime minister—just as Golovnin had told me he would.

On September 21, I watched CNN in awe as Yeltsin dissolved the Russian parliament and announced new parliamentary elections for December 1993. He also issued a decree that replaced the existing constitution with a new one granting him extraordinary powers.

The following day, the Constitutional Court ruled that Yeltsin had violated the Constitution and could be impeached, while Alexander Rutskoy, Yeltsin's vice president, accused Yeltsin of a coup d'état. Rutskoy was unremarkable in appearance, with thick gray hair, a bushy moustache, and small blue eyes behind frameless glasses. He certainly did not possess Yeltsin's magnetic charisma. Khasbulatov and the parliament convened all night in the White House and declared Yeltsin's decree null and void. They named Rutskoy president. Rutskoy promptly sacked Yeltsin, together with his powerful defense, security, and interior ministers. I was shocked that Khasbulatov had decided to betray Yeltsin and side with Rutskoy!

Yeltsin ignored this and had the electricity, phone lines, and hot water in the White House disconnected. Meanwhile, tens of thousands of anti-Yeltsin demonstrators rallied around the building, protesting about their appalling living conditions, the new crime wave engulfing Moscow, the corruption, the deterioration of medical services, the lack of food, and the small group of "Yeltsin-made" billionaires—the so-called oligarchs—who'd emerged from the ruins with Russia's riches. In other words, they blamed Yeltsin for everything.

This was the last thing we needed on the eve of asking corporations and the public to give us A$50 million for a project in Russia!

I could just imagine the scenes inside the White House. So, it felt surreal when, on September 25, Ian and I inspected an apartment in Kirribilli to rent. It was a gorgeous large two-bedroom ground-floor apartment with an expansive balcony right on the harbor. Ian rented it for a year without hesitation. I'd already sold my Bronte apartment for A$460,000, pocketing a nice profit of $175,000, so was ready to move in. We then walked down to the local sailing club for a celebratory lunch.

I wanted to be with Ian for the rest of my life, with no compromises. I wanted all or nothing with him. Every day, he promised we would be together soon, living in a beautiful home as a family.

That week, Lachlan and I settled into our divine Kirribilli apartment. We could hear the jingling of the yachts bobbing in front of the balcony, which was magical. I immediately placed an advertisement in the paper for a full-time live-in nanny. Marty, a mother of six grown-up boys, who'd retired from work, answered, and I hired her. I figured that after raising six boys, she would know what she was doing!

A copy of Frere Cholmeley Bischoff's legal opinion on the state of the Lenzoloto JSC was forwarded to me. It validated all my arduous work for the past three years. I was so relieved. In a way, it was like passing an exam with high distinction.

I celebrated this triumph with Fran. We shared a couple of bottles of chardonnay and a Thai home delivery. Very hungover the following day, I was lounging with fuzzy eyes, enjoying a greasy hamburger, when I received a call from Graeme Ellis, Ian's friend and Central Mining's financial director, whom I'd met only once before.

"Ludmila, Malcolm has called a meeting at his offices this afternoon at 4 p.m. and specifically asked that you attend. Are you free?"

What was it about Malcolm Turnbull and his timing? "Yes," I said.

I finished the burger and raced to the nearest chemist to buy eye drops. Then I rushed home, showered, and put on my favorite Armani suit, a chocolate brown. I wore my hair as usual in a high ponytail and studied myself in the mirror. Not bad for a hungover, breastfeeding, out-of-shape first-time mum.

I rang Ian, who was back in Aspen.

"I'm so glad you called, little girl. I know you're on your way to meet Malcolm. They are finalizing the underwriting and placement documents, and he has some queries."

"I'm sure I can sort him out."

"I'm sure you can."

At 3 p.m., I caught a taxi to the offices of Central Mining in the city center. Graeme was waiting for me at the entrance. As we walked together toward Malcolm's offices, I asked what Malcolm was like. "I will refrain from saying anything. You will see for yourself," he replied.

At Turnbull & Partners, we were led into a boardroom and offered tea by Sam, Malcolm's busty blond secretary. I was dehydrated and dying of thirst, so tea was welcome. A few minutes later, Malcolm's associates walked in. I recognized Christian, a good-looking man with a friendly disposition. We all chatted politely, waiting for the man himself.

Ten minutes later, the door was flung open, and Malcolm Turnbull steamrolled into the room. The room suddenly felt small and crowded. He was undeniably attractive, although he looked like he enjoyed his food a bit too much. He had a mass of thick, dark-brown hair tinged with gray at the sides; huge, sexy dark eyes festooned by long eyelashes; and a roundish face capped off by a double chin.

"Malcolm, I would like you to meet our main player and one of Star's directors, Ludmila," said Graeme.

Malcolm walked over to me, shook my hand formally, and said, "I've been waiting patiently to meet you for a long time. I've been told you know everything there is to know about the project."

"Yes, I hope I do," I replied. "Malcolm, I have to say, the Russians will love you."

"Why?"

"Because you look like a big Russian bear."

The room went silent. Malcolm grinned. "Splendid," he said.

He then got down to business, updating everyone on the legal opinions and on where the fundraising was at before asking me how I saw the current political situation in Russia.

"Yeltsin is locked in a battle with parliament," I said. "But I have no doubt he'll win. There could be some fighting in the near term, but long term, this is a good thing. The parliament is full of old Communists who block all of Yeltsin's reforms. I've attended many sessions, and it's a hopeless deadlock. Yeltsin plans to hold new elections, and this should result in a new and more progressive parliament, which can only be seen as favorable to Star."

Malcolm said he agreed with me. Then he had another question. "No one seems to be able to tell me exactly how the preference shares are paid out. I'm told the Lenzoloto preference shareholders are entitled to 6.9 percent of the face value of their shares, paid as yearly dividends, which would be sixty-nine hundred rubles per preference share. But the Lenzoloto charter and, in fact, the legal opinions I commissioned say something entirely different; they say that the workers are entitled to 6.9 percent of the yearly profit."

Everyone began arguing about this, until Malcolm ordered us all to be quiet.

"We have John Mitchell on speakerphone from Russia," he said. "Let's see what he has to say."

John Mitchell, a director of Turnbull & Partners, was currently in Russia with Chris MacNee and John Thomas.

"Good afternoon, Malcolm," came his voice on the speakerphone. He had a very upper-class English accent. "From what I understand, preference shares are paid on face value—that is, sixty-nine hundred rubles per share."

I cut him off. "You're wrong."

He, in turn, cut me off. "I assure you I'm not wrong. I've been in Moscow for three days now, and I've examined this issue carefully. The shares are paid on value. It's absurd to think they receive 6.9 percent of the yearly profit. That's a huge amount of money."

"Well, sir, unlike you, I've been in Moscow for three years," I said pointedly. "And I'll be going back there again soon. And I assure you, you're wrong. I dealt with this personally. The Russian law on privatization states that all privatized companies must set aside a percentage of the yearly net profit to pay an annual fixed dividend to its preference shareholders, who are the workers. The workers are only entitled to preference shares and not ordinary shares. This is to exclude them from any voting power. But to make up for that, they are guaranteed a yearly, fixed priority dividend. In Lenzoloto's case, the dividend equals 6.9 percent of the profit. I too realize this is potentially a large amount, but I'm afraid it's something left over from the Communist dogma that workers come first. This is also the opinion of Frere Cholmeley Bischoff, whose report, by the way, is spot-on."

I could swear Malcolm was grinning.

John Mitchell tried to argue again, but Malcolm hung up on him. It was brilliant. "Well, Ludmila, all I can say is thank God you have finally resurfaced," he said, before turning to Christian, who was looking rather pale. The reason became clear after Malcolm told him the "explanatory notes" had to be altered immediately, to reflect the correct payment on preference shares.

"I'm afraid the placement document with the explanatory notes has already gone out," replied Christian. "We released it this morning, after talking to John Mitchell."

Malcolm exploded. "Fuck!" he roared. "You fucking idiot! How could you release it without talking to me first? It's such an important document. Fuck!"

His face went bright red with rage. He got to his feet and started to pace the office, swearing and ranting. Then he suddenly grabbed a Yellow Pages directory (a very thick book listing all the businesses in Sydney) and hurled it with all his might at Christian, hitting him smack in the head. Christian's face contorted with pain.

At this point, Graeme suggested we leave and let the two of them sort it out in private. We tiptoed out of the office like mice.

"He's not always like that," said Graeme, once we were back in the street.

I dismissed Graeme's comment with a wave of my hand. "Oh, the Russians will love him."

In fact, I thought Malcolm was perfect for us. He was just as passionate and unpredictable as Yeltsin.

Within a few hours of my meeting with Malcolm, the first bloody clashes broke out between Yeltsin's special police forces, sent by the interior ministry to seal off the White House, and the growing numbers of anti-Yeltsin demonstrators around the parliament building.

On October 1 Graeme Ellis announced to the market that Central Mining had entered an underwriting agreement with NatWest and Malcolm's bank to the tune of A$50 million. Meanwhile, in Moscow, demonstrators were constructing barricades and blocking traffic. I knew that Malcolm would be going ballistic over these scenes. So I sent him a quick fax telling him to hang in there and boldly predicting a Yeltsin victory.

He phoned me immediately. "You think Yeltsin will win?"

"Yes, he has the support of the army. There will probably be bloodshed, but it will be over quickly. Yeltsin is determined to cleanse the parliament of the last die-hard Communists and rule the country unobstructed, which is good for us."

"And you think he will do it?"

"I do. Malcolm, I've been through this before. Last time, it lasted a couple of days, and Yeltsin emerged as president. Russia really wants democracy."

"Okay. I believe you."

Two days later, the situation in Moscow exploded. Rutskoy and Khasbulatov appeared together on one of the balconies of the White House and urged the protesters to storm the pro-Yeltsin national television station—and then the Kremlin itself. They were calling for a revolution.

That afternoon, the protesters advanced on Moscow's mayoral offices and, after bloody clashes with pro-Yeltsin forces, seized the building. Encouraged, they marched toward the television and radio center. With people already dead on the street, Yeltsin declared a state of emergency. The pro-parliament crowds were met at the television center by Yeltsin's interior ministry units. Fighting followed. Sixty-two people died, hundreds were wounded, and the badly damaged station went off-air.

The next morning, as the sun rose, the Russian army—which still viewed Yeltsin as the ultimate authority—encircled the White House, and a few hours later, tanks started to shell the parliament building. At noon, the troops entered the building and went through it floor by floor, like locusts, shooting anyone who resisted. Ceasefires were called a few times, to remove the badly wounded and allow those who opted to leave the building to go.

I watched the whole spectacle live on CNN and saw my charismatic acquaintance Khasbulatov with his face white and his hands cuffed behind his back. Perhaps he should have been more loyal.

Yeltsin had won, but at an exorbitant cost. The official toll was 197 dead and 537 wounded. Unofficial sources claimed up to 1,500 had been killed inside the White House.

On October 8, Mostovoy was confirmed chairman of the Lenzoloto JSC, and Avlov the general manager. Alexei, who'd virtually saved the whole deal, became company secretary. It was well known that every foreign company had a Russian mole working in it. Alexei was our mole—a KGB informant, Katya claimed.

In Sydney, five days later, Central Mining held an extraordinary meeting at a business conference center in the city. Ian, Malcolm, and Graeme were already present in the auditorium when I arrived. Ian introduced me to his financial adviser, Bill O'Neill, who stood by the glass doors looking forlorn; Malcolm had insisted upon his resignation.

"I'm sorry we won't have a chance to work together," I said to him.

"Yes, I think the Lenzoloto mine has enormous potential. But Malcolm wanted me out to make way for himself," he replied.

The meeting started. Bill resigned, and Malcolm was voted in as a director. The Lenzoloto joint venture was approved, and a decision was passed to change Central Mining's name to Star Mining.

Malcolm, as a new director of Star, was granted 12,515,331 Star shares and 3 million options. His bank also signed a lucrative agreement to become Star's financial adviser, for a fee of A$1.2 million per year.

By this time, all our future fortunes were tied to what was happening in Moscow. Yeltsin had decreed that a national referendum would be held on the 12th of December to approve his new constitution. He'd (again) given himself sweeping powers.

Not very democratic, but necessary, according to Yeltsin.

If the people voted for the new constitution, and I was sure they would, this would be positive for Star. Malcolm was delighted about it.

On October 29, 1993, a stunningly sunny beautiful day in Sydney, I became a millionaire—on paper, anyway. The settlement meeting was scheduled for 10 a.m. Ian was due to fly in that morning. I hadn't seen him for a few weeks, so I was even more excited.

In all honesty, now that I was back home, I no longer minded his absences. In fact, I enjoyed the time alone and looked forward to our time together. That morning, I took extra care with my appearance. I spent more than the usual ten minutes applying my makeup, including my signature red lipstick, and put my long hair up in a high ponytail. I wore a new cream suit, a figure-hugging jacket with a long skirt split to the thigh, cream stockings, and red patent-leather high-heeled shoes.

I walked into the building at exactly 9:55 a.m. Ian, Malcolm, Graeme, and the lawyers were all seated around the table in the boardroom where the settlement was to take place.

Malcolm opened the proceedings with a short speech. He was dressed in a navy-blue Armani suit—and looked hot!

"As you know, Central Mining has changed its name to Star Mining," he said. "As you also know, the fundraising has been very successful. I received overwhelming support from the market. Today, Star Technology will become Star Mining's fully owned subsidiary, and its owners will be allotted two hundred million Star Mining shares, one hundred million options, and five million US in cash. While some problems remain in Russia, I'm confident we will overcome them and eventually become one of the world's greatest gold mining companies. Today, I'm releasing twenty million US to be wired to an escrow account in Lenzoloto's name with the Dialogue Bank in Moscow."

He spoke for about ten minutes before announcing that he and the directors of Star Mining—namely Ian, Graeme, and I—would be flying to Moscow on the 10th of November for a week. He then retrieved a bunch of checks from his pocket and handed them one by one to the lawyers. I was handed a check for US$75,000.

Turnbull & Partners' fees for fundraising expenses totaled A$5 million. During the fundraising, Turnbull & Partners had acquired

5,052,351 ordinary Star shares at a premium of thirty-five cents Australian a share, like all the other investors, totaling A$1.77 million.

By the time these deals closed, Star shares were trading at forty-four cents, so Malcolm did very well.

Afterward, we went to a celebratory lunch at the InterContinental Hotel, a glamorous five-star hotel housing one of Sydney's finest restaurants. I was seated next to Malcolm. At one stage of the afternoon, after he'd drunk a lot of wine, he took off his jacket, leaned back in his chair, and said, "You know, Ludmila, I think you and I are going to be *really* good friends."

I blushed and tried to hide it.

"And why is that?" I asked quizzingly, cocking a brow.

"Because I am extremely handsome, smart, and fabulously rich!"

I grinned. "Well then, I guess we will."

"I know we will," he said with conviction.

CHAPTER TWENTY-THREE

A Lovers' Spat

At 5 p.m., I made my exit from the high-spirited gathering at the InterContinental and, after a short stop at home to check up on Lachie, met Ian at 7 p.m. at the Ritz Carlton for our own private celebration. He was already sitting at a table when I arrived, with a very expensive chilled bottle of Cristal champagne, which he'd ordered in my honor.

"Isn't it all wonderful?" I exclaimed, kissing him warmly on the cheek.

"Yes, I'm glad it's all over. I was under a lot of pressure for it to happen."

He seemed on edge, but once we were sitting down, he raised his glass and toasted me. "After all, it was you who put the whole thing together," he said. Then he asked me what I thought of Malcolm.

"I think he's ideally suited to the cognac-drinking, meat-eating, basic masculinity of Russia's burgeoning business culture," I replied.

Ian laughed. "Yes, indeed. My only concern is that he might be difficult to work with. People say he likes to run things his own way and won't listen to anyone."

"Oh, I think he'll listen to us, since he knows nothing about Russia."

I told Ian that I would play the "Malcolm card" with Yatskevich, who was a mining snob. "He likes the rich and powerful. I'll leak that Malcolm is likely to be the first president of Australia," I said, before changing the subject. I wanted to talk more about today's meeting.

The night before, I'd studied the deed of acknowledgment and the preemptive rights deed. The list of institutional investors and their contributions was impressive. It included ANZ Nominees, FAI Insurance, Westpac, Australian Mutual Provident Society (AMP), and, of course, Turnbull & Partners. Malcolm's philosophy was that if he contributed his own money, everyone else would follow suit—and they had.

I'd also glanced over the names of the vendors and the number of Central Mining (a.k.a. Star Mining) shares and cash amounts they were to receive. Ludmila Melnikoff was there, along with eight other company names controlled by Ian, including Pan Pacific Sulphur Ltd., of which I owned 20 percent as a result of annulling my direct 10 percent shareholding in Star Technology. As a bonus, Ian had decided to allocate to me an extra, direct 1.5 percent shareholding of Star Technology; hence I was listed as a vendor owning 1.5 percent of Star in the rights deed, which yielded me US$75,000 plus 3 million Star Mining shares and 1.5 million options. Ian said it was a small bonus for all the challenging work I'd done in Russia. I certainly felt I deserved it.

But most of my vendor shares were held through my 20 percent share of Pan Pacific. All of Star Technology vendor shares, including mine and Pan Pacific's, were now locked up for twelve months, until October 28, 1994. The new director's shares issued to Malcolm were locked up for two years until October 28, 1995. Interestingly, Ian did not reveal who the actual owners of the vendor companies were, and legally Star Technology was not required to reveal anything at all, as it was registered in the British Virgin Islands. Earlier, Ian had told me he controlled all the vendor companies; thus, he could allocate the vendor shares to whomever he wanted, under a veil of secrecy. I hadn't questioned him further.

Over dinner, I asked Ian what his intentions were for Pan Pacific, which had received 100 million Star Mining shares and US$1.5 million at settlement.

"As I told you, we will keep it until the shares hit one or two dollars and then sell the whole company to someone," he replied. "I'd like to aim for one hundred million dollars US."

"That would be great, but there's a lot of work ahead of us before that could happen," I commented.

"I realize that."

"What's going to happen to the 1.5 million that Pan Pacific received today?" I then asked. Startled, I watched Ian's expression change to one of extreme displeasure.

"It will be used to extinguish debt," he said. "Do you have any idea how much Russia has cost me?"

"How much?"

"Close to two million Australian."

"You're kidding! On what?"

"Oh, lots of things. It all adds up, you know."

"Well, even if that was so, I should only have to pay ten percent of the expenses. If I had kept my direct ten-percent share of Star Technology, I would have received ten percent of five million US today. Even if we deduct my share of expenses, i.e., ten percent of two million Australian, I am still owed six hundred thousand Australian."

To me, this was indisputable.

Ian's eyes turned to ice. "You started with nothing when I met you," he said. "I pulled you out of the gutter and made you into what you are today."

I gasped and then said furiously, "That's fucking bullshit!"

"I see you still talk like someone from the gutter."

Who was this man? I felt as if a knife had plunged into my heart. I'd never seen Ian like this—scarlet-faced and spitting venom.

"Ian, I would like to remind you that when we met, I was running a very successful company and making lots of money. I owned a stunning penthouse-style apartment at Bronte Beach. I guess, by your standards, that's living in the gutter, which is fine by me!" I retorted.

By now, tears were rolling down my cheeks. I thought I had every right to ask about the Pan Pacific money. Now he was telling me that the whole US$1.5 million given to Pan Pacific that morning was gone.

"Look, that's why you got the extra shares this morning in your own name," said Ian tightly. "I told you and Greg that you'd have to pay your share of the expenses. You have no idea what it cost to run Russia. I had a lot of debt I had to settle. To make up for it, I allocated you the extra shares and cash. You will be able to sell those shares soon for a million or so. I thought the whole thing was really well done."

I just stared at him.

His voice became gentler. "Let's not fight, little girl. You know I love you and I will always take care of you. You really don't have to worry about anything ever again. I'm sorry about what I just said. I know you are a diamond. You're my rough diamond, and I love you."

Rough diamond? I tried to smile. Here was the love of my life, the father of our child, and my future husband. Why was I going on about money when all that really mattered was our love and happiness?

Our lovemaking was especially tender that night. Afterward, I told myself that I still believed in Ian. But the word "still" spoke volumes. My first serious doubts had sprouted. Could I trust him?

I told Fran about my fight with Ian over the shares. In Fran's pragmatic opinion, it wasn't worth jeopardizing my future with Ian over a "mill or two," as she put it. I wanted to believe she was right. However, I did ring Frances, Ian's accountant, to ask her how much Ian had spent in Russia. Her reply was prompt: "Oh, probably two million or so."

So, he hadn't been lying. I guess when you took into account the bribes Ian had paid, it sounded right.

All my life, I'd considered myself to be someone who dealt fairly with others. The one thing I hated was being ripped off. I tried to push the incident from my mind and resume my fairy-tale relationship with Ian.

He'd always been so cagey about how much he was worth. But considering I was family and soon to be his wife, I decided I had the right to know. As far as I was concerned, partners shared everything and trusted each other completely.

"Can I ask you a question?" I asked one night after we sat down for a glass of champagne before dinner.

"Oh no, not another question!" exclaimed Ian, smiling.

"Don't worry, it's not a zinger! I'm just curious to know what you're worth. Chris told me you had a nest egg in Switzerland but would never touch it under any circumstance."

Ian flinched slightly. "It's actually embarrassing," he replied. "It's in the nine figures."

"You mean one hundred million?"

"Yes. American dollars. I always wanted to reach half a billion. That's why I want Russia to work so badly," he added.

Little did I know that he would achieve this: to the astounding tune of US$464 million!

Ian then told me that he'd come across some gold bars a few years earlier and had bought them. They were in a safe deposit box in a Swiss bank.

"That sounds exciting. Do you have a secret number?"

"Yes, I do."

"So, is all your money in Switzerland?"

"Yes, I transferred all my money into Switzerland after I purchased the gold ingots," he replied. "I became friends with some Swiss bankers, and we set up a trust. They are the trustees now. SY is a trustee too."

Ian was referring to his accountant in Hong Kong.

"Is all this money tax-free?" I went on.

"Yes, it's all black money. No one knows about it."

"Does Bobby know?"

"No, but she suspects. She'll never find out."

"So, who controls the money?"

"I do, but the trustees have full discretion over how the money is invested. They have a target they must meet: ten percent per year. Lately, they have been doing really well, making twenty to thirty percent."

"Is this what you live off?"

Ian didn't seem to mind the interrogation. "Yes," he replied. "I mainly live off my credit cards, and the trustees pay the bills."

"What if you needed money for your projects?"

"It used to be much easier. I just had to ask SY to send the funds, and he'd oblige. Now I have to provide full details of the projects, and they decide whether to invest the funds or not."

"What if you really wanted to invest in something? Could you overrule them?"

"Of course. But it's hard to find something that does better than thirty percent on your money. It's cheaper to use other people's money."

"What will happen when you die? Who is going to run the fund?" It was a blunt question, but I thought it important to know.

"Well, the bank will go on forever. They all make so much money out of me, they will be happy to run it forever."

"But who will take your place?"

"At this stage, I'm hoping Angus will," Ian replied. "Chris is not capable. Lachie will get a chance too. You never know how your kids will turn out."

He added that Angus would manage the trust income, but he could never touch the trust's capital itself. He'd be obliged to distribute the trust's income to eight people nominated by Ian, including himself. According to Ian, the eight beneficiaries were me, Lachie, Chris, Angus, Bobby, Cathy, Cathy's daughter, Grace, and Ian's first wife, Jan. "But when they die, that's it. The money stops. So, Angus, in effect, will be working for the family."

"And if Angus is not suitable, then Lachie will run it?"

"Yes."

"So, Lachie is not in your will?"

"No, but you are."

"Is this the nest egg Chris was referring to?"

Ian paused. Then he said, "Did Chris really tell you this?"

"Yes," I replied. "I asked him why money had been so tight. There were all those times when my wages weren't paid, and I came close to losing my Bronte Beach apartment. You were very short of cash."

"And what did Chris say?"

"He said you were pretty broke, but you have this nest egg in Switzerland, which you would never touch."

"My cash flow varies," replied Ian. "I have many projects all over the world that I'm trying to fund. I use the monthly income from the trust fund to carry on my businesses, and sometimes there's not enough to go around in any one month. Everybody does get paid eventually. I have to prioritize."

I asked my last question. What was his ultimate aim?

"I have always wanted to own a bank," he replied. "That's what we're working on."

"A bank in Switzerland?"

"Yes, it's the only place to be."

Years later, I would think back to this conversation, aghast.

CHAPTER TWENTY-FOUR

Altercations and Explosions

On November 6, 1993, I left Sydney for Moscow with Ian, Malcolm, and Graeme. We flew first class to London, arriving at 6 a.m. During the four-hour stopover we enjoyed showers and Bloody Mary cocktails for breakfast in the first-class lounge, which would become a ritual. Refreshed, we landed in Moscow at 3:30 p.m. It was dark already, and the temperature had plunged to minus ten. Thick snow enveloped the city.

We checked into the historic five-star Marco Polo Hotel, a deluxe business hotel with a cozy lobby bar and two on-site restaurants, located in the heart of downtown Moscow. We discussed our schedule over dinner. As well as meetings with Mostovoy in Moscow, there was to be a formal reception at the Australian embassy. There was also a Lenzoloto board meeting that we had to attend in Bodaibo.

Malcolm had a fear of flying and refused to fly Aeroflot. In fact, most foreign companies had recently banned their employees from flying Aeroflot within Russia because there'd been so many fatal crashes. Chris arranged a private charter plane to fly us to Bodaibo the following morning.

On board Lenzoloto's private cargo propeller plane the next day, a feast of salami, ham, salmon, caviar, bread, cheese, and cognac awaited us. Malcolm looked pale and nervous until his first few swallows of cognac. I could see he really liked food and alcohol—a man after my own heart!

Avlov was waiting on the tarmac to greet us when we disembarked. He was positively beaming when we introduced Malcolm as *his* new banker. He escorted us to a newly refurbished lodge, which lacked a sauna but had a glorious fire raging in the lounge room.

The board meeting was held in the Lenzoloto hall. Avlov chaired it. His figures representing Lenzoloto JSC's economic and financial situation were, as usual, incomprehensible. He'd also managed to spend US$37 million on construction (most of it only half finished because the money had run out) and was claiming this amount from Star. At the end of his speech, Avlov handed out copies of his twenty-page financial report. It might as well have been written in Egyptian hieroglyphics.

Later that evening, back at the lodge, Avlov's spending spree was discussed at length. Malcolm's rage boiled over, and he threw his copy of Avlov's report into the fire. "Ludmila, we have to get rid of that maniac. He's going to bankrupt Lenzoloto—and Star with it. Fuck this idiot!"

I told him that someone else shared this view of Avlov. "That person is Yatskevich. So you two have something in common already," I said. "But things must be done carefully. Avlov is very powerful in Bodaibo. Frankly, we wouldn't be here without him. He has been our fiercest ally. You must also remember he has ruled over Lenzoloto in this way for many years. His job was to spend the funds sent to him every year from the central government on construction and on the employment of virtually the whole town. Profit never came into it. Now he's expected to adopt the new market conditions, which are wildly at odds with the old Communist ways."

"So how do we solve the problem?" asked Graeme Ellis.

"The board must rule that he cannot spend one cent unless it's approved by the board," I replied.

"That will be done tomorrow at the board meeting," cut in Ian. "We've drafted a contract which stipulates that the board has power over all financial management, and monies must be spent strictly according to budgets. Avlov has agreed."

Malcolm brooded over this. "Well, I hope it's not too late," he commented finally. "But will he restructure Lenzoloto the way we want? Thousands of people must be sacked, and Lenzoloto must dispose of its noncore assets, like its shops, schools, restaurants, factories, auto workshops, hotels, hospitals, and transport facilities and fucking roads and power stations! Can he adapt in order to make these changes?"

"No, it's like asking a Russian to stop drinking vodka," I replied. "That's why there's a step two. We have to move him sideways, eventually, to a nonexecutive position. Something like president of Lenzoloto, with no actual power but a good salary."

"Oh, that's ridiculous. He's a dead weight and must go. Now, when are we going out to eat?"

That was the end of the subject. Malcolm had ruled. I knew that from a purely business point of view, he was right, and in Australia, someone like Avlov would be sacked by the board immediately. But this was Siberia, and I was gravely concerned that if we got rid of Avlov, it would be the end of us too, given his importance in the town. Also, my conscience gave me pause, as he had been Star's most loyal defender.

That night, we had dinner at Tanya's restaurant. Malcolm greatly enjoyed the evening, as well as Tanya's company. Tanya introduced her new guest to a great Siberian delicacy called *raskolotka*, a rare white Arctic fish eaten frozen and raw, sliced very thinly, and dipped into a spicy sauce. The Russians call it "ice cream of the Arctic."

The vodka and cognac flowed liberally, as usual—but the mood became less lighthearted as Tanya described how the townsfolk had suffered under Avlov's rule.

"Avlov and his cronies live like kings, while the rest of us live in poverty," she said. "Most of the men are alcoholics. The most common cause of death is freezing to death in the snow in the middle of the night. Our shops are empty, and even if they were stocked with goods, no one has the money to buy anything."

"Hopefully things will change when we restructure Lenzoloto," replied Malcolm.

A lot of people had great faith in Star, Tanya told him. "Anything is better than Avlov," she added.

Malcolm raised his glass. "To Star—and to Tanya!"

The board meeting continued the next day. Avlov was appointed chairman of Lenzoloto, to Malcolm's displeasure, and Avlov's cronies were appointed associate directors, representing the workers. There was nothing we could do about this. Avlov ruled Bodaibo and the board meeting.

At the grand formal dinner hosted by Avlov after the meeting, there were dozens of toasts. To keep up with the Russians, Ian kept throwing his vodka into the plant behind him and refilling his glass with water. Malcolm soon caught on and did the same.

The next morning, we flew from Bodaibo into Irkutsk for refueling. Malcolm suggested we try to see Nozhikov while we were there. I considered this risky, but Malcolm insisted.

Nozhikov, we were told, was in Moscow, and Yakovenko (his first deputy) was on holidays. However, his second deputy, Suitkin, agreed to a meeting.

"I don't like it," I said nervously to Ian. "Malcolm isn't aware of the deep-seated hatred toward us in this town. I'm worried Suitkin will say something really horrible."

"I really don't think they would have agreed to see us if there was still bad blood between us," replied Ian, always the optimist.

When we walked into the boardroom of the Irkutsk government, six men were already there, waiting for us. I had no idea who they were. One of them—a short, fat, balding man with beady eyes—stood up.

"My name is Suitkin. Welcome to Irkutsk."

"Thank you," replied Malcolm. We sat, but Suitkin remained standing.

"I would like to start by informing you that I speak on behalf of the Irkutsk government," he said. "Nozhikov is in Moscow discussing Lenzoloto, so I'm here to meet with you."

Malcolm thanked him again and then explained that we'd just come from Bodaibo and were very concerned about Lenzoloto's pending financial crisis. "This crisis can very simply be avoided, as Star has deposited an amount of twenty million US into the Lenzoloto JSC account in Moscow, but we need to control how this money is spent because—"

"Mr. Turnbull," broke in Suitkin, "pardon my interruption, but I must put you on notice that we can't guarantee the security of any investment Star makes in our region. The Irkutsk government is against the joint venture, and my advice is for you to take your money and go home. Our position is that Lenzoloto JSC was founded illegally and must be dissolved. We fully expect to pursue the case through the courts until we win, and then we plan to hold a tender for the Sukhoi Log deposit on our terms."

I watched Malcolm's face turn the brightest shade of crimson and felt sick to the stomach. These creeps knew we were with our banker and had only agreed to see us to give us our marching orders.

"Let's go! This meeting is over!" roared Malcolm.

Once we were out of sight of the building, he gave full rein to his rage.

"Why wasn't I told of this? They basically said if we invest our money, we risk losing it. How the fuck can we work in this environment? I'm pulling the plug!"

He kept on raving about what had happened until we boarded the plane. Only then did I get a word in.

"Firstly, Suitkin is a nobody and is disposable," I said. "This is part of Nozhikov's game. There's a simple solution to this, as I've told you. We have to convince Mostovoy to give Irkutsk ten percent of Lenzoloto."

"Why won't Mostovoy do it?" Malcolm demanded.

"He keeps saying the orders come from above."

"Meaning what?"

"Meaning that the orders come from Chubais or Gaidar, or even higher, from someone like Chernomyrdin, the prime minister. These boys do not want to lose control."

"Well, they are about to lose everything!"

"Yes, and that's why now is the perfect opportunity to force them to change their stance," I continued. "Look, Malcolm, most Russians hate foreigners. Suitkin, who's a vodka-slurping male chauvinist pig, represents Russia's old style of business. Luckily, the government is full of young reformers who realize Russia urgently needs foreign investment to rebuild itself."

Malcolm listened and seemed to become calmer, although the rest of the flight was spent in silence.

After we returned to Moscow, Mostovoy agreed to urgently meet with us. But then, as usual, he kept us waiting in his reception area.

His young, pretty secretary, Lena, tried to appease Malcolm with offers of tea, which he declined. She offered him cognac, which he also declined. He was growing angrier by the minute.

"Fuck this place!" he finally erupted. "I thought the deal was done! I can't believe what just happened in Irkutsk! Why wasn't I told of the Irkutsk problem? I would have never committed to the fundraising. Fuck, Ludmila!"

He started to pace, then turned and hit Mostovoy's old-style Soviet plywood safe, next to Lena's desk, with his fist. Lena stared at Malcolm in sheer horror, and then hurried off to see if Mostovoy was ready for us.

Ian's eyebrows were raised in disbelief. But I knew that Malcolm's passionate nature would open doors. It was very Russian. Lena returned, gave Malcolm a quick smile, and announced that Mostovoy was ready to see us.

Mostovoy had already heard what happened in Irkutsk. "We will have to reach a compromise with Irkutsk within one month. I will talk to Chubais," he said.

At this, Malcolm settled down completely. I thanked Mostovoy warmly and gave him a hug and kiss on the cheek.

On November 11, Cavan Hogue, the Australian ambassador, hosted an evening for Malcolm at the embassy. There was a raging snowstorm that night, and the temperature plunged to minus fifteen. Little did we know that a storm was about to break inside the embassy as well.

We were all gathered around the fireplace in the embassy's new hall. Alexei and Katya were also there, along with Lucy, Malcolm's wife, who had flown in that day. Malcolm, now in a jovial mood, was chatting with the ambassador about Lenzoloto. Suddenly, the doors flew open, and two men in black suits marched in. They said they were Gaidar's representatives. One introduced himself as Dr. Sinikov, a member of the board of Gaidar's think tank. The other one, a Mr. Chao, was also a board member and Gaidar's adviser. They said they had urgent private business regarding Lenzoloto to discuss with Malcolm Turnbull and Ian MacNee.

The ambassador immediately led all four into a private meeting room. The huge double doors closed after them.

My heart leaped into my mouth. "Katya, what's going on?"

"I don't know. But they're Gaidar's people, so the dog may have betrayed us again."

"Nozhikov has been in town."

"That could explain it."

The wait was agonizing. Finally, after one hour, they emerged. Ian was grinning, but Malcolm looked thunderstruck. Malcolm came straight back to the fireplace.

"They were sent by Gaidar to give us a message," he said. "Gaidar is in favor of a tender for Sukhoi Log. Therefore, they said, there won't be a Lenzoloto JSC, and the Russian government will be holding a tender in the near future. Star could participate in the tender—or it could sue the Russian government if it so wishes. They wanted to tell us this before we put any money in, since they're aware we've deposited the twenty million into the Lenzoloto account in Moscow."

"They're scared that once we put the money in, there's no going back," I said firmly. "If the Russian courts were to dissolve an operational joint venture, it would cause an international scandal. Gaidar would never live that down."

I couldn't understand why no one could see this. I guessed my understanding of doing business in Russia was becoming more refined.

"You're right. That's what the visit was about, to bully us into pulling out of Russia," said Malcolm. He was gazing at me with a great deal of respect. "I pointed out to them it was already too late," he went on. "I explained the whole fundraising process and listed the banks involved. They were familiar with most of them. I told them there are absolutely no legal grounds to dissolve the Lenzoloto JSC and hold a tender.

"I also said that we would fight them in every local and international court available to us if a tender was ever held. The press coverage would be enormous, and it would affect Australia's relationship with Russia. I then described our plans for the development of Sukhoi Log, including the total commitment by Turnbull and Partners to raise the balance of two hundred fifty million US and provide further loans of seven hundred fifty million."

My body tingled with delight as I started to realize that Malcolm had saved the whole deal. I think this was the moment a small part of me fell in love with him. He was charismatic, devilishly clever, and passionate, not to mention very handsome.

Malcolm also told Gaidar's men that Star planned to create one of the world's greatest mining companies, and that Star's investment was of utmost importance to the development of a market economy in Russia.

At that stage, the visitors completely changed their tune. They said they hadn't realized that Star was backed by so many important people, and accordingly, they would report back favorably to Gaidar. However, there was one nonnegotiable, critical condition they revealed, which Gaidar was adamant about. Nozhikov had been demanding it too.

Avlov had to go.

"I told them I couldn't agree more," continued Malcolm. "So, they insisted that we sack Avlov when the time is right and wanted Star's commitment, which they got from me."

"This is great news!" Katya exclaimed.

"Yes, it is," agreed Ian.

It was a huge relief, knowing that Avlov was regarded as the problem and not Star. Even so, I felt terrible about Avlov.

The next day, Katya spoke to Gaidar behind closed doors. He wanted a letter of guarantee for the full US$250 million from our bankers.

"Ludmila, neither NatWest nor any other bank would ever sign such a guarantee," said Malcolm when I told him this. "They couldn't. It could potentially expose them to a huge legal battle."

"Gaidar has asked for it. I really think the whole thing hinges on this. It's make-or-break time."

"It's impossible."

"Why can't you sign a guarantee on behalf of your bank?"

"I can't!" he shouted. "That's absurd. I can't possibly guarantee that much money."

"But, Malcolm, if Gaidar doesn't get our guarantee, Sukhoi Log will go to tender. Surely you can see that?"

"Even if you are right, I can't sign such a letter," he replied.

"Can't you word it in some way that doesn't expose you?"

He brooded over this. "Let me think about it," he said, finally.

Malcolm drafted a letter guaranteeing that Turnbull & Partners would organize the raising of US$250 million for Lenzoloto JSC conditional upon the Russian side fulfilling its obligations, including the secrecy lifting. It spelled out the fact that Star's total commitment of US$250 million was the largest foreign investment in a Russian enterprise to date. He also got another letter from Cavan Hogue strongly supporting Star and its activities in Russia. I was thrilled. I knew this would do the trick and tip the balance in our favor.

On November 12, after Malcolm had flown home, Katya delivered both letters to Gaidar. I was sure Gaidar would be impressed.

A few days later, I made an appointment to see Mikhaylov, the minister of atomic energy. As soon as I sat down, he said, "My colleague in charge of precious metals, Krotkov, tells me I should support a tender for Sukhoi Log and that the ministry should participate in the tender, because we're the only ones with the technology and the money and would win."

"My dear Mr. Mikhaylov, I assure you any tender is illegal, as Lenzoloto already has the license to mine Sukhoi Log," I replied.

Mikhaylov said he believed me, but he'd like me to convince his comrades at a meeting he was setting up for the following day.

Mikhaylov, Krotkov, and his whole team were present when Chris and I arrived for the meeting—late, after being caught in a traffic jam. I counted ten men present. This was going to be tough.

Krotkov immediately launched into an attack. Geolkom had told him Lenzoloto JSC didn't hold a license to mine Sukhoi Log, and in any case, Geolkom was going to tender the deposit shortly.

"Mr. Krotkov, I assure you Lenzoloto JSC does own a legal license to mine Sukhoi Log. Here, let me give you a copy," I replied and flung the old license onto the boardroom table.

"And here's Gaidar's ordinance ordering Geolkom to reissue the Sukhoi Log license to Lenzoloto in the new format," I continued. "Here are Mostovoy's ordinances, also ordering Geolkom to reissue the license to Lenzoloto. And lastly, here are our founding documents, which also confirm that Lenzoloto owns the rights to mine Sukhoi Log!"

I tossed all the documents into the middle of the table.

Krotkov read through them silently. I then proposed that we join forces and work together.

I looked over at the minister, who was smiling. He stood. "I, for one, would like to take Ludmila up on her offer. But we must insist upon a ten-percent shareholding. This is nonnegotiable. Mr. Krotkov, is this your position too?"

Krotkov looked uncomfortable. "Clearly, I wasn't given all the facts," he said. "I can see now that Lenzoloto does indeed have the license to mine Sukhoi Log. I would very much like to work with Lenzoloto."

Chris and I stood and shook hands with everyone present. The minister looked as pleased as punch, and I was ecstatic. It was a huge coup to win over the Ministry of Atomic Energy. I couldn't wait to tell Ian and Malcolm.

December came. Malcolm was working hard in Sydney on the Star deal and the funding of Lenzoloto. On December 15, he was appointed director of what was now Star Mining's British Virgin Islands registered subsidiary, Star Technology Ltd.

Back in Russia, on December 12, the people voted in favor of the Constitution of the Russian Federation, giving Yeltsin sweeping powers. But they also delivered a stunning blow to his economic reforms by not voting for Gaidar's party, Russia's Voice.

Meanwhile, I was still very concerned about Yatskevich and decided that the time had come to bribe him, as nothing else had worked. We also needed to market Malcolm Turnbull to the Russians—especially to Yatskevich—as the man who stood to become Australia's first president if the country voted in favor of becoming a republic.

I told Alexei what I was plotting. I asked him to visit Yatskevich and then, over a few vodkas, tell him about Turnbull and say that Star wanted to reconcile and work together. Alexei did this—and let me know that Yatskevich had agreed to meet Malcolm.

While we were busily courting Yatskevich, Malcolm was courting Paul Keating, Australia's prime minister, a staunch labor man and advocate of Australia becoming a republic. Keating wrote to Malcolm, asking to be kept informed of any new developments regarding the important stage Star had reached in its negotiations. He also said that his office would be contacting the Russian ambassador to Australia to make sure that the Russian authorities were aware of Canberra's interest.

I copied the Keating letter and attached biographical details on Malcolm, then delivered the lot to Mostovoy so he could present them at the government meeting on Lenzoloto the next day.

Deputy Prime Minister Gaidar chaired the meeting. There were more people for Lenzoloto than against. The meeting was rowdy, with Yatskevich and Suitkin doing most of the yelling. In the end, everyone (except Yatskevich and the Irkutsk people) agreed in principle that Lenzoloto JSC should be allowed to operate properly. However, Gaidar, after listening to everyone's opinion and forever the coward, moved a resolution still questioning the legality of our license and saying he'd seek further legal opinion. He really was a two-faced toad.

CHAPTER TWENTY-FIVE

Malcolm Opens Up

I returned to Sydney for Christmas and the New Year, desperate to be with Lachie. Two days after Christmas, the Supreme Court in Moscow reexamined the Irkutsk government's claim against Lenzoloto JSC. The court date was reset for January 10, 1994.

The machinations in Moscow seemed a long way away when I drove to Malcolm's rented holiday house in Palm Beach on January 8. It was the type of house famous rich people rented for A$35,000 a week in summer. Malcolm had invited me to go with him and Lucy to a party up there.

A hospitable Lucy greeted me when I arrived, and then Malcolm and I took a bottle of Veuve champagne out on the balcony. We were discussing Russia when the phone rang. Malcolm declared, "Ludmila, it's Paul Keating. Please excuse me." He chatted to the prime minister for thirty minutes or so about the Republic Movement and Russia.

After Malcolm hung up, I quizzed him about his political aspirations. "So, I guess you plan to be the first president once we become a republic?"

"No, not at all. The president will have little power. I want to be the next prime minister."

"What about Keating?"

"Keating will be our president, and the plan is for me to replace him when he retires before the next election in 1996."

I told Malcolm I thought he would make a stellar prime minister.

"Thank you, Ludmila. Then you will definitely have to come and work for me."

The glorious Sydney summer continued. But in Moscow, all sorts of changes were afoot. Prime Minister Chernomyrdin had become increasingly powerful. He declared that Western economic advice had done more harm than good for Russia and the era of market reform was over. He announced a new cabinet of hardliners. Chubais was the only exception. Gaidar resigned in disgust.

CHAPTER TWENTY-SIX

Changing Sides

In early February, Malcolm and I flew Qantas first class to Tokyo and then to Moscow to attend a Lenzoloto JSC shareholders meeting on February 8, 1994. Ian, who was in Aspen, was meeting us there.

Alexei had arranged a private meeting between Yatskevich and Malcolm. Alexei and I waited in the bar of the Marco Polo Hotel while it took place. Eventually, Malcolm walked in, looking triumphant. He ordered a bottle of Moët and sat down.

"The meeting went well. I actually quite liked him. You described him as resembling a rat, Ludmila, but I thought he was good-looking."

"Okay," I said impatiently. "But what did he say about Star?"

"He is willing to work with Star and was keen to befriend me. But he said straightaway that working with Ian would be hard. He hates Avlov and said he must go. He spoke highly of you, though. He described you as a classic Russian beauty."

"That's nice."

"Yatskevich thinks we should call a conference in a neutral location and thrash out all the problems with Irkutsk. He said that first, though, we had to submit our application for our license renewals to Geolkom. Ludmila, why haven't we submitted our applications yet?"

"Oh, just maybe because before Yatskevich decided to be your best friend, he said that the application would be approved over his dead body. So we decided to hold off," I answered sarcastically. "Avlov has had the application ready to go for ages," I added.

At this point, Ian walked into the bar and Malcolm repeated the news, omitting Yatskevich's ill feeling toward Ian. We continued celebrating into the evening.

Lenzoloto JSC held its shareholder meeting. But Malcolm understandably was concerned about the continued failure of the government to lift the secrecy.

He decided to write a letter to Chernomyrdin. Malcolm clearly laid out the investment schedule by Star, making it contingent upon the licenses and lifting of the secrecy. Katya hand-delivered the letter and asked Chernomyrdin to read it in front of her. He admitted that the Lenzoloto JSC must be allowed to exist.

Malcolm got on the plane back to Australia a more relaxed man.

I stayed on in Moscow to spend an extra few weeks with Ian. I missed Lachie madly but knew I had to finish Russia for his sake as well as mine. I hoped one day he would understand the reason for my long absences and thank me for it.

On March 24, Alexei came over. He told me that Yatskevich was now saying that Sukhoi Log should be mined by a group of Russian mining companies with no foreign involvement and that Russian businessmen like Chugaevsky, an example of Russia's new elite, had funds to mine Sukhoi Log.

"I can't believe they can get their hands on two hundred fifty million," I said.

"Not yet. But time is running out," Alexei replied. "Yatskevich liked Malcolm very much, but more needs to be done."

"Are you referring to a bribe?"

"Yes."

He then revealed he had tentatively planned to meet Yatskevich at his place that night.

The following day, Alexei walked into the office with a smile. Yatskevich had spoken to the Irkutsk branch of Geolkom. They wanted a "contribution" of US$30,000. Yatskevich himself wanted US$70,000.

I was surprised he didn't want more. Then again, this might just be the first round. I knew Ian would agree to the plan, but to clear it with Malcolm, we needed to send him a carefully worded fax to make it sound like a legitimate expense.

Chris, who seemed to have become the bagman, went off to the Dialogue Bank at the Radisson Hotel to get the money. I was in the Star office when he returned with the cash. Alexei was also in the office, and we separated the money into two brown bags, one for Yatskevich and the other for Irkutsk Geolkom.

Alexei then sent Malcolm the following fax:

Dear Malcolm,

As per STAR's request, I would like to inform you that I met with the mentioned person, and he didn't accept any of our proposals. Any further negotiations with this person using these tactics are useless.

In order to properly prepare for further negotiations and to make them successful, I believe it is necessary in the near future to organize a campaign to collect information about the activity of the persons in question and exert some public pressure on them.

To organize such a campaign we need:

In Moscow, US$70,000
In Irkutsk, US$30,000

This money will be paid to private detectives, gifts and for newspaper articles.

If you agree with my proposed plan, please approve the budget.

Sincerely yours,

[signature]

Alex Mihailov

Alexei delivered the bags to Yatskevich's apartment that evening and stayed for dinner. Yatskevich told him that he would now support Star.

Forty-eight hours later, I flew home to Sydney and went to see Malcolm in his office the very next day to explain Alexei's message. Malcolm told me that it was the most bizarre fax he'd ever received and demanded an explanation. I said that we'd worded it carefully because the KGB read all our faxes. We were actually asking him to approve the money for Yatskevich, who needed it to finish building his mansion on the outskirts of Moscow.

Malcolm wasn't happy. He only accepted the situation after I made clear that Yatskevich would never give us the license to mine Sukhoi Log without the payment.

Ian, holding the fort in Moscow, went to a meeting at MinAtom. Mikhaylov was there, along with Yakovenko, first deputy head of the Irkutsk government, and Mostovoy. The outcome was dazzling.

Irkutsk agreed to drop their resistance to Star's participation in Lenzoloto JSC. Everyone agreed to meet in Angarsk (a city forty kilometers from Irkutsk, to avoid the press) at the end of April to finalize matters and sign one last agreement settling all unresolved issues.

Could the small matter of US$100,000 have been a factor?

Ian advised the Star board to release the US$20 million to Lenzoloto immediately. But Malcolm still wasn't happy. He wanted a letter from Geolkom confirming their prompt reissue of licenses.

The next evening, I had dinner with Malcolm and Lucy in their house in Paddington, where they still lived even though they had just bought a beautiful mansion in Sydney's most expensive suburb, Point Piper. They were waiting for renovations to finish. Their three-story Paddington house was also opulent, though, with a formal dining room boasting high ceilings, dark-brown walls adorned in paintings, and a massive oak dining table. The kitchen was modern and vast, leading to a pretty backyard with a pool. I'm sure the rest of the house was just as grand.

Malcolm seemed in a much brighter mood. After dinner, he asked me to outline the Star situation as I saw it—and then hesitantly agreed to travel with me to Irkutsk in a few days for the Angarsk conference.

"What astounds me, Ludmila," Malcolm went on, "is that the prime minister signs an ordinance ordering Yatskevich to issue the licenses to Lenzoloto, and it means nothing. Yatskevich has simply refused to do it, with no repercussions."

"That's Russia for you," I told him. Oddly, I got the feeling that Malcolm was secretly enjoying all this. Outfoxing our political enemies was right up his alley.

CHAPTER TWENTY-SEVEN

A Drunken Hero

On April 22, 1994, a Friday, we left Sydney at midday for London. Ian, Malcolm, Graeme, and I sat together in first class. Malcolm was attentive and flirtatious. He kept telling the others how beautiful and smart I was, and what a pleasure it was to work with me.

Ian looked jealous, but of course he couldn't do anything as we were still a secret—and he was still married.

Malcolm again refused to travel on Aeroflot from Moscow to Angarsk, so we booked the same private plane we'd flown in last time. Our group included Mostovoy, Kuranov (the Lenzoloto director representing MinAtom), Krotkov (head of precious metals under MinAtom), and a few Irkutsk politicians.

Yatskevich had planned to come but couldn't in the end, because of work commitments. However, he said he would be available on the phone anytime during the conference.

Once we'd taken off, Malcolm grabbed my arm. "Let's go over to the Russians," he said.

We made our way to the front of the plane, where all the Russians sat in a group, and spent the next couple of hours bonding over lots of cognac, our party growing rowdier and rowdier with each nip. Ian and Graeme remained at the back of the plane, watching. After a while, I couldn't drink anymore and retired for a snooze. When I woke up, Malcolm was still partying. He was sculling vodka by now, as they'd run out of cognac. He looked very jolly. Most foreigners can't handle vodka, but Malcolm looked fine. I dozed off again and woke just as the plane was landing in Angarsk. It was pitch black outside. I gathered my belongings and made my way down the aisle toward the exit. The Russians had already disembarked.

"Where's Malcolm?" asked Graeme.

We didn't see him. Graeme and Ian searched the plane. Malcolm was nowhere to be found.

"I'll check if he got off with the others," I said, disappearing through the door.

A delegation headed by Yakovenko awaited us on a large square of red carpet on the tarmac, lit up by floodlights. Yakovenko was dressed in a smart navy suit. Avlov stood alongside him, wearing the suit Ian had bought him in Paris. A Russian folk band played a traditional Russian song, "Our Glorious Lake Baikal," referring to the great lake in the Irkutsk region. Avlov had decided to greet the great man in style. The only problem was that Malcolm was nowhere to be seen.

I raced back onto the plane.

"We've found him," said Ian. "He's asleep on the floor in the back row."

"Is he okay?" I asked in a panicky voice.

"No. He's unconscious. We can't wake him up."

"Shit! How much did he drink?"

Ian fired back, "You should know—you were with him."

I went back to Avlov and told him Malcolm was airsick but would be down soon. Avlov raised his eyebrows disapprovingly. I stood by his side, patiently waiting for Malcolm to appear. The scene was an exact replica of when Yeltsin had recently gotten drunk and failed to emerge from his plane to meet the German president, who awaited him on the red carpet. The whole world had watched the scene on TV in utter disbelief!

After thirty long minutes, Ian and Graeme finally appeared, holding Malcolm up by the arms. Malcolm staggered down the steps and gave Avlov a huge bear hug, then said, "Mr. Yakovenko, it's a huge pleasure to meet you."

Yakovenko half smiled and said cordially, "Likewise, Mr. Turnbull."

Then Malcolm saw me. "Ludmila," he cried, staggering in my direction. "I want to go with you to the hotel. Don't leave me!"

We climbed into a van waiting to take us to the Angarsk Hotel, an old white Soviet-style building and the only hotel in Angarsk. Graeme handed me a vomit bag—luckily, as Malcolm threw up twice.

When we arrived at the hotel, we dragged Malcolm out of the van and managed to get him to his room. He was sobering up, so thankfully he managed to shower himself and get into bed. We forced him to drink as much water as possible and then left him to sleep it off.

In the morning, Malcolm felt so sick he was unable to get up. When I went to see him, he was sheepish and apologetic. I told him not to worry. We'd start the meeting without him. He could get some more sleep, and we'd come and get him after lunch.

"This is terrible, Ludmila. What am I going to do?"

"Just relax. It happens to all foreigners," I replied. "The Russians call it 'the christening.' Plus, if Yeltsin can get away with it, so can you!"

Malcolm smiled weakly.

We started the meeting midmorning in the hotel's boardroom, and at about 2 p.m., Malcolm appeared looking anything but dazzling. Yakovenko asked if they could have a private conference. I accompanied the two of them into another room.

"Mr. Turnbull," said Yakovenko.

"Please call me Malcolm."

"Malcolm, I've done everything to help Star. This morning, we've agreed that MinAtom and the Irkutsk government should be granted a ten percent holding each in the Lenzoloto JSC."

"Okay, but what about the secrecy?" asked Malcolm immediately.

"Regarding the secrecy, I also assure you all 106 licenses will be reissued to Lenzoloto JSC imminently, including Sukhoi Log, and, as shareholders, you will have access to all previously secret data."

"I understand. But do you have the authority to release all the data Star requires?"

"Yes. Irkutsk Geolkom has a copy of the data, and we have the right to release the data to you with the licenses. We only need Moscow's approval to release the data on Sukhoi Log."

"Well, that's a start," said Malcolm.

"Yes. So you can start mining gold immediately. But first you must invest the twenty million US without further delay," added Yakovenko.

"I agree, as long as you can guarantee the licenses and all geological data for all the deposits excluding Sukhoi Log will be given to Lenzoloto JSC."

"Yes, I don't see a problem with that. I will give you a letter today, guaranteeing the issue of the licenses and data."

After lengthier discussions, including certain assurances demanded by Malcolm, Yakovenko said he'd ask Star to consider investing a second US$20 million under the strictest conditions to prop up the alluvials. "Maybe even as a loan to Lenzoloto JSC."

"Well, something like that I would certainly consider," said Malcolm.

The two of them talked some more. Yakovenko then asked Malcolm to transfer the US$20 million to Lenzoloto in the next few days, promising he'd get a letter guaranteeing the licenses—after which he would want Malcolm to arrange another US$20 million for the alluvials.

"What do you think, Ludmila?" said Malcolm, turning to me after Yakovenko briefly left the room.

I replied that all our problems seemed to have been solved, apart from granting Lenzoloto access to Sukhoi Log data, which our new shareholders, Irkutsk and MinAtom, would now help us to resolve.

"Yes, I agree." said Malcolm.

The deal, recorded in what was named the Angarsk Protocol, was sealed not over the usual cognac and vodka—due to Malcolm's fragile state—but over a bottle of Mumm champagne. Yakovenko proudly produced his letter of guarantee. And as a show of good faith, Star agreed to release US$5 million to Lenzoloto the next day. Malcolm and Yakovenko shook hands, and together they told the good news to the other parties. Malcolm then called Yatskevich in Moscow to share the news with him too.

"Malcolm, this is great progress. I can't see you failing now. I see only success," he said.

Malcolm beamed. "That's great to hear from you," he said.

"I have also read Yakovenko's letter confirming that all the licenses, including the Sukhoi Log license, will be reregistered in the name of the Lenzoloto JSC by July 1, 1994. I can provide you with a similar letter. I am even happy to fly to Sydney and confirm all this to your shareholders in person."

"That would be wonderful!" I exclaimed, hardly believing what I was hearing. Was this the same Yatskevich we'd fought for so many years?

Yatskevich said he was meeting with Mostovoy that evening. He wanted to ensure Mostovoy accepted the Angarsk Protocol and agreed to transfer the GKI shares to MinAtom and to Irkutsk, giving them 10 percent of Lenzoloto each.

"I would welcome that, as so far Mostovoy has been against doing so."

"I will try my best for you."

The next day, Nozhikov asked Malcolm to join him, alone, in Moscow's beautiful Gorky Park to discuss the latest developments.

Malcolm was booked to leave Moscow that afternoon. We dropped him at the wrought-iron gate and watched from our car as he disappeared around a path into the formal gardens. He reappeared almost an hour later and had a smile on his face. The walk with Nozhikov had been extremely pleasant, he told us. "We also chatted about how his daughter would like to live in Australia for a while and study law. I said we could definitely help with that."

"I hear his daughter is his greatest love," I commented.

"Yes, he spoke very highly of her," Malcolm replied, before adding, "He warned me as well that nothing happens in Lenzoloto without being known in Irkutsk within hours."

We took Malcolm to the airport—and then, later that night, Ian and I made our way to Mostovoy's office, arriving at 10 p.m., armed with cognac and his favorite Cuban cigars. He'd let us know rather mysteriously that the time had finally come for us to meet someone.

CHAPTER TWENTY-EIGHT

Held Over a Barrel

Mostovoy and another man were sitting in semidarkness at the conference table. The only light came from a couple of lamps.

"Welcome," said Mostovoy, gesturing for us to sit down. "Firstly, I want to tell you that I met with Yatskevich. By the way, I don't know how you managed to convince him to support you, but well done! I have agreed to transfer the GKI shares to Irkutsk and MinAtom. I now would like to introduce you to Lopukhin, the Moscow representative of the famous French investment house Lazard Frères."

Lopukhin was about fifty years old, with gray hair, wrinkly skin, and piercing blue eyes. We exchanged greetings and toasted Lenzoloto with cognac. Mostovoy then lit a Cuban cigar and sat back in his dark-red leather chair, letting his guest do the talking.

"I have been following your progress with great interest," said Lopukhin. "I must congratulate you on how far you have come. But now, as I understand, you are at a critical point where you must not let Sukhoi Log slip away from you."

He suggested that Lenzoloto JSC appoint Lazard to give it financial advice on organizational structure and raising loans, to assist it in the reissue of the Sukhoi Log license, and to obtain preferential tax status. This appointment would be exclusive, he added.

"And what is the cost of these services?" asked Ian.

"Before we go into that, I'd like to convey to you how important this is to the future of Lenzoloto," interrupted Mostovoy. "We still have a lot of enemies, and we cannot proceed without the help of Mr. Lopukhin and Lazard Frères. This was planned right from the very beginning. Again, the orders came from above. I assure you this is vital for our success. Lenzoloto must sign this contract with Lazard."

Lopukhin smiled. "I can guarantee that you will be given the Sukhoi Log license, but our work goes beyond that," he said. "We will protect you from certain things and ensure the mining of the gold and payments go smoothly."

"Well, that would be very useful," admitted Ian without, naturally, asking for clarification on the "certain things."

"Our fees are standard. We would ask for an up-front payment of two hundred thousand US dollars, plus per diem fees with a cap of one million US, and our success fee of two million US—less any other fees already paid. Success will be defined as Lenzoloto or any party in which Lenzoloto has a majority interest receiving the Sukhoi Log license.

"We also charge a one percent fee on any investment loans provided to Lenzoloto, other than by its shareholders, regardless of whether Lazard procures them. Lastly, if Lenzoloto sells any equity to any party other than an existing shareholder, Lazard will get a percent of the equity contributed, again regardless of whether we have procured the equity. This fee structure is our standard and is used by Lazard across the world. I have a contract draft for you to take away and discuss with the other directors."

Smooth. Very smooth. It was a vehicle for Mostovoy & Co. to be paid for all their vigorous work.

"Malcolm won't like this one bit, as Lazard will virtually replace Turnbull and Partners," I said to Ian after we'd left.

"It's not up to him. The directors will decide, but I agree it's quite unsettling," replied Ian.

We departed Moscow a couple of days later and flew to London to spend a few precious days together. Then I returned to Moscow while Ian stayed on in London at his Knightsbridge townhouse.

CHAPTER TWENTY-NINE

Dissension

On May 9, 1994, I left Russia for Sydney, planning to return to Russia at the end of the month.

I got home to find an alarming fax from Ian. He was concerned that he was losing control of the company to Malcolm. He praised Malcolm for his achievements but then started making allegations. Malcolm, he said, went outside procedures. His ego would get in the way after his success with Irkutsk, and he would probably ignore advice from the other directors. Ian added that he and I, and Chris, should start to back away and allow the others to handle the day-to-day operations.

It was the start of Ian's growing jealousy of Malcolm.

Ian knew that Malcolm had offered me an office on his floor at Turnbull & Partners, to keep me close to him. He was right that Malcolm was acting without consulting the other directors—all of them, except for me. The two of us worked very closely together and were achieving remarkable results. From the outside, it looked as if Malcolm and I had taken over the company and were running things as we saw fit. In truth, when it came to solving problems with the Russians, the others were clueless. Malcolm knew it, I knew it, and the Russians knew it. They respected only two people—Malcolm and me.

On May 12, I walked into Malcolm's office full of beans, ready to review Irkutsk's demands. Malcolm's angry expression stopped me in my tracks.

"What's wrong?" I asked.

"Everything. I just got off the phone from Ian. He told me about Lazard. I can't believe that Ian is even contemplating signing with them. No one seems to know what they are doing. Ludmila, I'm so sick of it."

"Malcolm, calm down."

"I can't calm down. We're due to fly to Moscow in one week to finalize the agreements reached in Angarsk, which I'm about to cancel, because if Ian signs with Lazard, I will walk away from Star."

"Oh, Malcolm, it's just a vehicle for them to get their money out of Lenzoloto, legally."

"It's bribery! I think they're toying with us. They have no intention of ever working with Star. When I agreed to underwrite the deal, I thought the deal was done," he went on, his voice rising. "But nothing is further from the truth. I can't keep doing this. It's really getting out of control!"

He stood, grabbed the books on his desk, and hurled them across his vast office, hitting and breaking a very expensive-looking lamp.

"I can't do this anymore!" he repeated.

"Malcolm," I said evenly, "what's really the matter?"

"Okay, I'll tell you. I am losing the bank because I'm spending too much time on Russia and neglecting our other projects."

"Is it really that bad?"

"Yes."

"What if Russia comes off? And I know it will, because it's in our hands now. It will be all worthwhile."

"It's taking too long. That's the problem!"

I sat next to him and hugged him like a child. Malcolm put his head on my shoulder and sobbed like one. The pressure on him was enormous. Russia produced problems almost every day. Some were ripples; others turned into tidal waves. He was giving his all to save Star, at the expense of his bank.

"Malcolm, we're so close to success. We can't give up now."

"You know, if not for you, I'd throw in the towel," he replied.

I grinned at him.

"Ludmila, I'm serious. You're the only reason I'm still in this. You're the only one holding all this together."

The two of us were due to leave for Moscow on May 23. About a week before our departure, the prime minister instructed Chubais (head of GKI) to submit his draft of the ordinance on Lenzoloto, ordering GKI to transfer 10 percent to Irkutsk and 10 percent to MinAtom. Malcolm and Mostovoy would then finalize the amendments to the Lenzoloto founding agreement and charter in accordance with the Angarsk Protocol.

Malcolm was pleased and booked our flights to Moscow, first class.

CHAPTER THIRTY

A Birthday Celebration

In Moscow, we were locked into meetings that lasted for three days. Each amendment was painstakingly argued over a hundred times between Mostovoy and Malcolm. They were both lawyers—and acted like it. Finally, a compromise was reached. Star would have eighteen months after the secrecy lifting to contribute the balance of the US$250 million, which was plenty of time to raise the funds. Irkutsk and MinAtom would get their 10 percent each.

For the first time, everyone was happy.

On the 27th of May 1994, these amendments were signed at the Lenzoloto shareholders' meeting. To celebrate, Yatskevich and Alexei invited us, together with Ian, Chris, and Tim Razzall, Star's newly appointed London-based director, to the elite Writers' Club for drinks to celebrate. We gathered in the same private room where we'd had our private dinner with Poltoranin a few years earlier.

Toward the end of the evening, I noticed Malcolm and Yatskevich huddled together. Malcolm turned and beckoned me over. As soon as I was close enough, he grabbed me and kissed me passionately on the lips. Shocked, I pulled away and looked over at Ian, who was talking to Tim Razzall and hadn't noticed anything. I walked away with Malcolm following.

"Malcolm, are you drunk?"

"No. Ludmila, they want me to go to a high-class brothel with them, and I really don't want to. The only way I could get out of it was to tell Yatskevich that you're my mistress. You have to play along with it."

We left the Writers' Club, and Ian, Malcolm, and I caught a cab to our hotel, the Radisson. Now that I was constantly traveling between Sydney and Moscow, I no longer needed the apartment.

On May 28, the day before my birthday, Malcolm, Ian, and Chris and his new Russian girlfriend, Tanya, took me out to celebrate. Tanya worked for the United Nations and spoke excellent English.

I wore a sexy, low-cut black satin top with wisps of see-through chiffon spilling down from my waist over black satin pants. As Moscow was still chilly, I had to cover the top with a leather jacket.

Before we went to meet the others, Ian gave me a stunning necklace crafted from Russian gold.

Chris had booked a dinner and show at a Brazilian club. We enjoyed many cocktails, a Brazilian BBQ, and a dazzling dance extravaganza. Afterward, Ian and I went with Malcolm to a nightclub called Night Flight, one of Moscow's oldest and best-known nightspots. It was always packed with foreign businessmen and gorgeous Russian women. Some of the women were prostitutes; some were just girls who would do anything to marry a foreign man and leave Russia.

When we walked into the club and I took off my jacket, Malcolm's eyes about popped out of his head.

"You look amazing," he said.

We made our way upstairs and settled in at the bar. A group of Russian bombshells immediately surrounded Malcolm and Ian. After the third bottle of Moët, Malcolm grabbed my hand and said, "Let's dance." He led me downstairs to the dance floor, leaving Ian to talk to the girls. We partied until 2 a.m., then called it a night and headed back to our hotel.

My birthday continued the next day when Ian and Malcolm took me to lunch at the Hotel Metropol, the scene of my very first date with Ian. It was a lovely lunch—Moët champagne (hair of the dog) and the best beef *Stroganov* (succulent slices of beef with mushrooms and onion in a sour cream sauce) I have ever had.

Then Ian drove Malcolm and me to the airport; we were flying home to Sydney. As Malcolm and I passed through the gates and I waved back at Ian, I thought he looked a little jealous.

By the time we landed in Tokyo, I was nursing a severe hangover, made worse by the jet lag. We both slept most of the way to Sydney, and at the airport, we caught separate taxis home. My taxi was behind Malcolm's. His taxi took the turnoff to Paddington and disappeared—and mine continued north to Kirribilli.

CHAPTER THIRTY-ONE

Another Hurdle Overcome with Help from a PM

Mostovoy delivered a draft of the decree on Lenzoloto, signed by Chubais and Shokhin (now the minister of economics), to Chernomyrdin for him to sign and issue. The decree directed the transfer of 10 percent of Lenzoloto JSC shares, currently owned by the Russian government (held by GKI) to the Irkutsk government, and another 10 percent to Atomredmet (Precious Metals, a department of the MinAtom). It ordered Geolkom of Russia to issue Lenzoloto JSC with licenses to mine its deposits and ordered the KGB to give access to geological data on the Sukhoi Log gold deposit to all Lenzoloto specialists (including its foreign specialists). This was a far cry from declassifying Sukhoi Log and decreeing the reserve data as public, but it was palatable for now.

On June 20, Chernomyrdin sent a letter to Yeltsin agreeing in writing to all the proposals in Mostovoy's draft of the decree, as reported to us by Katya.

The Star board agreed to consider releasing another US$5 million to Lenzoloto, on the condition that a Star representative cosigned every single payment and expenditure. Avlov quickly agreed. Mostovoy urged Ian to transfer the money immediately. He also said that the Lazard contract needed to be signed in the very near future. In other words, it was time to cough it up. Ian assured him he would take care of both issues. Unfortunately, Ian always did this—guaranteed things he had no authority to guarantee. But at least it bought us time.

When Malcolm heard about Mostovoy's demands, he exploded like an atomic bomb—again.

"We are being screwed by the Russians. I'm so sick of this, Ludmila!" he yelled. "I find this nauseating! It's been agony for me. I came into this last October under the impression the deal had been done, but the deal had not been done and is still not done."

"Look, Malcolm, I thought it was all over on April 9, 1992, when Gaidar signed our stupid ordinance; I also thought it was all done on August 29, when we signed the founding documents with GKI; as I did on October 4, when Lenzoloto JSC was registered with the Ministry of Finance; and again last Wednesday when Chernomyrdin signed his letter to Yeltsin," I said hotly. "Malcolm, you are rubbing salt into all the wounds I have collected over the last few years. I *do* understand your position and can only say how sorry I am Russia has proved to be such agony for you. I also owe everything to you, because without you, the deal would have been long lost."

"Ludmila, the whole thing can now be fixed by the stroke of a pen, yet it's still not happening!" he responded.

"Mostovoy, whose whole political career is at stake, is playing an intricate game, trying to outmaneuver all interested parties, which is why his requests should be taken seriously; you should reconsider Lazard."

"Lazard is a scam, and Mostovoy is off the wall!"

"Yes, but he's very clever," I argued. "What gives Mostovoy the leverage he needs is the fact that Star is gradually contributing more and more funds to Lenzoloto, making the deal increasingly irreversible. The KGB isn't counting the money in Star's account, only the money Star is contributing into Lenzoloto's account. This is the Russian mentality."

"Yes, I know, Ludmila. Where to from here?"

"Frankly, I think two things will facilitate the signing of the ordinance at this stage," I said. "The five million US and a letter from Keating to Chernomyrdin supporting Star Mining, as per Yatskevich's suggestion."

"Well, a letter from Keating is possible, though highly unusual, as prime ministers don't get involved in private business ventures," replied Malcolm. "But I'm not sure about the immediate release of more funds. We should keep the pressure on. I've organized a conference link with all Star directors to discuss the issue."

The Star board meeting took place that evening. It was decided to release the $5 million to Lenzoloto upon the signing of Chernomyrdin's decree.

On June 24, we had a victory. Malcolm triumphantly produced a letter from Paul Keating to Chernomyrdin. It read in part:

> The Australian Government is keen to promote investment between Australia and Russia and I have no doubt many other potential investors in the Russian gold mining industry are closely watching the development of the Lenzoloto project. It seems considerable progress has been made by the relevant parties to resolve the outstanding problems associated with Lenzoloto. I would be most grateful

for any assistance you can give to finally resolve these problems so that the project can proceed with the co-operation and support of both Russian and Australian participants.

Malcolm invited me into this office to see the letter. I told him I thought it was brilliant and that I was sure Chernomyrdin would now sign the decree.

"I hope so, Ludmila," replied Malcolm.

He told me he and his people were having drinks after work and suggested I stay and join in.

"I'd love to," I said.

I was drinking Moët with Malcolm, Sam (his secretary), and a few others when the phone rang. It was Ian, calling us from the top of the Sukhoi Log mountain. He'd acquired a powerful long-distance Soviet military transmitter to make the call. Ian had taken Drs. John Thomas and Bryce Wood, the senior geologist, there by helicopter to have champagne on top of the deposit and had planted the empty bottle in the snow, symbolically claiming the deposit.

"You're absolutely mad. How cold is it up there?" laughed Malcolm.

"Oh, about minus forty, snowing with gale-force winds," shouted Ian.

"Oh, Ian," I cried. "You're mad!"

"That was Ludmila," said Malcolm. "She's here too, having a few drinks with us."

"Good," replied Ian in a suddenly restrained voice. "Okay, see you in Moscow. I'm signing off now."

We all yelled: "Bye!"

An hour or so later, everyone had left except Malcolm and me. Then he glanced at his watch.

"Oh, damn, it's eight o'clock. I'm supposed to be home by eight. Lucy and I had a dinner party tonight. Damn, I have to go."

"Don't worry," I replied. I was a little relieved to escape.

CHAPTER THIRTY-TWO

Dare We Hope?

On June 28, 1994, I departed for Moscow to join Ian. The next three months proved extremely stressful, though everything initially looked good. We were told that all interested parties were urging Chernomyrdin to issue the Lenzoloto decree. Malcolm and the Star board then released the second $5 million to Lenzoloto, bringing Star's total contribution to US$11.5 million.

But by the end of July, Chernomyrdin still hadn't signed the decree. On August 3, Chris reported that Chernomyrdin had ordered a committee to present yet another report on Lenzoloto JSC.

Ian and I were enjoying a few days' holidays in Nice with Chris and Tim Razzall. The days were glorious, filled with French champagne, sun, beaches, long lunches, even longer dinners, and much lovemaking. My love for Ian flourished. He was so charismatic, so engaging, so exciting and so loving—he was my family.

The south of France was enormously relaxing, in sharp contrast to the tensions of Moscow, and I felt alive. I wished that our time in this carefree, happy, magical part of the world would never end, but it did, and abruptly so. An urgent fax arrived from Katya. She had read the draft of the committee's latest report to Chernomyrdin—and it was bad.

The report recommended that Chernomyrdin stop the signing of the decree. The committee wanted an additional geological investigation of Sukhoi Log because the Geological Institute in Irkutsk suspected the presence of platinum apart from gold and silver and recommended a new valuation of Sukhoi Log be carried out.

Katya asked us all to return to Moscow immediately. We packed and went straight to the airport. I felt sick. How much more of this uncertainty could I take?

Ian called Malcolm, who was in China chasing another gold deal and planning to go to Russia in the next few days. Malcolm was beside himself with anger when he heard the news. Ian, the eternal optimist, guaranteed Malcolm the problem would be fixed and said that he should still plan to come to Russia to celebrate the signing of our decree.

Katya met us when we arrived. She had a copy of the signed report. I was stunned to read that the committee had claimed Sukhoi Log was full of platinum.

Katya then said the word on the street was that Nozhikov had sent a letter to Chernomyrdin claiming Sukhoi Log contained platinum and calling for an investigation. Stabbed in the back once again by Nozhikov the Knife!

On August 27, I left for Sydney for a short break.

Chernomyrdin made his decision three days later, on September 1, by convening yet another meeting to resolve the Sukhoi Log platinum issue. The same day, Lebedev, Ian's nuclear scientist friend, called me at home and asked to talk to Ian. He was somehow involved in the platinum issue. He sounded anxious and said that

Ian should come to Moscow ASAP. I located Ian in Aspen and passed on the message.

Ian arrived in Moscow a week later. By that time, I was back there too. He said we were going to meet Lebedev in the tunnel below the office, to discuss something of critical importance.

Lebedev was already waiting in the dark, damp tunnel when Ian and I arrived. He kissed me on the cheek and said, "Ludmila, this is a conversation I need to have with Ian in private."

I immediately understood that the conversation would involve some sort of bribe and left them alone. Lebedev spoke excellent English and didn't need a translator.

Later, Ian revealed what had happened. Lebedev told him the platinum issue was under control. In Lebedev's opinion, there was platinum in Sukhoi Log, but it was impossible to extract. He explained that when the Sukhoi Log samples were fire-assayed, the platinum seemed to disappear into thin air, literally.

"So why didn't Chernomyrdin just sign the decree?" Ian asked him.

"That's why I've requested this meeting. It's a very delicate matter, and I have been designated as the in-between man," came the reply.

"How much will it take?" said Ian.

"One million dollars, deposited into a Swiss bank account. I have the numbers here," Lebedev added, handing Ian a folded piece of white paper. "I don't need an answer, but I must tell you that once this is done, the decree will be signed."

Ian, after telling me all this, asked me never to mention it again.

Remarkably, on October 1, as I was getting ready to go out to dinner with Fran and her husband in Sydney, Avlov rang.

"Ludmila, the decree has been signed! You are the first to know. It's incredible!"

I screamed. "We did it!"

"Yes, Ludmila, we did it. We did it together and now are going to create the best gold mining company in the world!"

I called Malcolm, who was in London.

"Malcolm, it's done! Chernomyrdin has signed our decree!"

"Ludmila, that's fantastic!" Malcolm sounded over the moon with happiness. "You're amazing!"

I told him I couldn't have done it without him. "It has been thrilling working with you," I added.

"In more ways than one, Ludmila."

"I hope I will now be given a directorship on the Star board. I think I've earned it," I commented.

"You sure have. I have absolutely no problem with that."

Next, I called Ian, who was in Aspen.

"My little girl, we did it. I'm so proud of you. You made this happen. I love you so much."

"Darling, I love you too. I can't wait to see you to celebrate."

"Me more than you!"

On Sunday 2, I received a fax from Malcolm.

> Ludmila,
> I will be back in Sydney on Tuesday morning (I am leaving tonight). I am currently planning to come back to Sydney and go to Moscow next week. I rang Yatskevich and told him the good news. He was VERY excited!
> Much love,
> Malcolm

On October 3, 1994, the decree was officially published. It was dated September 30 and signed by Chernomyrdin, prime minister of the Russian Federation. Star transferred another $8.5 million, bringing the total to US$20 million.

The joy! The triumph! The glory!

CHAPTER THIRTY-THREE

A New CEO and an A-List Party

Star started searching for a CEO, someone who would relocate to Bodaibo and manage the alluvial and hard-rock mines, including Sukhoi Log. Ian and Malcolm finally settled on Michael Bates, ironically ex-CEO of RTZ's gold mining operations in North America.

The burning issue for me now was to become a director of the Star board. After all, I'd brought the deal to the table in the first place. But when I tried to discuss this with Ian, his reply stunned me, though he'd said something similar before.

"I really think both you and I should step away from Lenzoloto," he said. "I would prefer us to do other things now. Let the others take over. Chris, Malcolm, and Graeme."

"Are you saying you're making Chris a director?"

"Yes. He can represent our interests."

I was dumbfounded. "Ian, that's so unfair. He has nothing to do with running Lenzoloto. He's just the office boy."

"He's much more than that, Ludmila."

"He only became involved toward the end! The Russians don't have any respect for him."

"That's quite enough," said Ian abruptly. "Look, the real reason I don't want you on the board is that I don't wish to fight with my wife during our board meetings."

"That's a ridiculous reason," I said furiously, despite the surge of joy I felt at the thought of becoming Ian's wife.

"I must go now. I'll talk to you further when you have calmed down." He hung up.

Every time there was some disagreement between us, Ian would end the conversation and then disappear and remain totally uncontactable for a time, leaving me to stew. The only option was to write him a fax over a few glasses of white wine—which I did. I asked for a one-year appointment, after which we could reassess.

Ian wrote back, informing me that he wanted Michael Bates on the front line and suggesting that perhaps I could be based in London. This pacified me somewhat, but I began questioning my whole relationship with Ian again.

It was a relief to forget Russia briefly and set off for Malcolm's fortieth birthday party a week later. The party—a formal sit-down affair with fireworks and Kate Ceberano singing "Happy Birthday" Marilyn Monroe style to Malcolm—was held on October 22 at Michael McMahon's exclusive Catalina Restaurant in Rose Bay. Situated on the shores of Sydney Harbour, Catalina was a beautiful, airy, light-filled restaurant and bar with floor-to-ceiling sliding glass doors opening out onto a long, curved balcony overlooking the water.

I wore a body-clinging burnt-orange designer dress and satin stilettos of the same color, with my hair swooped up in a high ponytail.

Early into the night, a handsome man came up to me. He had long silvery hair and a seductive manner. He introduced himself as Rob and wanted to know who I was.

"My name is Ludmila."

"Ah, you work for Malcolm."

"No, in effect he is working for me. He is doing the fundraising for my Russian gold project."

"Yes, he talks about you constantly. Do you know you are exactly the type of woman I love?"

"And what's that?"

"Long hair, full lips, and big brown eyes."

At this point, the food arrived, and Rob returned to his table. After dinner, I saw him dancing on the floor with a tall, slim, attractive woman.

"Who is that man on the floor?" I asked one of the women at my table.

"That's Rob Hampshire, the celebrity psychiatrist, and the woman he is dancing with is his wife." *Typical*, I thought. *All the interesting ones are married!*

The room was full of famous people, all social A-listers, and a few politicians. Malcolm strolled around with a huge smile on his face the whole night. Then he disappeared.

I was sitting at the bar drinking a blue lagoon made personally by Michael when Lucy approached and sat next to me, looking distraught.

"Ludmila, do you know where Malcolm is?" she asked.

"No, I haven't seen him for ages," I replied.

"I can't find him anywhere." She was close to tears. "Where is he? Who is he with? Do you know?"

"Lucy, I don't. Have a blue lagoon."

"Excellent idea."

I sat drinking cocktails with a sobbing Lucy for the next hour, after which I made my way to the bathroom and bumped into Malcolm.

"Where have you been?" I asked him.

"I've been here all the time," he answered convincingly.

"Well, Lucy couldn't find you."

"Come and show me which is your present. I want to open it."

We went to the huge pile of presents, and I found mine. It was a telephone in the shape of a pair of large red lips.

"I gave you this so that you'll think of me every time you pick up the phone."

"Thank you, Ludmila. I love it," said Malcolm.

CHAPTER THIRTY-FOUR

Turmoil in Star

Two days after Malcolm's birthday party, Ian, Avlov, and Yakovenko met in Irkutsk. The result: The Irkutsk government promised to ensure that Lenzoloto's licenses were reregistered by the end of November.

But within twenty-four hours, a man called Ilyukhin, head of the security committee in the Duma (the lower house of the Federal Assembly of Russia, which had replaced the old parliament), had declared the Lenzoloto JSC illegal. He ordered his committee to examine the whole issue of Sukhoi Log and report back to the entire Duma.

Once again everything was being rewound. I felt like we had been thrown from the eye of the hurricane back into the storm.

On October 29, Malcolm asked me to come into the office. He wanted me to meet a Russian woman called Natalia Sokolova. Natalia was the niece of none other than Vladimir Zhirinovsky, the leader of the ultranationalist Liberal Democratic Party (LDP) and a presidential candidate in the elections to be held in mid-1996. She was also an associate of Varenikov—the Siberian miner with a vendetta against Avlov and Star. Since Natalia had dual Russian/Australian citizenship, she lived in both Moscow and Sydney.

I arrived at Malcolm's office and waited in the boardroom. A few minutes later, Malcolm came in with a well-dressed blond woman, who sat by his side.

"Natalia, this is Ludmila Melnikoff," he said. She nodded in my direction.

"Natalia is keen to work with Star. She says we have enemies in the Russian parliament who are still trying to stop the project."

Natalia interrupted him and came out with a whole spiel about Ilyukhin's actions. She further claimed the incorporation was illegal because the old Lenzoloto Association had been liquidated, so we'd lost all the licenses, including Sukhoi Log. The only option was to hold a tender.

"And Mostovoy, whom you clearly bribed, is now being investigated by the prosecutor general of the Russian Federation," she finished.

"And where, Ms. Sokolova, did you get all this information?" I asked sarcastically.

"From my good friend Varenikov, who is honest and hardworking, not like the other idiots who run Lenzoloto."

I was never one to back down when inconvenient truths needed to be told.

"Well, I want to inform you that you're both misinformed," I said.

"What would you know? You're just a translator!" Natalia then turned her back on me, shouting, "Malcolm, I refuse to discuss this with a translator!"

"Natalia, calm down," replied Malcolm. "Ludmila is a director of Lenzoloto JSC and of Star Technology. She founded the whole project with Ian MacNee."

"Yes," I said, almost at the same time. "I brought the Lenzoloto project to the table."

Natalia's expression changed. She looked embarrassed and apologized profusely.

I put her right about everything, and she changed her tune. "Ludmila, I can help you and Malcolm," she said. "My uncle is a very close friend of Ilyukhin. He will do as my uncle says. They all know Yeltsin's time is over and my uncle will be the next president."

"Do you really think that?"

"Yes, the people don't want to go back to Communism, but they're sick to death of Yeltsin the drunk. The only real alternative is my uncle, who's a good man with a great love for Russia. I'll introduce Malcolm and you to him. But first Malcolm must write a letter describing the project and showing how good it is for Russia. I can guarantee you his support after that."

"It's a good idea," commented Malcolm.

"Yes," I agreed. "We need as many friends as possible."

Malcolm hired Natalia on US$2,000 per month to lobby for Star in the Duma, which was still controlled by Communists, and to promote Star within her uncle's party. Natalia's job was to convince the hard-line deputies to vote in favor of Star and the secrecy lifting—if the matter ever reached parliament.

There was no doubt that we needed her. In the 1993 Duma elections, the LDP had gained substantial representation, threatening Yeltsin's candidacy. Ilyukhin also believed that gold was a matter of national security and a state secret. His committee would be instrumental to our secrecy lifting.

Problems were developing within Star itself as well. Ian frequently asked me to deal with Malcolm on my own. This was partly because of Malcolm's growing anger that Star was taking up so much of his time at the expense of his bank. But as well, a rift had opened between Ian and Malcolm, which was really a power struggle on two fronts.

Firstly, the Russians wanted to deal with Malcolm and met with Ian only if they had to. As for the new CEO, Michael Bates, they simply did not acknowledge him. The Russians adored Malcolm and regarded me as one of their own.

Secondly, Ian had sensed the closeness between me and Malcolm.

For my part, I adored Malcolm, but Ian was my man.

The tension Malcolm was under was evident yet again when I walked into his office on November 1.

"Ludmila, I'm sick and tired of this," he ranted. "The only solution is to farm the project out to a large mining company. I'm fed up, and I want out!"

"Malcolm, we're so close," I pleaded. "It would be madness to flog Sukhoi Log off to an RTZ."

He sat next to me on the couch, put his hands over his face, and broke down.

What could I do? I was on the same roller coaster ride. It was true that dealing with the Russians was a nightmare. At every turn we were blocked and then confronted with demands for bribes to "unblock" us. The mental strength it took to never lose sight of our goal was overwhelming.

I put my arms around Malcolm and held him once again.

"I know how you feel and I'm sorry it has taken so long, but since you came on board, we have achieved amazing things," I said. "Without you, Star would have failed by now. The Russians love you and me. We'll finish this together. I know it."

Malcolm stood and went to his desk.

"Do you know who is selling shares now? Is it Ian?" he asked suddenly.

"I have no idea. Why do you think it's Ian?" I asked.

"It can only be him. He's doing it through one of his offshore companies. Do you know he's completely broke? He asked me for a loan against his Lambruk property in Victoria. I did a check, and it's triple mortgaged."

I was stunned. "Really?"

"Yes, that's why I had to decline him."

I said that all of Ian's money was hidden in some foundation in Liechtenstein or Switzerland, and Malcolm said yes, he'd heard about that too.

Finally, Malcolm agreed to continue with Star.

On November 2, Malcolm received and subsequently gave me a copy of an internal cablegram circulated within the Australian government, reporting that the Duma has begun hearings into the Lenzoloto gold mine project, in which an Australian company has a significant share. It further stated,

> The Russian State Duma will hold closed hearings on the government's decision to establish the Lenzoloto Joint Stock Company with Australia's Star Technology to develop the Sukhoi Log gold deposit (Irkutsk region) on November 16, 1994. Chairman of the State Duma Security Committee, Viktor Ilyukhin (note: Communist faction) said the hearings must assess the benefit for Russia of establishing the joint venture and examine gaps in Russian legislation which permit foreign companies unhindered access to Russia's natural resources.[6]

Malcolm read the cablegram and exploded. Natalia calmed him down, advising that she would arrange a meeting between him and her uncle and pull Ilyukhin into line. However, before

---

6   Inward Cablegram, O.MS3422 WJKI, 02.11.94; TO PP CANBERRA/ PM. MOSCOW/ FA REF O.MS3216, CM Waller.

she did anything, Natalia asked Malcolm to give her 800,000 of his Star shares. Malcolm agreed, as it was vital to stop Ilyukhin in his tracks. And though it was unlikely, it was possible that Zhirinovsky could one day become president. Natalia later confided to me that Malcolm also gifted her A$50,000, as she lived in low-cost housing in Sydney with her son and was experiencing financial hardship.

At this point, I started to discuss my future role in Star Mining with Malcolm, Graeme, and Ian—since I'd given up the fight with Ian to become a Star director. Graeme informed me that Bates, as CEO, was preparing my contract, and I needed to discuss my future with him.

On November 6, I flew from Sydney to London with Malcolm, Ian, and Graeme. We checked into the Ritz and met in the bar for drinks with Chris, who'd flown in from Moscow, and Michael Bates, whom I'd not yet met in person.

Bates was plump and bald, with beady eyes and a fat chin. He smoked cigars and acted like he was the crème de la crème of the mining world because of his RTZ past. He ignored me for the most part, apart from a few lecherous looks, and came across as sexist and racist.

My misgivings about him grew when Chris let me know quietly that Bates wanted him to become my boss.

"You are kidding!" I said with great indignation.

"He did, but I set him straight."

I felt wretched. Russia had been my brainchild, and some ex-RTZ playboy wanted to take it away from me. I decided to watch him closely and to engineer his departure if need be.

We all flew into Moscow two days later for the Lenzoloto board meeting on November 10. Katya picked us up from the airport and, as usual, was full of stories. Yeltsin, she said, was drinking too much. Together with Poltoranin, he'd been partying with some girls in his private cabin outside Moscow when his wife turned up. Yeltsin ran out the back door in his jocks and jumped into the creek—which, to his surprise, was only knee-deep. He had to be pulled out, drunk and unconscious. Naina was furious and went to Katya for advice.

"I told her all men were pigs, even presidents, and I'd know!" said Katya, giggling like a little girl.

The board meeting went smoothly, and a resolution was passed to implement Chernomyrdin's decree.

While Malcolm continued to do all his excellent work, Ian and Michael Bates were busily running him down. I was present and reminded Ian later that Malcolm's only aim was to turn Lenzoloto into the world's greatest mining company. I also expressed how irritated I was at his constant criticism of Malcolm. "We have enough enemies. We don't need to make enemies of our own people! We must all work together," I said.

The night after this conversation, Ian, Chris, Michael, and I had a drink at the Radisson bar. Afterward, Michael invited Ian and me up to his room for a nightcap. He poured Ian and himself a glass of French cognac and lit a cigar—I stuck to champagne—before stretching out on his bed.

"I've got your contract here," he said, looking at me. "I'm pretty sure you'll still be happy with it. I'm offering you eighty-five hundred US per month. The only condition is moving to London, and as Chris will also be living in London, you'll be answering to him."

I could hardly contain my anger. This was my company and my project. Chris had reported to both Ian and to me, up until now, and I thought Chris had set him straight. However, since I didn't want to argue with Bates directly, I said the money was great and I would certainly consider moving to London. I'd talk to my family and would let him know in a couple of days.

At this point, Ian said goodnight and left, winking at me, which was our code to come to his room. Bates promptly offered me a large cognac to celebrate my contract. I accepted reluctantly. He poured two glasses, gave one to me, returned to his bed, and patted his hand on the cover.

"Come over here. I'll give you a massage."

Horrified, I took a swig of the cognac and told Bates I really should call it a night. Then I charged out of his room and fled to Ian's.

"Ian, I can't believe what Bates just did; he wanted to give me a back massage on his bed."

Ian grinned. "Can you blame him?"

"Shit, Ian, I can't stand him—and look at this contract. I wanted eleven thousand five hundred per month, not eighty-five, which is fair if I stay in Sydney but not if I must move to London."

"Don't worry. I'll take care of it. Come to bed."

The next morning, I looked at the contract again and was astounded to see that it prohibited me from ever talking to Malcolm or Ian about Lenzoloto. This was beyond all absurdity— and it also prevented me from doing any other business in Russia. Was this guy serious?

There and then, I decided I didn't want to work with Bates or sign his contract, let alone live in London and answer to Chris. I would stay in Sydney and consult on the Star board for a fee of US$10,000 per month. They could take it or leave it.

On November 14, Malcolm met with members of the Duma, including Zhirinovsky. His report of the meeting was riveting. Zhirinovsky had told him our problems were entirely political because our "partners" were Chubais and Mostovoy. Malcolm made the obvious point that our contract was with the Russian Federation and that while politicians come and go, government business must continue. He stressed that as foreigners, we had no interest in playing politics or taking political sides in Russia and didn't wish any politician or political faction ill will. For his part, Zhirinovsky confirmed that he supported Star.

The Duma committee hearing was held, and Natalia reported that it was concluded that Lenzoloto JSC had been incorporated incorrectly, but Star shouldn't have to suffer for this. Her uncle had made it clear that he and his party supported Star and regarded us as a serious investor. He'd also said that Australians were welcome in Russia, since Australia, with the Labour Party in power, was semi-socialist. Ilyukhin didn't utter a word during the whole hearing.

On November 18, I flew home to Sydney.

December 1 marked a huge victory for Star; Yatskevich and the Irkutsk Geolkom formally awarded 106 gold mining licenses, including Sukhoi Log, to the Lenzoloto JSC.

But the Sukhoi Log license came with a price tag of US$3.5 million dollars, which, for a change, wasn't a bribe. It was owed due to an official clause in the licensing agreement, based on the gold content of Sukhoi Log and calculated in accordance with the new laws on licensing.

Malcolm and Ian decided they had to wear it and not give the Russians another excuse to postpone the long-awaited piece of paper. Ian suggested this was a good time to sell the small bundle of shares I'd received at settlement in my own name. I agreed, and soon after, a fax arrived from the brokers. They'd deposited a sum of A$1,068,120 into my bank account in Hong Kong. I squealed with delight. My first million!

I was on top of the world. I also felt rewarded, finally, for the hard slog in Russia all these years. I later found out that Ian also sold a huge volume of his vendor shares—about half his original holding in Star Technology—but at the time didn't share any details with me.

My issues with Bates continued. Ever since he'd joined Star, the dynamics of the company had changed dramatically. Ian and Bates had formed an alliance and were conspiring to get rid of both Avlov and Malcolm, while Malcolm was desperately trying to get rid of Avlov. Three huge egos were involved: Bates, Malcolm, and Avlov, all jostling to rule Lenzoloto. Only one of them could survive, or so I thought. I was becoming extremely anxious about the plan to sack Avlov. If Star took part in his sacking, it would be a fatal error, in my opinion.

At the same time, I acknowledged that Avlov was incorrigible. He was like a runaway train. One of his latest acts had been to apply for a loan of US$50 million from a local bank called Bam Credit, and he'd committed Lenzoloto to various other debts without board approval. He was also making noises about being granted Star Mining shares. Clearly, Avlov wanted some of the riches and the recognition for all his hard work over many years of managing Lenzoloto. I knew I had to convince Ian and Malcolm of the value of rewarding Avlov and moving him sideways by offering the role of president of Lenzoloto. As for Bates, I wanted him to disappear.

Malcolm was fed up with Avlov's antics and took it out on me. "The madman must go! Not even you could make me change my mind."

"Malcolm, I'd like to point out, it's *me* he rings constantly demanding more money, which frankly is becoming very unpleasant for me. Even so, I still think it's a grave mistake to get rid of him."

"Ludmila, he is bankrupting Lenzoloto!" said Malcolm furiously. "He's spending Star's money at his own discretion. I will not put in another cent if he isn't replaced."

"Okay, okay, you'll probably get what you want, as the whole board wants him out. But there are ways to do it without making an enemy out of him."

"I'd be happy to discuss that with you later. I have to go to a meeting now."

Off he went. I'd survived another "Malcolm hurricane." How many more could I weather?

Back in Moscow, Kuranov from MinAtom had introduced Ian to a banker called Weinberg, the chairman of Bam Credit. He offered to arrange a much-needed gold loan for Lenzoloto against Lenzoloto's 1995 gold production.

Star embraced Weinberg and started to work with him to put the loan into place. Bam Credit had also applied for a license to buy and sell gold to foreign banks and institutions—and wanted Star's support. If granted, Lenzoloto could sell all its gold to Bam Credit for world prices without any hitches.

In the New Year, I received a lovely message from Malcolm: "Happy New Year, and nice job on a next-to-impossible task, All my love, Malcolm." His recognition of my work meant a lot.

On January 26, I received another fax from Malcolm:

> Ludmila,
> I will be at my farm in Scone tonight and until Sunday. I would love to have a chat before you go to Russia.
> Love, Malcolm

I did carry a torch for him.

CHAPTER THIRTY-FIVE

World's Greatest Mining Company

On January 28, 1995, I flew to Moscow to attend a conference for European investors organized by Bates, who had prepared a snapshot of Star Mining for potential investors, outlining its prospects. It painted an impressive picture:

Star Mining
- An Australian listed company with a 31% interest in Lenzoloto JSC, a Russian gold miner
- Existing alluvial operations and hard rock deposits
- 110,000 sq. km concession area
- Undeveloped Sukhoi Log—60 million oz. confirmed (1,700 metric tons)
- Potential +80 million oz. reserve (+2,267 tons). Total gold: +4,000 tons.
- Largest known undeveloped resource in world

- Star could potentially become the largest gold miner in the world!

Lopukhin, representing Lazard, was a guest speaker at the conference and made the point in his speech that even the hardline Communists were, in principle, in favor of privatization and the Star/Lenzoloto project.

It was interesting to see that Lopukhin was still jockeying for Lenzoloto. Clearly, Lazard wasn't going away. Malcolm had said bluntly that if Lazard was appointed as Lenzoloto's banker, he'd resign.

I was on the verge of resigning from the Lenzoloto directorship myself. Bates and Mel Williams, Star's new chief finance officer, were as thick as thieves, along with Chris. Mel seemed like a nice guy and was certainly a competent CFO, but he was Bates's man. The three of them were running the show in Moscow, and I was constantly fobbed off. But I also knew that if I stepped aside, they would destroy everything that had been achieved in Russia. Malcolm shared my view.

In February, the Avlov situation flared up again. Avlov had acquired a credit of RUB ₽24 billion, equaling US$6 million, from Komdragmet (Committee for Precious Metals) in forward gold sales and was spending it without Yatskevich's knowledge or board approval. At the time, we could only sell our gold to Komdragmet, as no other Russian entity had a license to buy and sell gold. Yatskevich finally cracked when the two of us met on February 2.

"Ludmila, enough is enough. Avlov must be sacked. I have the power to withdraw the Sukhoi Log license at any time, and the way things are going, you will make this easy for me. The secrecy may not be lifted for months, in which case you won't be able to complete the feasibility study by May, June, or July—which means you will lose the license."

"Fine. What if we supported your demand to sack Avlov?" I responded.

"Then I would be happy to extend the licensing agreement if indeed you fall behind schedule," replied Yatskevich.

It was an impossible situation, but at least Yatskevich always laid his cards on the table. I started to believe Avlov must go.

Bates and Chris became more and more secretive about Star's activities both in Russia and in London. Every time I contacted Bates with suggestions on how to resolve an issue, I was told, "Don't worry, Chris now handles everything." It was obvious Bates no longer trusted me, as he knew I'd relay every word to Malcolm.

As per my request, I'd remain in Sydney and become an official consultant to the Star board on US$10,000 per month plus expenses—plus first-class travel to Russia. I had to remain in communication with all the Russian players and regularly report to the board with my updates, observations, and conclusions. For now, I remained a director of Star Technology and Lenzoloto JSC but had appointed Mel Williams (the only palatable option for me) as my proxy whenever I was unable to attend a Lenzoloto board meeting. I admit it was a cushy setup, but well deserved.

Meanwhile, on March 6, 1995, America's *60 Minutes* aired a fascinating story about the journalist John Helmer.[7] On the program, two former KGB operatives at the Russian embassy in Washington said that Helmer had been a Russian spy, code-named Socrates. John denied it on air, but the two KGB men sounded more convincing. Of course, Katya had told me long before that John Helmer was a double agent working for both the KGB and the CIA. It was all very intriguing. I'd worked with John for many years in Russia and could certainly picture him as a spy; he knew too much!

---

7   *60 Minutes*. Season 27, Episode 25, "Derivatives/The Language Factor/Washington Station." Aired March 6, 1995, on CBS.

CHAPTER THIRTY-SIX

Must Get Rid of Malcolm

Avlov kept calling me every day, pleading for money. He sounded desperate.

"Ludmila, I'm telling you our joint venture is finished," he said. "Everything we've worked for together for the past few years is dead in the water. You must provide twenty-nine million immediately, even as a loan, to save Lenzoloto. It's the only chance left."

"Mr. Avlov, I will try, of course, but you must see it's impossible for Star to give you so much without any guarantees. You must see this."

"Well, it's the end then."

"It's not. We still have Bam Credit and Weinberg."

"Their money will not come in time. I can't talk more right now. Goodbye," he said, abruptly hanging up.

I didn't know how much longer I could take the pressure from everything that was going on.

Things went from bad to worse. Ian and Bates, together with Sir Tim Razzall (he had been knighted by the queen), put together a demand for Malcolm to resign from the Star board, claiming that certain merchant bankers in London had made negative remarks about Turnbull & Partners and would not deal with Star if Malcolm remained on the board.

After a large volume of faxes were exchanged, Tim Razzall sent Malcolm a conciliatory response suggesting they continue to work together for the sake of Star and its shareholders.

I was acutely aware that if Malcolm resigned from the board, it would be the beginning of the end for Star. So I was very relieved when the spat resolved itself. If Tim Razzall's accusations were true, though, it was a concern, as Star had to raise another US$225 million.

But how true were the allegations? Did all the merchant bankers in London hate working with Malcolm that much? Was Lazard mixed up in a plot to damn Malcolm's reputation? Or was his alleged reputation (fiery, self-indulgent, arrogant) truly the cause?

Or was Ian behind the whole thing out of pure jealousy?

In mid-March, I joined Ian in Moscow. He and I met with Avlov privately at the bar at the Sheraton Palace Hotel, a modern five-star in Moscow where we were all staying. I'd already discussed with Mostovoy the idea of "promoting" Avlov. There were many examples of so-called "red directors," i.e., general directors of government-owned enterprises from the Soviet era, who could not adapt to Gaidar's new Western economic models of company management and were pushed out via "promotion" to the role of company president. I thought it an elegant solution—one that would not make an enemy out of him.

"Mr. Avlov, I feel the time has come to really understand each other," said Ian. "Success is near. It's vital we remain united. It's important for you to acknowledge that Western needs are different from Russian needs, particularly in accountability. We must work together to show everyone we can make Lenzoloto an enormous success."

We needed to restructure Lenzoloto into a Western-style profitable mining company, Ian went on. A president would be elected to oversee Lenzoloto. "I think you'd make a fine president," he said.

Avlov smiled briefly and said all he wanted was to pay wages so that his people could eat.

"Very important," agreed Ian. "And we will help you."

"I hope so," said Avlov.

I had a sinking feeling that he was never going to agree to the puppet position of president.

The Lenzoloto board meeting took place on April 4 in the Palace Hotel. Malcolm spearheaded all the negotiations. It was decided the US$29 million would be a loan through Bam Credit Bank and that Lazard Frères would become the financial advisers to Lenzoloto (Malcolm had finally conceded to Lazard, as he just wanted all matters to be finalized). Star would contribute US$5 million charter capital to Lenzoloto immediately, and a further US$25 million by the 31st of May. NatWest would do the fundraising for the US$30 million. All the pressing problems seemed to have been resolved.

Everything, though, was still entirely conditional on the lifting of the data secrecy.

I flew back to Sydney the next day to be with Lachlan, who was almost two years old by now. My motherly instincts were finally in full swing, and I yearned to spend every minute with him.

I faxed Malcolm from Sydney, praising him for his fine work in Moscow. I told him he was my hero and a wonderful friend, and how thankful I was that he remained part of Star.

I knew, though, that Malcolm was sick of traveling to Russia and solving the never-ending crises. Lucy, too, was very unhappy with the Russian venture—and possibly with the close relationship between Malcolm and me—and urging him to resign.

Reflecting on all this when I got home, and on how my love for Ian was becoming frustrated by his inaction when it came to us living together with Lachlan as a family, I called him in Aspen to get some of these things off my mind.

As usual, he wooed me. "My darling, I love you very much. You are like a drug. I can't live without you, but I don't know if I want to live in Sydney. I do want to live with you, but I need more time."

"Time for what?"

"For Angus to settle in at Geelong's Grammar."

I wanted to scream. I was so sick of hearing about Angus. But sanity prevailed.

"What about you? Are you staying in Aspen?"

"Yes, Aspen is my place now, but of course I will visit Angus during his school breaks."

"Are you saying we'll be able to live together later this year?"

"Absolutely, my darling. I want that as much as you."

I wasn't convinced. I brought up the issue of Lachlan's birth certificate. "He's almost two, and we need to register it," I said.

"Yes, I agree, but let's wait until Lachie turns two."

I felt a wave of anger. Ian's excuse for not registering Lachie's certificate at birth was that we could not agree on whether to christen Lach Russian Orthodox, as per my wishes, or Presbyterian, as Ian had wanted.

"Ian, this is not negotiable. You said we would sign it when you arrived home for Easter. Look, if this doesn't happen, I don't want to see you ever again. It's over."

"Ludmila, I do what I can to please everyone. Maybe we just aren't good for each other. I seem to enrage you all the time lately. Maybe we should separate for a while."

And there it was. I hung up on him, opened a bottle of wine, and cried for hours. Then I wrote Ian a letter. I listed all his broken promises, which included us living together openly as a couple after Angus finished primary school; signing Lachie's birth certificate; and buying family homes in Sydney and Byron Bay, a stunning sea resort on the north coast of New South Wales in Australia, where we had holidayed many times. Byron Bay, a mecca of sun, sand, and serenity, housed an eclectic mixture of dope-smoking hippies, bohemians, and the rich and famous. It also boasted hatted restaurants, glamourous bars, and five-star hotels.

I further wrote that I wasn't prepared to continue the relationship if he wouldn't make a serious commitment. I signed the letter, "Farewell, Ludmila."

Half an hour later, Ian rang, swearing eternal love and promising that nothing would ever separate us.

He was coming back to Australia for Easter, he went on, and should be in Sydney for a few hours on Good Friday. "So, if you can organize it, I'll be happy to sign Lachlan's birth certificate. Also, book another trip to Byron Bay for us, and we can look around for a property. I know how much you love going there."

I fell asleep that night with visions of Ian and me walking around a magnificent estate on the shores of Byron Bay, with little Lachie frolicking at our feet.

The next morning, I searched for a justice of the peace (JP) to witness Ian's and my signatures on Lachlan's birth certificate and quickly realized, of course, that everything was closed on Good Friday. Ian would have known this. I started to suspect it was another tactic to stall the registration of the birth certificate.

Fran knew of a JP who owned a real estate agency. I called him, not feeling very hopeful, but he agreed to do it. I made an appointment for 11 a.m. on Good Friday and thanked him profusely. Later, I found out he was Jewish, so Good Friday wasn't a problem.

I didn't get another chance to speak to Ian until his plane landed in Sydney early on Good Friday. He called from the airport and asked what our plans were.

"I found a JP who will see us at 11 a.m., and then we can go home and celebrate with champagne and hot cross buns," I told him.

"Sounds perfect," he answered, sounding a bit subdued.

At 11 a.m., we were both standing in front of the JP with Lachlan's birth certificate in hand and a bottle of champagne for our benefactor. Both of us signed it. I felt relieved and very happy. This was a big step forward for us and for little Lachie.

We went home to my Kirribilli apartment and shared a bottle of Moët and buttered buns. Then Ian left to fly down to Lambruk to see Angus—and, obviously, Bobby. The minute the door shut behind him, I started to cry. I knew I couldn't endure this for much longer.

He must have sensed this too, because soon afterward, he came up with the idea of going to the Greek island of Hydra in early June. Lachie and our current nanny, Anna, would come too. Lachie had grown into a gorgeous kid. The black hair he was born with was now the color of white gold. He had huge brown eyes, long eyelashes, and sun-kissed skin. The idea of vanishing to Greece and leaving everyone else to deal with Lenzoloto was appealing indeed. I began counting down the days.

However, Moscow was still uppermost in my mind in the weeks beforehand. Malcolm was reluctantly renegotiating the Lazard contract, but the negotiations did not end well. Malcolm said he had never heard of such absurd terms.

He yelled, "So if NatWest or I raise two hundred million US, they will get two million for doing fuck all. Plus, they still want a success fee of two million for helping Lenzoloto acquire the Sukhoi Log license when we obtained it with no help from them. It's blatant theft! I am going to call Antoine, the chairman of Lazard, in Paris to discuss this."

Malcolm did call Antoine, who denied having any knowledge of Lopukhin or this proposed contract with Lenzoloto. He agreed that the terms were uncommercial and said he would be happy to negotiate a new contract with Malcolm if Malcolm needed Lazard's help in raising future funds for Lenzoloto. Malcolm promptly reported his conversation with Antoine to the Star board, who decided to have no further contact with Lopukhin or Lazard.

I had no solution to this. I knew Lazard was "their" vehicle to get money out of Lenzoloto—"their" meaning Yeltsin, Chernomyrdin, Gaidar, Mostovoy, Chubais, Shokhin, and maybe Yatskevich, the main players involved in the creation of Lenzoloto. Thanks to Malcolm, the Star board would now never sign the Lazard contract; there would be consequences. I could only guess that the government would now stall the release of Sukhoi Log data to Star until another method to extract money was found.

Satisfied with the Lazard outcome, Malcolm started to raise his concerns over limiting access to the secret Sukhoi Log data to a small group of Star experts as per Chernomyrdin's decree. Malcolm told the Star board they needed to prepare a comprehensive statement of the disclosure requirements of Western stock exchanges and financiers for the Russians in preparation for the secrecy lifting. He said Star should tell the Russians bluntly that unless this level of disclosure could be achieved, there would be no prospect of raising the project finance.

Sometimes, Malcolm forgot he was working in Russia, a wild, corrupt country still bogged down by old Communist laws. The fact that the reserve data was a government secret on par with Russia's nuclear bases proved to me that Sukhoi Log contained much more than the 1,100 tons officially published. Katya, who claimed to have sighted the reserve estimate when she met with Chugaevsky, told us it was four times that amount. Avlov had often hinted to me that Sukhoi Log contained at least three times the reserves quoted.

But my biggest concern was the number of Russian companies now emerging, owned by oligarchs who were becoming overnight billionaires by grabbing Russia's wealth. Like Chugaevsky they could probably get their hands on the secret Sukhoi Log data.

Star had been given an amazing window of opportunity in 1990 to grab Russia's greatest gold deposit because the Russians simply didn't have the funds to mine it. But that window was rapidly closing on us.

CHAPTER THIRTY-SEVEN

Yatskevich in Australia and More Bribery

I hadn't spoken to Avlov for weeks. He'd ordered Lenzoloto's press center to start a campaign against Star and was openly suggesting Star's shareholding should be decreased in proportion to its contribution of US$25 million, representing 3.1 percent of Lenzoloto. Yakovenko, in the meantime, was fired up about saving Lenzoloto's alluvials and was being backed by Nozhikov. I spoke to Yakovenko's wife, Mara, who told me that her husband was being groomed to be the next governor of Irkutsk and would do whatever was necessary to make Lenzoloto a success story.

Four days later, I finally spoke to Avlov. He sounded despondent and said that Bam Credit had advanced Lenzoloto a total of US$6 million, but this barely covered urgent bills and some wages. I told him the contract with NatWest had been signed and money was imminent. This cheered him up, and he stressed that we needed to remain friends. Otherwise, the joint venture would fall apart.

NatWest was indeed very close to handing US$30 million over to Star and wanted the directors to lock up their vendor shares for one year.

Malcolm wasn't keen to lock up his shares, so in a private and confidential fax to Ian (which was later published in the 2016 *Financial Review* article written by Neil Chenoweth, mentioned in the prologue), dated May 7, 1995, he wrote that he and his bank owned twenty-one million Star shares. He proposed selling ten million of these to a third party and transferring the remaining eleven million to himself. He noted that, of the eleven million, only six million were vendor shares.

In the same fax, Malcolm asked for his advisory mandate to be extended until December 31, 1996, with sixty days' notice of termination. He also wanted his monthly fee increased to US$45,000.

The Star board had no choice but to accept Malcolm's terms. Ian also agreed to lock up his vendor shares—though, as he owned his shares through a string of offshore tax haven companies owned by other offshore tax haven companies that in turn were owned by a string of trusts, his shares were impossible to track.

Much later, it was reported in the *Financial Review* that in Star Mining's 1996 annual report, Malcolm declared 8 million options, including the 3 million he had received in 1993. But the glaring question was, where did these options come from? Star Mining only had half a million options on issue in 1992 before the big fundraising of October 1993, during which 200 million Star Mining shares and 100 million options were issued to the vendors of Star Technology, i.e., Ian's British Virgin Island companies. The number of shares issued was double the number of options, so the 8 million options acquired by Malcolm were tied to a whopping 16 million secret vendor shares, which could only have come from Ian's "hidden" BVI companies. I concluded that Malcolm had made a secret deal with Ian to keep the majority of his options (5 million) in a tax haven.

On May 9, 1995, Star made an announcement to the Australian Stock Exchange. Star Mining had appointed NatWest Securities to raise approximately A$50 million to allow an advance contribution of charter capital to Lenzoloto of US$30 million, subject to Bates, CEO of Star, becoming director of Lenzoloto. He'd be traveling immediately to Siberia to take up his position.

On May 10, I decided I wanted my Star Mining shares transferred from Pan Pacific back into my name, through Carson Investments, an offshore company Ian had set up for me with the help of his Hong Kong accountant, S. Y. Hui. My name did not feature anywhere on the account. It was totally controlled by SY and some directors I'd never heard of. As Ian completely trusted SY, and I trusted Ian, I had agreed to this arrangement. And that's how the rich get away with not paying taxes.

Since I was about to retire as director, I needed control of my Star shares, and as I would no longer be directly involved, I wanted the option to sell them at any time. I also wanted to be financially independent.

I'd now definitely decided to invest in a wine bar and my own beach house in Byron Bay, using the A$1 million I'd received from the sale of my portion of Star shares the previous December. Byron Bay was where Ian wanted to live, so I needed to create something for me to do.

First, though, I had to organize Yatskevich's visit to Australia, which had been postponed from April to May. Malcolm had already proposed we give him a parcel of 80,000 Star Mining shares to thank him for his undying support of Star. Now, though, Yatskevich was suggesting that instead of the shares, he could get a full cosmetic makeover of his teeth in Australia during his visit, which would end up costing Star A$45,900. Both Ian and Malcolm agreed.

Yatskevich arrived in Sydney on Sunday morning, May 21. We had arranged a fully catered harbor cruise to welcome him to Australia. I left my car at Malcolm's house in Paddington, and together we drove to Double Bay wharf in Malcolm's black Mercedes. Double Bay was a ritzy suburb on the harbor in the eastern part of Sydney. Malcolm was in an extremely good mood.

We were joined at the wharf by Yatskevich, Graeme, some bankers, and the rest of the Star staff. Everyone was in high spirits, especially since Yatskevich said he was certain the secrecy was soon to be lifted. On board our boat, the Veuve champagne flowed. We ate lobsters, oysters, crabs, prawns, Balmain bugs, and smoked salmon. Malcolm and I, as usual, did not leave each other's sides.

The next day, I took Yatskevich to Rod Wills, one of Sydney's best cosmetic prosthodontists, for a full oral makeover. He was there for most of the day—the first of three full days. On Tuesday, we flew with Malcolm to Canberra to meet the minister for resources, David Beddall.

When we arrived at Parliament House, we were treated like royalty thanks to Malcolm's close relationship with Paul Keating. After a formal three-course lunch, we flew back to Sydney and continued partying in a private suite in the elite, very plush Qantas Chairman's Lounge at Sydney Airport. Membership to the lounge was by invitation only, extended to the "powerful and famous"; money alone did not get you in. Of course Malcolm was a member. We nibbled on an array of delicious gourmet finger foods and sipped glasses of Moët. We called it a night at 10 p.m., and Malcolm and I reluctantly retired to our respective homes.

On Wednesday, Yatskevich met with NatWest, Hambros, Mercury Fund, and AMP. He declared that the Russian government would imminently issue a decree declassifying all Sukhoi Log data for everyone to access—not just a group of Lenzoloto experts. In the afternoon, he called a press conference at the Russian consulate in Woollahra, a leafy upmarket suburb in Sydney's east, and stated that he was so sure that the secrecy was about to be lifted from Sukhoi Log that if it wasn't, he would call another press conference and put a gun to his head. Dramatic, but effective!

That Friday, Malcolm and Lucy took Yatskevich and me to their farm in Scone in the Hunter Valley for the weekend. The Hunter Valley is one of Australia's premier wine regions. Originally, I'd refused to come on the trip, as I suspected I was being taken there for Yatskevich's pleasure.

"There's no way I'm sleeping with Yatskevich," I told Malcolm.

"Why?" Malcolm asked.

"Because I find him physically very unattractive, with his ratlike eyes and pointy nose," I said spitefully.

"Ludmila, no one is expecting you to sleep with him, but from another man's point of view, I actually think he's quite attractive!"

We'd had this conversation before. "You sleep with him then."

Unfortunately, there was an electricity blackout in the valley. Some wires had come down in an earlier storm. By the time we rolled up the driveway to the residence, the farm was dark. The electricity was off till the morning.

Malcolm and Lucy guided us into the residence, and while Lucy lit a few candles, Malcolm started the fire to fight off the freezing cold. We stood in the main lounge room, admiring the surroundings. The kitchen and dining room were huge, with high wooden cathedral ceilings. The dining table could sit thirty people and was hand-carved from red cedar.

The fire and the candles created a romantic, cozy scene. I couldn't take my eyes off Malcolm. At one stage, he grabbed a candle, took my hand, and said, "Come, I want to show you something."

He was talking about the giant portrait of himself on the wall beside the kitchen table. As we stood in front of it, he said, "This won the People's Choice Award in the Archibald competition last year. What do you think?"

"The artist missed those long black eyelashes of yours!" I replied.

"You are right," he said, smiling at me.

I slept that night in the bedroom belonging to Malcolm and Lucy's daughter. Without power, though, it was an icebox. I slept with my clothes on and still shivered through the night.

After breakfast the next morning, Yatskevich and I went for a stroll around the farm, admiring rolling grass fields as far as the eyes could see, horse stables, and a grand fountain in the middle of the garden. We sat on the edge of the fountain, and Yatskevich looked at me.

"Why didn't you come to my bed last night, Ludmila? I waited for you all night."

I was taken aback by his directness.

"I realize in Russia it's perfectly normal for a man to have a mistress to prove his manhood, but here it's not," I replied.

"We may never get another chance. You should seize the moment!"

Thankfully, Malcolm appeared at that instant to give us a guided tour of the farm.

We walked across the grass meadow and eventually came to a grave. Malcolm explained that it was his father's. "It's why I kept the farm, even though it's a nightmare to manage and very expensive," he said.

"Were you close to your dad?" I asked.

"Yes. He raised me. My mother ran off when I was very young, so it was just the two of us."

After the tour, it was time to head back to Sydney. Malcolm, who was driving, dropped me off at my Kirribilli apartment. Lucy said they were having a dinner party that evening for some business associates of Malcolm's. Paul Keating was the honorary guest. She said they had functions every evening for the next month.

I thought, *I would hate to live like that*. I was so looking forward to kissing my beautiful boy on the forehead before Anna, the nanny, put him to sleep, then having a long bath with a glass of champagne before ordering my favorite Chinese home delivery and watching the latest blockbuster movie. Heaven!

But a few minutes after I entered the apartment, Ian phoned. He wanted to make sure I'd gotten home—and that I hadn't slept with Yatskevich. After I reassured him, we discussed our forthcoming trip to Greece in early June.

Ian said he wanted to really splurge on this trip. He told me to book a first-class ticket for myself and business-class tickets for Anna and Lachie, and he'd booked us into the Miranda Hotel. Ian recalled how he'd stayed there and partied with Sophia Loren when she was filming *Boy on a Dolphin*.

The evening of May 29, my mother and my two beloved sisters, Veronica and Marina, came to Kirribilli to celebrate my birthday with me. Malcolm was due to join us for a drink on his way home. I was excited, though not as much as my mum and sisters, who looked forward to meeting him.

I'd bought lots of delicacies from an upmarket French patisserie and a dozen bottles of Moët, one of which I placed in the center of the table, in an ornate silver cooler—a birthday gift from my mum. Malcolm arrived with a black Chanel handbag and a big hug for my birthday. He got along famously with my family. We were just about to open the fourth bottle of champagne when Lucy rang and demanded to know where he was. Malcolm said he would be home shortly, and after we finished the fourth bottle, he reluctantly left. I walked him to his car and watched him drive away in his black Mercedes.

Yatskevich was still in Australia. We'd sent him to the Gold Coast for a short holiday, and he'd fallen in love with it and said he wanted to live there. Malcolm and Ian said that they would be happy to arrange Yatskevich's permanent residency in Australia—although this favor was dependent upon Yatskevich fulfilling his promise of persuading the KGB to lift the secrecy from all Sukhoi Log data.

On June 3, I met Yatskevich at a bar in the city for a farewell drink, as he was leaving that afternoon for Moscow. His teeth looked spectacular—straight out of an "after" shot in a TV commercial.

He said he'd be all over the secrecy-lifting decree the moment he was back in Moscow. I told him I'd be there soon too, in only a few more weeks. We hugged and parted.

CHAPTER THIRTY-EIGHT

War in Bodaibo

The very next day, I flew with Lachie and Anna to Athens, from where we made our way to Piraeus Port and caught the *Flying Dolphin*, a fast ferry, to Hydra. Anna was an amazing nanny; she loved Lachie to bits!

The first thing I noticed after we arrived was that there were no cars anywhere. The main method of transportation besides the water taxis was by mule or donkey. The town was constructed on a hill and dotted with exquisite stone mansions and elegant monasteries; crimson bougainvillea lining its cobblestoned streets. Below, the port glittered with deep, crystalline-blue water. It was simply delightful.

It was very hot as we dragged our luggage up the hill to the allegedly five-star Miranda Hotel. To my horror, the hotel looked more like a youth hostel. The rooms were just as bad. Worst of all, there was no air-conditioning, and it was thirty-eight degrees Celsius.

I didn't want to stay there a second longer and decided to find another hotel. Eventually, after calling my travel agent in Australia, I managed to get us into the Bratsera, a gorgeous hotel with a trendy bar, a magnificent garden, and a pool surrounded by flowers.

Ian flew in. We spent all day on the sandy beaches and dined out every evening on fresh-caught fish and drank white wine and ouzo. Then, one evening, after we got back to the hotel room following a pleasant dinner, Ian insisted I call Avlov and offer him money to resign. I exploded. Firstly, it was 2 a.m., and secondly, bribing Avlov to resign was the most idiotic idea I had ever heard, and I said so.

After a shouting match, I stormed off to the bar by myself to calm down over a glass of ouzo and ice. When I got back to the room, Ian was asleep with all his bags packed, and when I woke in the morning, he was gone. I felt shattered, as I always did after our fights, but since I still had two weeks to spend in Hydra, I was determined to enjoy the holiday.

On June 10, there was a nasty incident in Bodaibo. Mel Williams, Star's finance director, was assaulted by some men after leaving Tanya's restaurant. He required hospital attention and remained in the Bodaibo hospital. We all knew that Avlov was behind it. Mel had been convinced Avlov was ripping off money by attributing it to construction and pocketing it instead, as he knew his days were numbered. Yatskevich thought the same.

From then on, the tension only got worse. At the board meeting in Irkutsk, Bates shouted at Avlov that the funds provided by Star had been misused, sending Lenzoloto into bankruptcy. Mostovoy walked out of the meeting and flew back to Moscow to sort out the Avlov issue with his superiors. It was decided that the shareholders' meeting on the 28th of July would be held in Moscow for security reasons, since safety could no longer be guaranteed in Bodaibo.

I was asked to call Avlov and try pacifying him. I called him from Hydra, which by now had become a place that I never wanted to leave. Avlov was very guarded when he answered.

"Ludmila, the situation is very complicated, and I can't say more over the phone."

But he finally opened up to me and said we'd betrayed him and his management team. It had all started when Bates and Mel joined Star, he said. "One thing is for sure: If we no longer work in Bodaibo, we will always live here. We were born in Bodaibo, we grew up here, and we will never leave," he went on. "Remember this—if you sack me, your money will be buried in the sands. I'll make sure of that. I've fought so many years for Lenzoloto, and now it has come to this. Wages remain unpaid since February. Two hundred and twenty-five billion rubles [US$44 million] are owed. I don't know what to do."

Then he added, "Mark my words. If I'm eliminated from Lenzoloto, I guarantee no one will ever mine Sukhoi Log."

Avlov clearly knew he was finished and was devastated. The morning after our conversation, the steps of Star headquarters in Bodaibo were covered in white calla lilies. In Russia, white calla lilies symbolize death.

In Hydra, I felt increasingly melancholy. Before Greece, I hadn't seen Ian for ages, and because of our fight, I hadn't seen him since. He was at his Knightsbridge house in London, so I faxed him there. I said that all our fights were over Russia, and if he continued to spend all this time away from me, our relationship would die.

I ended the fax by announcing that I was buying a restaurant called Mexican Mick's in Byron Bay for A$400,000 and wanted an undertaking from him that he could lend me the money for the renovations, as he'd earlier promised. Mexican Mick's was Australia's first Mexican restaurant and an icon of Byron Bay but was tired and needed a facelift.

The holiday in Greece drew to a close. On June 25, the day before we left, I finally spoke to Ian. He was at home in Aspen. He told me he loved me very much and missed me tremendously, and then he gave me a road map of our future. Our work in Russia was almost complete, he said. Lenzoloto JSC was in good hands and the secrecy almost lifted. We'd successfully created Russia's first gold mining joint venture. We could retire from Russia and spend our life together in Byron Bay.

When we'd last visited this balmy, sun-kissed town, we'd inspected an expansive country estate for sale in Ewingsdale, which we both fell in love with. It had six bedrooms, a large lounge room with a fireplace, an alfresco dining area overlooking a resort-style pool and spa, and a tennis court.

"I'm buying it," said Ian now. "We settle on July 17. In winter, we can travel to Greece, and in summer we can go to Aspen. What do you think?"

"Oh, Ian, it's a dream come true. I love it!"

"And I love you, and Lachie, of course. Oh, by the way," added Ian, "I can confirm that I'm totally committed to helping you develop Mexican Mick's."

It was a wonderful phone conversation. I couldn't wait to see him in Moscow for the shareholders' meeting.

Meanwhile, Bychkov, head of Komdragmet, had signed the draft of the decree "Lifting of secrecy from Sukhoi Log data without limitation" after arguing with Yatskevich over the lack of a bribe. Yatskevich indicated to him "something" would be arranged shortly. The only remaining missing signature was the KGB's.

On the day of the board meeting, Avlov flew into Moscow and met Weinberg in private. Avlov agreed at their meeting to become Lenzoloto JSC's first president. He would get a US$100,000 golden handshake, 25 percent of which would be paid upon him signing off on the terms of his "promotion." He'd step down immediately and stop all the anti-Star rhetoric.

The day after Avlov accepted the post of president, he broke his word. He appeared on Bodaibo TV and declared that the shareholders' meeting on July 28 should remove Star. He was planning to hold a workers' union conference on July 20 to vote on replacing Star's unpaid shareholding in Lenzoloto JSC with alternative Russian investors unless Star contributed its full US$250 million by September 4. He then threatened to deliver the minutes of this meeting to Chernomyrdin.

In the Communist days, if the workers sent a signed petition to any of the Communist leaders, the request was usually granted. But those days were long gone, and the current Russian government didn't pay attention to the workers' union. Despite this, Avlov was determined to deliver his petition and push his grievance against Star. On top of this, we discovered he'd been lobbying the KGB not to sign the decree lifting the secrecy from Sukhoi Log, claiming that Star had no money.

Finally, I accepted that Avlov had to go—immediately. The plan was to bring it on at the meeting.

Unexpectedly, Ian told me he'd had a serious discussion with Bobby in Aspen about commencing proceedings for their divorce. His lawyers in Melbourne would start the ball rolling on August 14. Everything seemed to be happening at once!

My future with Ian now looked bright. We planned to live permanently in Byron Bay after selling our involvement in Star Mining once the secrecy was lifted. I would run the restaurant. Ian would continue his other businesses around the world, including a lucrative winemaking joint venture in Oregon with Brian Croser, the internationally renowned winemaker and owner of the award-winning Petaluma winery in the Adelaide Hills of South Australia. Ian had apparently known Brian for years.

The continuing unrest in Bodaibo made our Byron Bay plans look even more enticing. Lenzoloto failed to meet June's loan repayment to Bam Credit. Weinberg warned of potential recovery proceedings against Lenzoloto. And Bates was clashing with Malcolm. Was that jealousy too? Star Mining was widely known as "Malcolm Turnbull's company."

I arrived in Moscow on July 23 in the heat of summer. Malcolm and Ian arrived two days later, straight from London. I'd already informed the board that Nozhikov's daughter, Anastasia, would travel to Sydney in October to be trained as a PA for Star Mining.

The extraordinary shareholders' meeting to address the sacking of Avlov started at 10 a.m. on the 28th.

Avlov was the first item on the agenda. He sat, looking thunderous, with his secretary, a striking young brunette who'd recently become his mistress. Alexei stood and read the first resolution, to dismiss Avlov from the post of general director.

There was a deathly silence. Slowly the shareholders began raising their hands. Alexei declared the resolution passed. Avlov got up and marched out of the hall with his secretary, his head held high. The door shut behind them.

I felt a strange mixture of remorse, dread, and pity for Avlov. He, Ian, and I had created Lenzoloto against all odds, and he'd fought so hard for Star.

Malcolm was now our sole key to success. But he was becoming increasingly disillusioned with Yatskevich's promises. To cap it off, Malcolm had told me that Lucy gave him an ultimatum: "Make your latest trip with Ludmila your last and pull out of Russia for good, or I will divorce you."

In Moscow, the decree draft on the secrecy lifting was now in the hands of KGB newcomer Barsukov. Kuranov had met with Barsukov's aide. Apparently, Barsukov was in favor of releasing all data—except the gold reserve data. Why were the Russians so adamant about keeping the reserve data a secret? Who else did we have to bribe? Was it a grave mistake not to go ahead with the "Lazard" bank?

CHAPTER THIRTY-NINE

Knives Are Out

Out of the blue, I received a panicked phone call from Graeme. "I spoke with Ian in London last night, and they're planning a coup against Malcolm," he said. "Ian and Bates have convinced Tim Razzall to oust Malcolm from the board by forcing his resignation right there and then."

"You're kidding me! Ian didn't say anything to me about this."

"That's because he thought you would run to Malcolm and tell him."

"I would have," I said grimly. "Graeme, you know this would be a fatal mistake. We can kiss Russia goodbye."

"You don't have to convince me. You need to talk to Ian urgently and stop him getting rid of Malcolm."

Graeme informed me that Ian, Bates, and Razzall had met with NatWest at the bank's request in London. NatWest had apparently refused to continue working with Star if Malcolm remained on the board. They regarded him as a loose cannon who was rude and arrogant and did what he pleased.

"Do you believe them?" I asked. They had, of course, tried this move before, in March.

"There's probably some truth to it, but it's not worth sacrificing Malcolm."

I totally agreed. I called Ian and told him I knew what was going on.

"Darling, I have no choice," he answered. "NatWest won't deal with us if Malcolm's still there, which jeopardizes the thirty-million-dollar fundraising. His reputation amongst the London banking world is woeful—no one will touch him or any company he's involved in."

"Frankly, I find that hard to believe," I retorted. "Anyway, if you do this, you might as well kiss Russia goodbye. The Russians adore him. He's the only reputable person in Star as far as they're concerned."

"That's rubbish!"

I felt a fight coming on and toned things down.

"Okay, darling, but please reconsider. Just wait a couple of months. Please."

"It's not up to me anymore. Bates and Sir Razzall are adamant he has to go immediately."

I tried one last time. "Ian, please reconsider Malcolm. I truly believe it's a monumental mistake and spells the end of Lenzoloto for us. You know you can save him if you want to."

But it was hopeless. Ian told me to trust him, said that he loved me, and hung up.

I heard nothing more until the next night, when Malcolm rang.

"Ludmila, it's all over for me."

It had been a coup d'état, he went on. "Bates claimed none of the London banks would deal with Star if I remained on the board, which is absolute rubbish."

"Oh, Malcolm, I know it is. Bates has been scheming to get you out for a while now. I really hate him."

"I'm actually calling you from the balcony of my penthouse suite at the Ritz in Istanbul, drinking a glass of champagne and thinking of you. It's so romantic looking over the whole of Istanbul. You must come here one day," he added.

"Did you fly straight from London?"

"Yes, I decided to come here for a few days to relax. Lucy is joining me tomorrow."

I started to cry.

"Oh, Malcolm, you know that without you, it's all over for Star. The Russians will eventually pull their support and oust Star from Russia. I've lost all hope. I'll probably leave Star soon as well. I'm sick of all the traveling and the constant problems."

"You should keep going," said Malcolm. "The board decided to release the twenty-five million US to Lenzoloto now that Avlov is gone. You may get there. My advice is to get your three million back from Ian. If the shares fall, you will never see your money."

"Yes, you're right, but it's not easy."

"Ludmila, I have to tell you that even after what's happened, I have no regrets," he went on. "The best thing that has come out of all this is meeting you and working with you. It has been a delight. You made it all worthwhile."

"Thank you, Malcolm. We'll still see each other, won't we?"

"For sure," he replied. "I will call you when I am back in Sydney. Bye for now."

The line went dead.

From that moment on, I began asking Ian to transfer my Star shares from Pan Pacific back into my name. At settlement back in October 1993, Star Mining shares were thirty cents, so my shareholding of twenty million shares was worth A$6 million.

However, every time I asked Ian to transfer my Star shares from Pan Pacific to me, he would simply reply, "Darling, I don't want you to sell them. I want to end up controlling Star Mining, and I need as many shares as I can get my hands on. If you still really want to sell them, I will buy them from you."

Love is blind and deaf. I agreed to wait.

In September, I called Yatskevich to ask how he felt about Malcolm's departure. Predictably, he was very unhappy. However, he told me that the KGB had finally reached a decision on the secrecy. A final meeting was being held the following week to ratify the decree draft. This would pave the way for Chernomyrdin's signature.

How many times had I heard that before? The only good news was that the Star board directed Bates to either live in Bodaibo or resign. He resigned.

Meanwhile, Ian and I bought up a large slice of Byron Bay. Ian had purchased the sprawling estate in Ewingsdale, which became our family home, and I purchased a gorgeous timber beachfront house as well as Mexican Mick's.

Ian chose Byron Bay because he disliked living in cities, although I thought he also preferred to keep me hidden away from his and Bobby's A-list friends. But I was happy to live in Byron Bay for a while. It *was* one of the most tranquil, spiritual places on earth; in the days before the white people came, the Aboriginals would go on pilgrimages from the deserts to Byron Bay to heal from various ailments.

I missed Ian when he was away, even though he was in contact every day. He assured me that Bobby knew all about me and had long accepted their pending divorce. I signed my faxes to him, "Your loving fiancé," but I felt increasingly lonely. A few weeks later, I sent a fax telling him that for me in Byron Bay, nothing had changed, and I was frustrated. I wanted to tell *everyone* about us, to release the pain of the long years of secrecy. I wrote, "The next person who asks me, I will tell them."

Ian rang and assured me everything was fine, and he would never be with anyone but me. He promised to come home straightaway.

But he didn't. Instead, he left Moscow and went straight to Aspen. His excuse was that he urgently needed work done on his teeth. When I started screaming at him, he came back with what was becoming his standard reply when we fought: "It's all too hard. Maybe we aren't meant to be together."

I said I would die without him, and again we made up. But then, once again, I didn't hear from him for days and couldn't reach him by phone. I shot off another heartfelt fax, adding, "For the billionth time, I request my Pan Pacific shares be transferred back to me. I earned those shares with blood, sweat, and tears, and they belong to me—NOT YOU—so please transfer them. I really want to be independently wealthy and do what I want, like you."

Following his usual pattern whenever I set ultimatums, Ian rang immediately. He promised to transfer my shares—and to tell me everything from now on.

In Moscow, the new KGB chief, Barsukov, an unattractive, beady-eyed man with thin lips, refused to agree to the total declassification of all the Sukhoi Log data. He drafted his own version of the original decree. We were back at square one.

The situation was ludicrous. So far, we had invested US$30 million in Russia. We had acquired title to Sukhoi Log. We had introduced recovery technology. We had restructured Lenzoloto. We had spent A$10 million on a feasibility study on Sukhoi Log—all without knowing where the gold was, or even whether it could be extracted profitably.

Katya was right; the KGB wanted a bribe, but they had to be acting on someone's instructions—possibly Yeltsin's.

CHAPTER FORTY

Liquidity—Dividing Up the Spoils

On October 9, 1995, Star Mining released its annual report. Star's total contribution to Lenzoloto was enumerated. Under the section "Directors' Benefits," it stated that in 1993, Ian had acquired 200 million shares from the sale of Star Technology to Star Mining. In 1994, Ian had reduced this interest to 99.5 million shares.

This was a huge reduction and would have yielded more than A$35 million. Pan Pacific's shareholding had been reduced from 100 million to 36.5 million—without my prior knowledge or consent.

So where did the shares go, and who benefited? Who were the other vendors of Star? Was Malcolm one of them? Malcolm apparently owned 6 million vendor shares, which would balloon to 16 million vendor shares in 1996, according to Star Mining's 1996 annual report, released on September 27, 1996.

I had sold my 3 million shares to Ian in December 1994, raising just over A$1 million.

The fate of the rest remains a mystery to this day.

Ian eventually agreed to transfer my Pan Pacific shares, 6,550 of them, to my offshore company, Carson Investments Ltd. To pacify me, Ian signed both letters. Then, once again, he became unreachable by phone. Naturally, he didn't transfer my shares.

I didn't see him for many weeks—until he called and professed his eternal, undying love. All he wanted, he said, was a life with Lachlan and me.

"Darling, I can't wait to show you off," he went on. "I want to take you to Aspen and introduce you as my new wife. I'm about to settle on a little house at the foot of the mountains with an expansive garden full of fruit trees for us. Just be a little patient. Aspen is so pretty in summer. I actually prefer it to winter. I will take you there at the end of May for your birthday, but in the meantime, let's just finish Russia."

How did he always manage to talk me around? I was hopelessly in love. But I was also on the verge of a nervous breakdown.

In Moscow, Yeltsin had another heart attack. According to Katya, the secrecy-lifting decree was now lying on the table in his hospital room.

On December 1, I spoke to Yatskevich, who'd been appointed the new chairman of Lenzoloto. He said the secrecy decree would be issued before the end of the year and asked if I was coming to Moscow for Lenzoloto's first board meeting without Avlov and chaired by him. I said I couldn't this time and wished him luck.

The board meeting went extremely well, as Yatskevich was on the same wavelength as the rest of the Western "civilized" world. A proper business plan was formulated, and all agreed to increase production from the alluvials, to mine the Pervenets and Visochaishi hard-rock deposits (two of the smaller mines), and to settle Lenzoloto debt prior to tackling Sukhoi Log. I was so excited about this that I decided to talk about it with Sally MacMillan, a journalist who had come to Byron Bay for the official opening of my restaurant. The following article, titled " Life's Golden," appeared in the *Sunday Telegraph* on December 17, 1995:

> Byron Bay is about as far away as you can get from the vast, desolate tracts that make up the Siberian Region.
>
> Byron Bay is a balmy bath of a place, right now gearing up for holiday mode. Siberia, inhospitable in land and climate, though not in its people. Much of it remains uncharted waters to foreign investors. But not to Byron Bay's Ludmila Melnikoff, who has helped set up an Australian joint venture to mine the world's largest gold deposit in Siberia. This thirty-something entrepreneur has dived into both these golden places. And she's landed feet first.

The article went on to describe my various property investments, including Mexican Mick's; my first company, Labstaff; and my education; all leading up to my forthcoming crowning achievement: the Lenzoloto venture.

> The hard slog of working behind the scenes—involving big names like dealmaker Ian MacNee and, until recently, Malcolm Turnbull—looks set to pay off. . . .
>
> Ludmila Melnikoff *found* Lenzoloto and its owners; found Ian MacNee; nurtured the negotiations; helped frame the exciting joint venture and attracted Malcolm Turnbull. Today she acts as a consultant to Star Mining NL and is a director of Lenzoloto.

"It is a long time coming," the gold guru laughs, "but now, all we need is a Decree lifting the secrecy on the geological data—to happen any day—and we can steam ahead with the bankable feasibility study. This should be complete next April or May, and we can start mining pretty much straight after that."

And that means another Siberian foray for Ludmila. More terrifying Aeroflot flights—eight hours in propeller planes where engines give out, you bounce in the sky and skid-land on ice.

"I've learned to slug another vodka or cognac and not give up," she chuckles. She laughs a lot, this golden-headed whizz.

But December ended with no news of the secrecy decree.

Life's golden
Soviet wastes create a boom for Louise

By SALLY MACMILLAN

BYRON Bay is about as far away as you can get from the vast, desolate tracts that make up the Siberian wastes.

Byron's a balmy bath of a place, right now gearing up for holiday mode.

Siberia: inhospitable in land and climate, though not in its people.

Much of the former Soviet mining remain uncharted waters to foreign investors, but not to Byron Bay's Louise Mehnkoff, who has helped set up an Australian investment in mining the world's largest gold deposit, in Siberia.

This thirtysomething entrepreneur has dived into both these golden places. And she's landed feet first.

Byron Bay is her home country estate in the Ewingsdale hills; a Suffolk Park beach house; her just-opened Dick's Wild & Woolly Beasts and Grill in the heart of town.

Since August, she's dropped a cool $2 million investment into this hideaway for the stars.

For a girl who, little more than a decade ago, lived on $10 a week from nuns while occupying a BSc in biochemistry and biotechnology at the University of NSW, it's a fairytale come true.

"I still don't want to say it all loud," she laughs, cuddling her flaxen haired son, Lachlan, 2, at home where the evergreen hills roll out to the coast and the famed Cape Byron lighthouse.

This Australian-born daughter of Chinese-born Russian aristocracy makes things happen.

In 1985, straight out of uni, he and partner Anne Sabine set up Labstaff, Australia's first personnel consultancy specialising in scientific placements.

The company, which won a Small Business Award in 1991, today has branches in Melbourne, Adelaide, Perth and Brisbane.

Anne Sabine now runs Labstaff, but Louise remains 50-50 co-owner.

"I like going for the kill," Louise laughs. "Making it happen. But I'm not too good on the day-to-day stuff."

Louise ventured to her ancestors' homeland, obtained a diploma in Russian from Moscow University, then set out to find ventures new.

After five years living on and off in Moscow and Siberia, her ship is about to come in.

LenaInco — translated as LenaGold — is a joint venture between the Russians and Star Mining, an Australian company listed on the Sydney Stock Exchange.

The hard slog of working behind the scenes — involving big names like deal-maker Ian MacNee and, until recently, Malcolm Turnbull and Neville Wran — looks set to pay off.

The company was registered in September, 1992 and alluvial mining begun.

But it's taken three years of negotiation battles with the bureaucracy — from Boris Yeltsin to the KGB to just about every Russian minister — to get the final green light for this hard rock project to get under way.

Three weeks ago, it happened. Signed, sealed and delivered: a decree lifting the secrecy and giving the go-ahead to mine the world's largest gold deposit — the Sukhoi Log, in Siberia's Irkutsk region.

Sukhoi Log — a government secret since '71 and still not fully explored after 20 years — is estimated to contain something like 94 million ounces of gold. Huge stuff.

Louise Mehnkoff "found" LenaGold and its owners; found Ian MacNee; nurtured the negotiations; helped frame the exciting joint venture. Today, she acts as a consultant to Star Mining NL and is a director of LenaGold.

"It was a long time coming," the gold guru laughs. "But now, the decree lifting the secrecy gives us the full data and we can steam ahead with the bankable feasibility study.

"That should be complete by April or May, and we can start mining pretty much straight after that."

And that means another Siberian foray for Louise. More — terrifying — Aeroflot flights — eight hours to propeller planes where engines give out, you bounce in the sky and skid-land on ice.

"I've learned to shrug and slug another cognac," she chuckles. She laughs a lot, this golden headed wiuk. Better than crying, she says.

Others haven't had her in her fortitude. Some share holders couldn't stick it out.

She and partner MacNee reckon they'll come back in now.

"We've had the documentation for a long time and we've been alluvial mining there for some time. But it's understandable some people lose hope over time with the hard rock," Louise says.

"That's why I want to see this thing through, and why I'll go back to Siberia, even though I've really had enough of it — the place, not the people.

"My next dream is to take LenaGold the number one gold mining company in the world.

"I'd like the shares to be $2 because that is success and that should be success with production predicted at 60 tonnes of gold a year."

Lot of contacts have helped Louise Mehnkoff. Her journalist-poet mum's contacts in Russia — 78-year-old Russian journalist Katya Shiveleva, childhood playmate of Andropov and translator to Khrushchev. Katya introduced Louise to Boris Yeltsin and let the LenaGold venture in motion.

Louise and Ian MacNee's 20-minute meeting with Yeltsin won them official backing.

Yeltsin said then, 'Go and do it, and I will support you'. He has, to this day.

Louise contacted a specialised service to find a tucker for her Siberian project dream — alluvial mining, platinum, gold and the "whisper of diamonds" — and was project "wed" to MacNee. He had delved into Russia and mining a few years before, and had a "shop" company set up about '92 — today Star Mining.

While attending the 90th birthday of 'Mr' Aviov, the owner of the mining company in the village of Botalis, the pair heard the "secret" of the LenaGold lode. That began the cogs moving.

Malcolm Turnbull managed to raise the first $20 million without the feasibility study — although other documentation was there — in hand.

LenaGold today is 37.5 per cent owned by Star Mining, with the balance held by the Russians.

Louise laughs: "I was speaking to Aviov last Saturday and he said: 'Darling, I've got everything ready for you'."

This year, she consulted yet another service to find a general manager to run her new Byron restaurant and tourist Chris Joyce, then executive chef Alan Patzl and restaurant manager Brian Bevan.

Rounding it out are astounding murals and paintings, Tasmanian oak ceilings, recycled local timber furniture, wrought iron chairs made by local blacksmiths, sandstone walls, a brick-and-tile barbecue oven, seating for 250 and a super sound system.

'Some people lose hope over time...I've learned how to shrug and slug another cognac'

INSIGHT

CHAPTER FORTY-ONE

Broken Record

I started 1996 with a phone call to Katya. Russia was swept up in the fervor of elections. In her opinion, the three hottest contenders were Yeltsin; Zyuganov, the Communist Party leader; and, of course, LDP leader Zhirinovsky. We were about to have a great deal more to do with Zhirinovsky.

Ian left Moscow and came to Byron Bay, and the two of us actually spent a happy weekend together. But then we had a huge fight over the restaurant, which I was now subsidizing from the A$1 million I had received as a bonus back in 1993. Ian took off. As always, I was left hanging, not knowing if our relationship was over.

He eventually faxed to say he was in Denver on his way to Aspen, where he was about to settle on his new house there, with the fruit trees. He rang that evening and said loving things and that he couldn't wait for me to see our new home.

By late January, Ian was back in Moscow, staying at the extravagant Hotel National.

I called Katya for an update on the secrecy-lifting decree.

"The KGB is violently against it and is now demanding an international confidentiality agreement between the governments of Russia and Australia, as stipulated in Russian law of government secrets," she said.

"Oh, Katya, the Australian government won't get involved in this. To propose such a thing is preposterous!"

"Well, if it comes to it, we'll go and see Yeltsin again," she replied. "But it may have to wait until after the elections."

Then a mammoth problem surfaced. On February 17, Natalia called me from Moscow in a panic and said the general prosecutor, jointly with our old enemy from parliament, Ilyukhin, had initiated a court case against Lenzoloto JSC, to be held on February 21 in the Supreme Court. The general prosecutor was demanding that Lenzoloto JSC be dissolved, claiming its incorporation was illegal.

Our Russian lawyers weren't too concerned: After all the earlier amendments, our founding documents were now legal. However, Natalia was saying that things were more serious than anyone first thought. The general prosecutor was making comments to the press: Why was the Sukhoi Log license not tendered? Why was Star the only foreign investor?

I told her to speak to Ian urgently and tell him what she'd told me. She did—and consequently, the two of them struck the following confidential deal: Star would transfer US$100,000 to LDP's Swiss bank account. To make the transfer look legitimate, Natalia would sign a contract with LDP to publish her uncle's book in Australia for US$100,000 and be paid these funds. She would then call her uncle on a safe phone line at his dacha to let him know of the deal—and would ask for the court hearing on February 21 to be "taken care of."

If Zhirinovsky was indeed able to "take care" of the court case, we would contribute another US$200,000 in April in cash. Effectively, we were paying protection money. The Communists would have to leave us alone. We would then be able to work in Russia in peace.

And if Zhirinovsky did become president, Russia would be at our feet, according to Natalia.

Ian sent a fax to Graeme, explaining that it was going to cost US$300,000 to make the court case go away. On February 19, he flew to London to arrange the transfers and sent first US$50,000 to the LDP's Swiss bank account.

On February 21, the court hearing took place as scheduled.

The prosecutor got up and said that back in 1925, a foreign investor had also got hold of the Bodaibo alluvial mines. All the mines were transferred to an English company, Goldfields Ltd., under a thirty-year lease. But Stalin snatched the gold mines back from the Englishmen in less than five years. The same thing would happen to Star if the joint venture was allowed to proceed; Star would lose everything, the prosecutor warned.

The judge stopped the hearing at this point and said he'd reached a decision. The time limit for bringing the case to the court had expired. Therefore, the case was dismissed. The court also ruled out any further reexamination of the legality of the Lenzoloto JSC or Star's role in it.

The newspapers were filled with announcements of the outcome. People started predicting that the Office of the Prosecutor General might take the case to the Duma.

Mostovoy took advantage of Lenzoloto's prominence and gave an interview to the Kommersant Daily on the KGB and the secrecy-lifting issue. He told the interviewer that the KGB's stubbornness in continuing to torpedo the exclusion of Sukhoi Log from the list of government secrets was incomprehensible. They were buffoons, he said.

Natalia called to congratulate me on "winning" the court case and then asked about the second payment of US$50,000. I said I'd call Ian. A few hours later, he sent me a fax to say that he'd organized the second payment for Natalia.

Zhirinovsky was throwing his fiftieth birthday party in the State Central Concert Hall in Moscow on April 25. "We've been invited," Ian went on. "It's time for you to return anyway, as all the Russians are asking about you. From there, I'd like to take you to New York and then to Santa Fe."

"I'd love that so much," I replied.

Natalia called and asked again about the payment.

"Ludmila, I really need at least fifty thousand immediately. The delay makes it look to my uncle as if you have stopped paying. There is no time to send it to Switzerland. Please wire it to my account in Moscow; you have my account details. I plan to give my uncle this cash for his birthday, together with your secrecy documents. This is vital to get his respect and get the secrecy lifted."

As always, I promised to talk to Ian, but Ian had left Moscow and couldn't be found again. I sent him a fax. Tess, his PA, replied that Ian would speak to me soon as he'd just come out of "the wilderness." I had no idea what Tess was talking about, and I didn't hear from Ian until February 26, by which time he was back in Moscow.

When he rang, I demanded to know where he'd been.

"I can't talk to you while you are like this," he said, and hung up.

Days later, I received a fax from him, saying that he and Chris had just finished dinner with Yatskevich, who was concerned that the Communists would win the June elections. If that happened, Ian had promised to arrange Yatskevich's immigration to Australia. At the end of the message he wrote, "I trust you will be able to exorcise your anger inside you in time. I love you, Ian."

After the second payment went through in early March, I rang Katya for an update on the secrecy issue.

"When are you coming to Moscow?" she said immediately. "The KGB are still refusing to lift the secrecy without an Australian government guarantee that Star would not divulge the secret data to third parties and are refusing to even consider removing Sukhoi Log from the list of government secrets. They definitely want a bribe."

"Great," I commented dryly. "What should we do then?"

"Go to Yeltsin again. I will set up a meeting."

This was not my only problem. At home, I was struggling financially. My consultation fee of US$10,000 per month was disappearing into the restaurant, which was operating at a huge loss. I survived on credit cards while trying to juggle house bills—my own beach house bills as well as the Ewingsdale house bills—with no help from Ian. He kept promising to send funds. They never arrived. My demands that he either buy my Pan Pacific shares or give them back continued.

CHAPTER FORTY-TWO

Collateral Damage and a Trip to New York

It was early evening, and I was relaxing at my beach house in Byron Bay when I received a frantic phone call from Graeme, to tell me that Nic Krkovski was on his way to see me. "He's driving up to Byron Bay as we speak. He has a gun."

I'd met Nic at one of the annual shareholders' meetings in Sydney. A Croatian, he'd invested a lot of money into Star and lost it all. Graeme said that Nic had the address of the beach house and knew I was there. "Take Lachie and go to a hotel."

I told Gill, our latest nanny, to pack an overnight bag, and I drove her and Lachie to the Beach Hotel, where I knew they'd be safe. Afterward, I returned to the beach house and waited. After all, Graeme had said that Nic was after Ian, not me. As a precaution, though, I alerted the local police. They parked around the corner on standby.

When Nic knocked on the front door an hour later, I greeted him with a smile before glancing swiftly at his jean pockets. No bulge, so no weapon. He looked dreadful. Once a very good-looking man, he'd aged by ten years and was skeleton-thin with huge bags under hollow eyes.

We sat outside on the balcony and talked. Nic told me he'd been through hell. He'd spent all his money on Star. "Ian kept talking me into putting in more and more money, till he took it all from me, a total of 4.2 million dollars Australian. I lost my house, then my family. My wife left me and took the kids," he said.

I told him how sorry I was and how hard we'd all worked, while explaining how unstable Russia was. Nic wouldn't have a bar of it. He said he'd met Malcolm at Star's 1993 annual meeting and that Malcolm encouraged him to increase his shareholding in Star. "I've been complaining to Malcolm and to Graeme Ellis. Both men directed me to Ian," he added.

I promised to tell Ian that Nic wanted to meet with him and to sort out an arrangement. Nic hugged me and left. With great relief, I let the police know everything was fine.

Ian was very concerned when I rang him and told him what had happened. He said he'd call Nic and arrange to transfer over some of his Star shares and maybe even throw in a bit of cash.

Katya called to say that she'd set up a meeting with Yeltsin at 10 a.m. on Thursday, April 25. "He will only see you and me," she added.

It was an interesting time to be going to Moscow. Intrigue and rumors had risen to a fever pitch. Russian TV reported that the Communists were planning a coup on July 2, the scheduled date for an election runoff. Most Russians believed that Yeltsin and Alexander Korzhakov, his chief of security and a former KGB general who was considered the main power broker in the Kremlin, would cancel the election and declare a state of emergency, using Russian's skyrocketing crime as the rationale.

I set off for Moscow on April 23 and two days later walked into the Kremlin with Katya. We were taken to a room lavishly decorated with gold ornaments, oil paintings, and chandeliers. Twenty minutes later, Korzhakov, not Yeltsin, appeared, walked over to Katya, and kissed her hand. He was short and balding, with an egg-shaped head and small blue eyes, and he wore his eyeglasses halfway down his bulbous nose.

"Sincere apologies, Katya, but Yeltsin is not in good health today, so if you agree, I will take the meeting."

We told Korzhakov that Barsukov, the head of the KGB, was holding up the secrecy-lifting process. Katya, in her usual style, accused the KGB of wanting a bribe. Korzhakov promised to talk to Barsukov and expedite the secrecy lifting. We thanked him profusely, and as we were leaving, Katya asked whether we could do anything for Yeltsin. Korzhakov thought about it for a moment—and said he would let us know. We had signaled that we were offering Yeltsin a bribe, which Korzhakov acknowledged.

That evening, Ian and I attended Zhirinovsky's birthday party, which was quite a spectacle. The auditorium was packed with thousands of well-wishers, while Zhirinovsky himself, clad in a red jacket with gold buttons and black pants, sat on a throne on the stage like a tsar.

Yeltsin's birthday gift to him was a performance by the Russian National Dancing Ensemble and a custom-made Mercedes Benz.

At the end of the official ceremony, Natalia escorted Ian and me onto the stage and introduced us to her ultranationalist uncle. Zhirinovsky shook hands with Ian and kissed me on the cheek. He said that he totally trusted his niece's judgment and thus supported Star.

When I told Yatskevich about attending Zhirinovsky's party, he scoffed. "I wouldn't tell anyone if I were you, as there were no respectable people there," he said.

On April 29, Ian and I flew to New York for a short holiday. The plan was to stay there for a few days and then fly to Sante Fe and then to Mexico. When we arrived at our hotel, the five-star Waldorf Astoria, Ian told the girl at the desk that it was our honeymoon. I beamed, though I knew it was just to get an upgrade, which we did. The hotel was old-fashioned and dark but stately and luxurious. It still served the Waldorf salad, which had been invented there 100 years before.

From the moment we arrived in New York, I fell in love with the city and its almost tangible intellectual energy. I went shopping at the world-famous Saks department store on Fifth Avenue, and Ian took me to the Grand Central Oyster Bar, an old underground railway bar famous for its Manhattan seafood chowder. Ian ordered two bowls of the chowder and two glasses of Moët.

I was in heaven! But the next day, Ian unexpectedly left me in New York and flew to London after a distressed call from Chris urging his father to join him there. Ian said that Chris did not elaborate. I was understandably upset and told Ian that Chris should grow a backbone and solve the issue himself. This caused a bad fight, and after Ian left the hotel, I sat in the dark, lavish bar on the ground floor, sipping champagne while tears trickled down my cheeks. The only other person at the bar was an Arab, dressed in a white robe and headcloth, who wanted to know why I was at the bar by myself. I told him I was waiting for my fiancé. He asked me if he could buy me another glass of champagne, to which I replied, "No thanks" and left the bar in a very bad mood, blaming Ian for leaving me alone. I went up to the room and stayed there for the rest of the day and evening.

Ian called: "Hi, little girl, I'm flying out tonight and will meet you in Santa Fe, so please cheer up!"

I asked about the urgent problem in London. "Oh," he said, "it was nothing to do with Star. I will tell you when I arrive."

But he didn't.

In the morning I caught a plane to Sante Fe and spent three glorious days with Ian in that beautiful, historic desert city before flying to Mexico, where we had another three magical days at the fashionable new Ritz Carlton in Cancún. Then it was back to Australia—without Ian. He flew to Aspen to celebrate Angus's birthday.

Shortly after, Ian disappeared once again. I knew he'd gone to South Africa to hold discussions with JCI, a large South African mining company that was keen to invest in Star; but I could not contact him.

A week later, he got back in touch, claiming that it had been impossible to call. He said his meetings with JCI had been successful.

He had intended to celebrate my thirty-sixth birthday in Aspen with me but couldn't, as he was heading back to Moscow for an urgent meeting with Weinberg, at Weinberg's insistence. Instead, I received three dozen long-stemmed red roses on my birthday and a fax with a request. At some point, I'd mentioned to Ian that I was writing a book about my experiences in Russia, using my notes, faxes, reports, company documents, minutes of meetings, newspaper articles, and all the decrees and ordinances as material. He asked me to send him a few pages so he could "get a feel for it."

I didn't.

CHAPTER FORTY-THREE

The Biggest Sting of All

On May 17, Natalia reported that Zhirinovsky had met with the KGB to discuss the secrecy lifting. She asked for the balance of US$150,000 to be wired to her Moscow account and said that her uncle thanked us for his "birthday present" (the previous US$50,000 we had delivered to her in March). This was done, and Ilyukhin dropped his investigation into Star, but the veil of secrecy over Sukhoi Log reserve data remained.

The KGB was simply not capitulating. Barsukov dug up the old 1992 report on the other company called Star Systems and referenced the departure of Turnbull, plus other management changes—all proving Star's unreliability and instability, ruling it out as an investor for Sukhoi Log.

Ian met Weinberg in a private room at the Hotel National. It was quite a meeting. Weinberg told Ian that Yeltsin wanted Star to provide for his family when he retired from the presidency.

Weinberg's personal translator recorded and transcribed the conversation. It wasn't difficult to read between the lines.

"Which man is golden, Korzhakov or Barsukov?" asked Ian.

"Korzhakov," Weinberg replied.

Ian asked what percentage of Lenzoloto's income they were talking about.

"They did not say percentages. Approximately ten to fifteen million dollars per year. Sukhoi Log will bring one billion dollars' gross profit per year, so ten million is about one percent, and maybe shares," said Weinberg.

As Ian told me afterward, Yeltsin had targeted ten major enterprises in Russia, including Lenzoloto: Olympiada Gold, Norilsk Nickel, Sibneft (an oil company), Yukos Oil, MediaMost (a large media conglomerate), Inkombank, Alfa Financial Group, Stolichny Bank, and, ironically, a vodka refinery. All except Lenzoloto and the vodka refinery were owned by oligarchs. Yeltsin would take a cut from each once he retired from the presidency and become one the world's richest men, like it has been said that Putin is today. This hardly compared to the yearly A$500,000-plus salary for life that Australian prime ministers get when they leave office.

Ian explained that the first payment would be deposited into Yeltsin's "pension fund" and was the price Star had to pay for the secrecy lifting. "I suggested this money could be made when Star converts its investment of one billion dollars US into rubles," he added.

"You are kidding me! This is outrageous!" I said incredulously. "I guess at least we now know what the KGB was waiting for. So, how do we put this deal into place?"

"Weinberg is drawing up the papers. The deal will be done this weekend over lunch at a certain restaurant."

Ian did the deal and left Russia the same day, for safety reasons.

On June 30, Yeltsin abruptly fired two powerful political figures—Barsukov and his chief of security and closest ally,

Korzhakov. Yeltsin said on national television these people "took too much and gave too little"—or did they know too much?

Katya thought it was good the duo was gone. They had overstepped their authority, she said.

The big question was, what would now happen to our decree?

Yeltsin was trailing in the polls behind Zyuganov, the Communist leader. The Russian people had lost all faith in Yeltsin. Most were living in poverty while a group of extremely wealthy oligarchs owned 40 percent of Russia's assets.

However, Yeltsin narrowly won the election in a runoff vote on the 3rd of July. Years later, it was debated whether the 1996 elections had been rigged by the oligarchs. In January of that year, a deal had been struck amongst four oligarchs, known as the "Davos Pact with the Devil," at the World Economic Forum in Switzerland. The oligarchs were Boris Berezovsky, Vladimir Gusinsky, Mikhail Khodorkovsky, and Vladimir Vinogradov. Back in Moscow, four more oligarchs joined the pact: Vladimir Potanin, Alexander Smolensky, Mikhail Fridman, and Pyotr Aven (ex-minister of foreign economic relations, whom I'd met in 1992). They appointed Chubais, who'd just resigned from the post of first deputy prime minister, to lead Yeltsin's reelection campaign. The deal was to fund Yeltsin's campaign, ensuring victory, in return for acquiring whatever was left over from Russia's privatization process for peanuts, known as a "loans for shares" deal.

Under this deal, some of Russia's most valuable resources were auctioned off by oligarch-owned banks. Although they were supposedly acting on behalf of the government, the bank auctioneers rigged the process—and in almost every case ended up as the successful bidders. This was how Khodorkovsky got a 78 percent share of ownership in Yukos Oil, worth about US$5 billion, for a mere US$310 million, and how Berezovsky got Sibneft, another oil giant, worth US$3 billion, for about US$100 million.[8] The government was generally unable to exercise much control, and these "new Russians" paid little or no taxes on their purchases.

Interestingly, they were the same oligarchs who were chosen alongside Lenzoloto to contribute to Yeltsin's pension fund upon his retirement.

Ian returned to South Africa on July 17 to meet with JCI and disappeared yet again. JCI announced they would guarantee funding of US$200 million if the feasibility study stacked up.

Ian resurfaced on July 29 and called to say that he'd buy my shares for A$2,274,000. It was less than half the original value of A$6 million, but under the circumstances, I agreed.

Following the phone call, Ian faxed me a signed letter confirming the purchase of my shares. Settlement was set for October 1996. The proceeds of the sale of the shares were to be deposited into Carson Investments. I convinced myself that he did love me and, for the hundredth time, pushed my doubts aside.

In Moscow, Yeltsin restructured his cabinet. Chubais was brought back and appointed Yeltsin's chief of staff. Chernomyrdin once again became prime minister.

Bychkov's Komdragmet was divided between the Ministries of Finance and Industry and ceased to exist. Yatskevich's Geolkom was restructured into the Ministry of Natural Resources. Yatskevich's future was unknown. Surprisingly, Mostovoy survived as first deputy minister of GKI, even though there was a criminal investigation against him brought on by the Russian parliament. But he was truly one of Yeltsin's loyal soldiers.

---

8   Li-Chen Sim, *The Rise and Fall of Privatization in the Russian Oil Industry*, Palgrave Macmillan, 2008; Yasmeen Mohiuddin, "Boris Berezovsky: Russia's First Billionaire and Political Maverick Still Has It in for Vladimir Putin," *International Journal*, Summer 2007, p 681.

On August 26, I picked up the phone to hear Katya yelling, "Chernomyrdin signed our secrecy decree! It's being typed on official government letterhead!"

And on September 9, it really happened. Ordinance no. 1354-p was issued:

> GOVERNMENT OF THE RUSSIAN FEDERATION ORDINANCE
>
> #1354-p of 9th September 1996, Moscow
>
> To attract domestic and foreign investment to support the development of the Sukhoi Log hard rock gold deposit in the Irkutsk region and the social and economic development in the region, it was resolved:
>
> To approve the proposals of the RF Economics Ministry, interested federal executive authorities, and the Irkutsk Government, to lift the secrecy from the gold reserve data on the Sukhoi Log deposit.
>
> Prime Minister of the Russian Government
>
> V. Chernomyrdin

Those two small paragraphs had taken five long years and a massive bribe to Yeltsin to produce.

On September 16, Star Mining announced the news to the stock exchange. Ian and I celebrated over Dom Pérignon in Byron Bay. Malcolm was especially thrilled as he still held sixteen million secret offshore shares, conservatively worth A$5 million.

Back in Russia, Yeltsin understandably wanted Lenzoloto's debt extinguished (which meant an immediate contribution of US$50 million from Star) and for Sukhoi Log to be mined, as it now formed part of his "pension fund." However, his health was failing him; Katya told me in confidence that he'd suffered a heart attack in between the election rounds. The pressure had been too much for him. I called Yatskevich to find out exactly what was going on. Yatskevich didn't hold back.

"Star always said the lifting of the secrecy was the main stumbling block to the charter capital contributions, and I worked very hard to lift it. But since then, Star has done nothing. Turnbull and MacNee said the money was there, but now that Lenzoloto is desperate for it, Star can't raise a penny. MacNee told me there was fifty million dollars US put aside for contributing as soon as the secrecy was lifted."

For the first time ever, Yatskevich announced that he'd begun to have serious doubts about Star himself.

"Maybe Star cannot provide the money?" he suggested.

"You know that's not true!" I replied.

"I must also warn you that discussions have taken place on selling the Russian government shares to new Russian businessmen." He named Chugaevsky as one of them. "And trust me, they would be a lot harder to deal with, particularly as I would no longer be chairman. Please tell Ian he needs to do one more important thing if he wants Sukhoi Log gold. I will tell him when he arrives in Moscow," he added.

On October 28, Ian and Yatskevich flew together to Bodaibo for the Lenzoloto board meeting. Yatskevich told Ian that he needed to put up US$10 million "with eyes closed" as soon as he could. "You can't question where this money goes. If you do this, all will be good. This is the final step—I can assure you of that," he said.

Was this really the last bribe?

Ian, of course, swore he would do it and even wrote on the napkin beside his drink, "I guarantee US$10 million in cash by the 20th of November" and signed it. He and Yatskevich shook hands and (as ever) had more cognac.

Yatskevich also asked Ian to deposit half a million dollars into his bank account that he'd opened in Sydney when he was there, by January 10, 1997. Yatskevich had negotiated this money and

Australian residency with Ian and Malcolm conditional upon the secrecy-lifting decree.

Ian agreed, and the two of them drank to that too.

The problem was that Ian had absolutely no authority to commit this money without approval from the Star board, and when Ian did put this to the board, they categorically rejected it.

On November 6, 1996, Star announced to the Australian Stock Exchange that Star Mining had signed a memorandum of understanding with the South African mining group JCI Limited. This would make it possible for JCI to acquire shares in Star's wholly owned subsidiary Star Technology for US$250 million, giving it 30 percent in the Sukhoi Log project. Star Technology would be able to fulfill its charter contribution of US$200 million and repay US$50 million, which constituted its total debt to Star Mining. The deal made good sense.

On November 11, I called Yatskevich and asked what he thought of the deal. He said he didn't care as long as Star put in the money.

Three days later, Yatskevich was confirmed as the minister of natural resources, which was good news. But on November 17, a court case was opened in the Supreme Court in Moscow, jointly by the Russian parliament and the Russian general prosecutor, claiming that Star's share in the Lenzoloto JSC should be reduced to 4.88 percent and all the amendments to Lenzoloto JSC's founders' agreement and charter were illegal! The court hearing was set for December 26. This was clearly an attempt to force Star to contribute more funds to Lenzoloto.

November 20 came and went without even a sniff of the US$10 million.

However, there was a major development on the home front. Ian went to Lambruk to begin divorce proceedings with Bobby. For the next five days, he rang me every morning and every evening to report on the day's proceedings in great detail; he even described what she wore and which car she got into that morning on the way to the lawyers in Melbourne.

He would say, "It's a warm, sunny day. She's wearing a pale-pink suit and getting into her BMW. I am in my navy suit and will be traveling in my 1955 Bentley." He said all was going well and the divorce would be amicable because of Bobby's long-term relationship with another man. And indeed, as Ian eventually confirmed, the proceedings concluded peacefully.

I could hardly believe it. Ian was no longer a married man—at last!

On November 22, I received a letter from S. Y. Hui in Hong Kong, informing me that the legal purchaser of my Star shares would be Boyle Investments, a Hong Kong company controlled by Ian. The letter enclosed share-transfer certificates, which SY asked me to sign and courier back to him. The proceeds would then be deposited into my Carson Investments account in Hong Kong. When I wanted to draw on the funds, all I had to do was instruct SY how much I needed and where to send them.

Excitedly, I signed the certificates and couriered the documents to SY.

I wrote to Ian: "I'm in a spectacular mood, so please ring!"

He didn't.

The money didn't arrive the next day. Nor the next—nor the next. I was in a state of panic; I'd signed over my shareholding but hadn't received payment. Finally, Ian called and assured me that SY hadn't registered the share-transfer certificates and would only do so when he had the funds to pay for them. Ian then revealed that the Swiss bankers who controlled his trust (which supposedly had hundreds of millions of dollars in it) had delayed settlement. But the funds were forthcoming, he promised.

On December 6, Yatskevich took the astonishing step of phoning Colin Sr., chairman of NatWest in London, and threatening to call an extraordinary shareholders' meeting to decrease Star's interest in the Lenzoloto JSC if Star didn't provide US$50 million immediately.

Colin Sr. said that NatWest would be closely involved in organizing funds in accordance with the outcome of the feasibility study.

Yatskevich hung up on him.

I called Yatskevich, then Yakovenko, and finally Mostovoy in a panic. All three said they'd completely lost faith in Star.

The Star board knew the situation was serious. The board wrote to Yatskevich, inviting him to London to nut out a solution together with NatWest, JCI, and Star.

Yatskevich tore up the letter and flatly refused to travel to London.

On December 9, I spoke to Yatskevich. He was spitting with anger and said that he hoped we all choked on Sukhoi Log. "The fifty million US is a matter of life or death for Lenzoloto, and for me. The money is to save Lenzoloto and more specifically the alluvials."

News of the talk about Lenzoloto reducing Star to 4.88 percent and auctioning off its unpaid shares reached JCI, who voiced their grave concerns about doing business in Russia. The Star office in Sydney was flooded with calls from worried investors, and Star's share price plunged.

On December 19, I spoke to Yatskevich again and told him we were sending him a full funding schedule of US$50 million, which had been agreed to by our bankers, NatWest, JCI, and the Star board. I also suggested we meet in Moscow on January 13. He agreed but stressed that the schedule must show that the US$10 million would arrive in January 1997.

On December 26, the general prosecutor's court hearing against Star in Moscow was adjourned until February 26, 1997.

December 1996 ended uneasily for Star and for me personally. I had a phone conversation with Malcolm. He asked me straight out who had fathered Lachie.

"Please don't tell me that it's Ian," he added.

I knew that my relationship with Ian was becoming public knowledge and wondered whether Malcolm had heard about Ian's divorce through the grapevine.

I took a deep breath and said that Ian was Lachie's father.

There was a brief silence. And in that silence, I sensed Malcolm's absolute disgust. Then he shifted the conversation back to Star and told me to keep him updated. But he said it indifferently. There was no warmth in his tone.

It was like having a door slam in my face, and it really hurt.

CHAPTER FORTY-FOUR

More Smoke and a Lifeline

The year began more optimistically. To my great surprise and relief, SY let me know that he'd managed to sell three million of my Star shares—and had deposited approximately US$300,000 into my Carson account, as Star shares had plummeted to ten cents. He attached the bank statement to prove it.
I could breathe again.

On January 11, I flew to Moscow. Ian was already there. We went together to Yatskevich's office the next day to find an angry, impatient man who began railing at Ian for letting him down over the guarantee of US$10 million.

"Okay, but that's history. Can we save the deal or not?" I interrupted.

Yatskevich said it was possible but that we had a big problem. JCI wasn't welcome in Russia. His anger grew. The fact that JCI was getting 49 percent of Sukhoi Log and wanted an option to get more was only part of it. "You have sold Sukhoi Log to JCI for fifty million, to be pocketed by Star. I am livid about this. Star has no right to bargain away Sukhoi Log, especially to blacks," he said.

"Are you serious?"

"Deadly serious. Also, we will not accept the terms of repayment. Why should the blacks get all the profit out of Sukhoi Log for ten years? It's outrageous and unacceptable. I can't even talk about this anymore; I am so furious! Ludmila, the bottom line is that we will never allow blacks anywhere near Sukhoi Log or Russia. They're not welcome here. They should stay in the jungles of Africa where they belong."

I was stunned by his racial prejudice.

"What if we rescinded the memorandum of understanding and broke off relations with JCI?" asked Ian.

"Then everything would be on again with Star, if you can provide a total of fifty million dollars US by the end of March, starting with ten million by the twenty-fourth of January," replied Yatskevich. "This is the last deadline I have been instructed to offer you. After that, if no funds arrive, it's over. Oh, and I strongly advise you, Ian, to give Mostovoy some Star shares. That's all I'll say on this matter."

We thanked him and left.

Yatskevich had given Star a lifeline, I said. Ian, though, looked glum. I'd already noticed that he seemed unusually pale and tired.

"What's the matter?" I asked.

"Oh, I'm just so over Russia," he replied. "I'm thinking of resigning as director of Star. We don't need this, little girl. I think we should step back and let the others take it to the finish. I've been quite ill, as you know, with bronchitis. I need to recover in a warm climate. What about Hawaii for a while?"

I said I'd love to live in Hawaii and then turned the discussion back to the situation facing us. Did he think we could find the US$50 million in time? Ian said yes, and that the South African Standard Bank (JCI's bank) would be prepared to provide the funds directly to Star. He startled me by adding that the reason he left me alone in New York was to secretly meet with the oligarch Berezovsky in London, who had contacted Chris to request an urgent meeting without saying why.

"Ian, clearly it was about Sukhoi Log," I retorted, rolling my eyes. "Let me guess: He wants 'in' and has offered you a deal."

"Something like that, but don't ask any more."

January 24, the date of the first deadline in our agreement with Yatskevich, arrived. It came and went without Star paying the US$10 million. I urged Ian to pay.

On January 31, Ian revealed to me that he'd been in discussions over Sukhoi Log with a London bank called Chartwell International, introduced to him by Berezovsky.

Chartwell International, Ian went on, had offered to become Star's main adviser and bring the Lenzoloto saga to a successful conclusion. Then we could get on with the real job of mining gold. Of course, there was an up-front fee of US$3 million. Was Chartwell just another front for "Lazard"? I felt like there was no way out. Russia was like a giant python gradually strangling Star, squeezing every cent out of us.

Predictably, Alexei, Yatskevich, and the other Russian directors of Lenzoloto all gave the thumbs-up to Chartwell.

On February 1, since Star hadn't put up US$10 million in escrow, Yatskevich announced that the Lenzoloto JSC's share registry had been closed. Star's shareholding shrank to 4.88 percent.

Three days later, Alexei told me that Chartwell had managed to strike a last-minute deal with Yatskevich. It involved Star paying US$50 million and signing a contract appointing Chartwell as Star's main financial adviser. "Mark my words, without this, it's over for Star," said Alexei. Once Star signed the agreement with Chartwell, a copy would be forwarded to the general prosecutor, who would then drop all litigation against Lenzoloto JSC. The Russians had found another route to "legally" extract money from Star!

Lenzoloto called an extraordinary shareholder meeting for February 9. The day before, Ian and Graeme managed to get a letter from the Standard Bank guaranteeing to deposit US$10 million into an escrow account. The Standard Bank would also come up with a suitable loan structure to raise US$800 million for developing Sukhoi Log.

Star could do no more.

On February 9, a cold, blizzarding Saturday, the meeting of Lenzoloto shareholders took place in the auditorium of the elegant Hotel Metropol in downtown Moscow. When Ian, Graeme, and I walked in, the Russian side was already seated. We took our places, and Alexei, as company secretary, read out the agenda. Suddenly, the heavy double doors swung open, and three men dressed in black Armani suits marched in. The main one announced that they were representatives from Chartwell Bank. They made themselves at home around the massive table. None of the Russians blinked an eye. The meeting continued, but it was like a dream—a bad one.

Yatskevich asked Star to present its payment schedule to clear Lenzoloto's debt. After lengthy legal arguments by our lawyers, Star agreed to pay US$10 million by February 15 (with eyes closed), US$15 million by March 15, and US$25 million by March 25—all via the Chartwell Bank. Of course, the main bribe was Chartwell's up-front fee of US$3 million. I was glad Malcolm was no longer part of Star; he would have exploded.

The three gate-crashers from Chartwell took all this in, and when the meeting ended, they disappeared within seconds.

Yatskevich, who had become cold and detached, also left without saying a word to me. There was absolutely no trust left between us. Could Star's relationship with the Russians be salvaged? Maybe US$50 million would do the trick.

Once I was alone with Ian, I confronted him over Chartwell Bank.

"What the hell? Why didn't you tell me? Who exactly is behind Chartwell?"

"I couldn't tell you, but I can now." Ian revealed that Chartwell was partly owned by the oligarch Berezovsky. He has a team of people working for him in Moscow, out of the elite central hospital—including his head of debt collection, M, and his right-hand man, Andrei, the same hit man I had been besotted with. Apparently they did all of Yeltsin's dirty work.

I stared at Ian in disbelief.

"Aren't you pleased at the prospect of seeing Andrei again?" he asked. "I remember you fancied him."

"No, the guy is a killer. I thought we had moved on. Why are we working with these people again?"

"Because we can't end it without them."

On February 14, Sir Tim Razzall, by now one of Star's longest serving directors, abruptly resigned from the board. The issue, he said, was Chartwell. He refused to work with Russian mafia. Some of the lawyers and banks we'd been talking to had withdrawn from any involvement with Star because they'd been told to back away from Lenzoloto or suffer the consequences. Tim added that Chris MacNee had been threatened with death twice, as had Ian.

"If you want to live, pay up" had been the message.

In a panic, I called Ian, who confirmed he'd been receiving death threats. "Don't worry about it," he said.

On February 15, the Star board blocked the transfer of the US$10 million to the Chartwell Bank, even though the Standard Bank had already transferred the money into Star's account. I told Ian this was a grave error. Yatskevich was now refusing to talk to anyone from Star.

The Russians began demanding that we deposit US$50 million into Chartwell by March 30. If there was no proof that this money was on its way, Chernomyrdin ruled that Star would be thrown out of Lenzoloto and out of Russia itself.

On February 20, Ian resigned from the board of Star Mining but said he would remain as a consultant.

On February 22, Graeme Newing from NatWest astoundingly posted a "BUY" on Star shares and recommended that while the market appeared to have given up on Star Mining, Star was likely to end up with at least 19 percent of the Siberian gold deposit.

Immediately, Star shares began to skyrocket and within a few days reached twenty cents.

The March 30 deadline for the US$50 million came and went. I couldn't reach anyone in Moscow to talk to—nor in the Star Mining offices. No one was picking up the phones.

CHAPTER FORTY-FIVE

Rats and Sinking Ships

On March 31, 1997, the Supreme Court finally met to hear the prosecutor general's case against Lenzoloto and Star and ruled to liquidate the Lenzoloto JSC.
The founding documents of Lenzoloto JSC were declared null and void.

On April 4, John Helmer's article on the court hearing, "Court Attempts Re-nationalisation of Russian Gold," ran in major papers around the world.[9]

> In a decision legal experts and investment bankers are watching around the world, a Russian court this week said the State should re-nationalise

---

[9] John Helmer, "Dances with Bears: Court Attempts Re-nationalisation of Russian Gold," April 4, 1997.

a US$60 million foreign investment, claiming the founding documents violated Russian Law...

The Court has yet to issue a statement of its reasoning. The judgement released so far is brief. The General Prosecutor's office declined to comment, as did Russian officials involved in mining policy. They are reported to have said they have been "taken completely by surprise." The government thought this would be thrown out of court as the last one was.

Attorneys in Moscow said they know of no precedent for a Russian court to unravel an investment agreement with a foreign mining company.

That same day, the board of Star Mining asked the Australian Stock Exchange to suspend its shares with immediate effect.

We had come to the end of the road.

The court ruling, of course, was a direct result of us not releasing the US$10 million. I wondered who'd pulled the trigger. It was probably Yeltsin himself.

I decided to call Malcolm.

"Hello, Ludmila, what happened? Why did the Russian court rule against Star?"

"I blame Ian," I replied before telling Malcolm how Ian had promised Yatskevich US$50 million without approval of the Star board.

"Typical MacNee. Are you still with him?"

"Oh, Malcolm. I think he may be the biggest mistake of my life."

"I know he is, but you have the most beautiful son in Lachie. How is he?"

"He's actually great. He loves Byron Bay. You should see his hair. It's pure blond."

Malcolm then asked if I'd ever got my shares back from Ian.

"No, and that's the cause of all our fights," I replied. "He signed a letter back in July '96 agreeing to pay me around 2.27 million dollars Australian, but he hasn't."

"That's no surprise," said Malcolm dryly. "Good luck with that one. I guess there's no point in suing him as all his money is overseas. Ludmila, once Star starts trading again, he'll say Star shares have fallen in value and use this as an excuse to rip you off."

"He can't! We have a sales agreement. It's irrelevant that the Star shares are worth less now. Plus, Ian was the one who caused the delay, promising the Russians money and then reneging."

"You need to protect yourself" was Malcolm's answer. "My advice is for you to get legal advice. Anyway, what do you think will happen to Star? What does Yatskevich say?"

"Yatskevich told me that minutes before the court hearing, the general prosecutor had asked him whether we had deposited ten million US as a goodwill payment. Yatskevich had to say no. That's why the Supreme Court dissolved the joint venture," I added. "Yatskevich also told me no one cares about Star anymore. He keeps lamenting about you leaving Star and says if you came back, it would change everything, even now. Regarding Star, the only solution would be to immediately deposit fifty million US into Lenzoloto. But that's up to the Standard Bank, who probably won't now because of the court ruling."

"No Western bank would," replied Malcolm. "Ludmila, protect yourself and Lachie. I must go now. Bye."

I put down the phone slowly, dreadfully missing the intimate connection we once had.

Meanwhile, worried shareholders called the Star office, as Star shares remained suspended. Many people were concerned about losing vast amounts of money. So many calls came through that the phone lines got jammed.

I called Yatskevich. He was aloof in his response.

"I think Ian is all talk, Ludmila. The only person in Star of real substance was Malcolm, and you, of course. Time has run out for Star. The secrecy has long been lifted, yet Star has not deposited a kopek since. There are no more excuses. I am no longer willing to fight for Star or support it. I've resigned as chairman of Lenzoloto. Goodbye, Ludmila."

Yatskevich hung up.

On April 31, Star Mining announced to the Australian Stock Exchange that Star had reached an agreement with JCI about the future financing and development of Sukhoi Log gold deposits. It was signed by Graeme Ellis.

I decided that Graeme was delusional. There was no other explanation. Graeme knew that Yatskevich had resigned, that all the deadlines for Star's money had come and gone, and that any involvement with JCI was suicide for Star.

Meanwhile, investors and banks all over the world were up in arms over the latest events surrounding Star and Lenzoloto. Star's major shareholders—Mercury Asset Management, M&G, and Robert Flemming—delivered a written ultimatum to the Russian prime minister, demanding he resolve the Lenzoloto saga.

I decided to make one more trip to Moscow to say goodbye and collect my belongings.

I had lunch with Mostovoy, and in a totally unexpected twist, he said he'd divorced his wife—and asked me to marry him. I could only stammer that I would think about it.

I was eager to escape the cataclysm that Russia had become. On the way to the airport, I dropped into the Star office and collected all my faxes, my notes, and the fragments of memoirs I'd written, as well as articles and documents from 1990 until the present, and packed them into a large suitcase I'd brought with me. By now, I was determined to write a book about Lenzoloto; this incredible story had to be told.

Home at Byron Bay, I grew restless. In my heart of hearts, I was a city girl. I was also concerned about enrolling Lachlan in a private school. I still dreamed of a family life with Ian in a beautiful home, preferably in Sydney.

Ian knew this and finally agreed for us to move back to Sydney and rent for a couple of years until he decided where we should live permanently. I was thrilled. I started approaching a few schools, including Sydney Grammar, hoping that Malcolm would help, as he was an old boy.

On May 22, I dropped Malcolm a line. I let him know I was coming back to Sydney and that I had quit Star. I filled him in on everything that had happened recently, adding that Chartwell Bank was Russian mafia. I also told him that the Russians, especially Yatskevich, to this day lamented his departure.

Malcolm phoned me. We spoke about the current situation with Star, and he asked me to keep him posted, remarking, "You never know. Maybe there will be an opening to do something else in Russia and capitalize on all our experience."

On June 3, Chernomyrdin issued a decree on Lenzoloto. This time we did not bribe him. The decree confirmed Star's reduced shareholding in Lenzoloto as 4.88 percent and ordered an international tender for the Sukhoi Log gold deposit.

The next day, Star Mining announced to the market that the Russian government had passed a decree, signed by Prime Minister Chernomyrdin, concerning the Lenzoloto JSC and the development of the Sukhoi Log gold deposit, in which Star had "a significant interest."

Since when was 4.88 percent a significant share? The shocking truth was that none of the Star directors had announced Star's 4.88 percent share to the market, but even more shocking was that they omitted how Chernomyrdin's decree called for an international tender on Sukhoi Log.

Ian no longer cared. He was solely concerned with the Oregon winery in the USA.

On June 24, I faxed Malcolm to tell him that the Russian government had decided to take Sukhoi Log to an open international tender. I added that I would be in Sydney that week and would like to discuss a few matters.

Malcolm called immediately and said he'd love to see me. We met a few days later, midafternoon. I hadn't seen Malcolm for a long time, and my heart missed a beat when I saw him. We hugged, and I followed him into his office.

"So, what's going on with Star?" he asked.

"I think if Graeme keeps running the show, it's hopeless, so you should sell your shares," I told him.

"Ludmila, do you think Sukhoi Log has the gold in it the Russians say it has?"

"I think so. The Russians *did* lift the secrecy. The official reserves show eleven hundred tons of gold, but remember that Katya saw a totally different reserve estimate showing close to four thousand tons; that's the big secret."

"The data could all be fabricated," pointed out Malcolm. "Without testing it ourselves, we will never know for sure."

"You're right," I said ruefully, before asking him what his own plans were.

"Turnbull's Bank is virtually finished. I'm thinking about moving over to Goldman's," he replied. He then asked me how Lachie was, and in turn, I asked Malcolm if he was still happy to be Lachie's godfather as we'd once discussed.

"I am godfather to too many kids with single mums and have been accused of being the real father too often," he replied.

"Well, they can't accuse you of being Lachie's dad, as I met you after I had him."

I kissed him and left. But the familiarity between us felt hollow. The day I'd finally admitted that Ian had fathered Lachie was the beginning of the end.

A comment Malcolm had made back then still echoed. "I'm disappointed in you," he said. "I know," I replied quietly.

CHAPTER FORTY-SIX

Ripped Off by One, Dumped by the Other

On July 9, 1997, Malcolm rang me in a panic.

He'd received an official letter from L. A. Rawson, an agent with the Australian Federal Police.

It read:

> Dear Sir,
> The General Prosecutor's Office of the Russian Federation is currently conducting investigations in relation to Mr. Mostovoy and Lenzoloto JSC. The Russian authorities have requested assistance in relation to this matter by way of recorded interview and have requested replies to the attached questions. Should you be willing to assist, and I suggest you do, I advise the evidence is required by the Russian authorities solely for the purposes of the proceedings against Mr. Mostovoy.

I calmed Malcolm down and told him, "This is all about the Communists trying to nail Mostovoy for alleged corruption during all his privatizations, of which Lenzoloto is but one," I said. "The general prosecutor has accused Mostovoy of giving Star an interest in Sukhoi Log at a substantial discount. The general prosecutor's office regards GKI as the main center for corruption and claims Mostovoy cost the state an enormous amount of money by allowing Star to buy shares at an artificially low price.

"They're wrong, of course, as they're referring to that amendment Alexei and Mostovoy made to our founding documents in June 1993, assessing our contribution in rubles, which converted to 892,857 dollars US instead of 125 million. But we all know that was because the Russians hadn't lifted the secrecy from Sukhoi Log, and Star would have defaulted on its charter capital obligations. Star's total contribution was always to be two hundred fifty million, within eighteen months of the secrecy lifting; you wrote that clause."

"Oh, what a fucking mess!" said Malcolm. "I so wish I'd never met MacNee and got involved in Russia. It almost ruined my life and is still ruining my life."

The next time we spoke was in August. I was in Sydney, looking for an apartment to rent, and called Malcolm's mobile.

"Malcolm, I'm in the city and wanted to know if I could drop by."

"Ludmila, I'm on another call. I'll call you back shortly."

I waited and waited. I even got my face made up at the Chanel counter at David Jones, to fill the time. Nothing. Malcolm didn't even bother calling me back as he'd promised.

I understood that the business side of things had gone sour, but clearly, he didn't want to continue the friendship either. Perhaps he was the sort of man who was only interested in people with something to offer. I could not provide neither financial gain nor social stature.

Shortly after this, Ian found a stunning two-story waterfront apartment in Double Bay and signed a two-year lease in the name of Mr. and Mrs. MacNee.

I was overjoyed, even though our fights continued over my Pan Pacific shares. In one of our most bitter fights to date, I again demanded payment of A$2,274,000, which had been our original agreement.

"You know the share price has dropped since our agreement," he shouted at me. "Your remaining shares are now worth only 929,200 dollars Australian."

This rip-off was exactly what Malcolm had predicted. Nevertheless, we agreed he would pay me A$100,000 by December, and the balance of A$829,200 by January 1998.

On September 1, Lachie and I moved into our apartment in Double Bay. I hired a wonderful nanny called Natalie, who fell in love with Lachie. We couldn't have been happier.

I decided to give Malcolm one last shot. I called him at his Point Piper residence on the 6th of September.

He answered in a sleepy voice.

"Malcolm, it's me. Guess where I am?"

"Where?"

"Just opposite the harbor from you. I reckon I could even see you from here."

"Are you on a boat?"

"No, I've moved into an apartment on the water at Double Bay. I am finally back in Sydney and very excited to be here."

"Ludmila, can I call you back? I must have a sleep before an important function tonight with John Howard. I really need the sleep."

"Yes, of course. I'm sorry for disturbing you," I replied, thinking, *Why is Malcolm romancing the Liberal Party when his loyalties have always been with Labour?*

I then remembered him telling me that he might have to switch over to the Liberals to give himself a better chance of becoming prime minister. He felt waiting for Labour to regain power could take too long.

Malcolm never returned my call, and I never tried to contact him again. Years later, though, I would once again pick up the phone and hear Malcolm's voice.

Now that we were out of Russia, Ian became very loving and was promising marriage. Toward the end of the year, he suggested that I plan a big New Year's Eve party at the apartment, where I would "come out" in front of all his friends and family members. I can't describe how happy I was at that moment—and how much in love I felt. Even the fact that his promised deposit for the purchase of my Pan Pacific shares hadn't materialized in December wasn't worrying me too much. Soon, I would be Ian's wife.

On December 19, there was a meeting of Lenzoloto shareholders. Star was absent, even though it still owned 4.88 percent of the JSC. Yatskevich announced that he'd met with Western mining companies to discuss Sukhoi Log and the terms of the tender. In a huge blow to Star, none of the terms included any compensation to Star for the US$30 million in lost charter capital contributions, nor the A$10 million Star had spent on the Sukhoi Log feasibility study—a total loss of A$60 million.

New Year's Eve arrived. I put on a beautiful black-and-white lace designer gown and waited to be introduced to Ian's friends and family as his future wife.

An hour before our guests were due to arrive, Ian opened a bottle of Dom Pérignon, which I'd always referred to as "God's nectar." We went up to the balcony off our main bedroom for a private drink before the evening began.

That's when he told me that no one was coming. "I'm sorry. I just found out myself," he added.

I just looked at him. "Why?"

"They all have their own commitments. A lot of them are away up at Noosa or overseas. C'mon, little girl. I'm with you and I love you; that's all that matters tonight."

His story made no sense whatsoever. I blotted everything out by sculling my glass of Dom—followed by the drinking the entire bottle.

I'd so hoped that 1998 would begin differently. But obviously, it wasn't to be. So, in January, I brought up the issue of payment for my Star shares again. As usual, Ian made excuses about why this hadn't happened. Then he made a new promise: full payment into my Carson account by the 30th of January. Ian confirmed, in a phone call to me, "The money will be there—it's set in stone. I'll be there in a few days. You should buy a case of Dom to celebrate with me." I did, of course.

A week later, Ian disappeared again. I began making inquiries in Hong Kong about the money. Nothing had reached Carson. The discovery was devastating. I hated Ian for the con man he was revealing himself to be. I'd ignored my own instincts all this time because I loved him! But now I felt trapped. I couldn't leave him, but I was slowly going insane.

Ian had ensured nothing was ever in our joint names, or in my name. He had locked up my Star shares in a company he controlled. He admitted to me once that he was paranoid I'd run off with a younger man if I were independently wealthy. The irony, of course, was that I would have been very wealthy if I'd only kept my Star shares in my own name. But then, he would have come up with some other scheme to steal the shares. Now all I had was an almost bankrupt restaurant, my beach house at Byron Bay, worth A$450,000, which I had to sell to survive, and my recruitment company, Labstaff.

It was impossible for me to pack up, take Lachie, and walk away. I'd invested so much emotionally in the three of us. Ian was the father of my child, and I was acutely aware of Lachlan's needs and wanted him to have a proper father in his life.

So, I persevered.

Nor was I able to sever the tie with Russia. On March 25, a frail Yeltsin stunned the world by sacking his entire cabinet. I watched his heavily edited brief address on SBS, the Australian public service channel. He was tired and glassy-eyed. Many saw the hand of Berezovsky, Star's silent partner in the failed Chartwell Bank partnership, behind Yeltsin's decision.

One victim of the cabinet sacking was Mikhaylov, minister of atomic energy and Russia's nuclear tsar. He'd been one of Star's most loyal supporters and a friend of mine. But Mikhaylov had been involved in secret nuclear deals with Iran and China. This may have been the reason for his downfall—as well as his support of Star.

Soon after sacking his cabinet, Yeltsin appointed a successor: Putin. The world would soon hear a lot more about this dark, enigmatic figure. But few in the West likely took much notice when a few years later, on June 16, 2001, Putin fired Yatskevich for reasons that have never been fully disclosed. Putin had recommended Yatskevich's dismissal back in 1997 when he wrote a report on corruption, claiming that Yatskevich had granted mining licenses to Lenzoloto JSC while serving as the chairman of the company.

Putin emphatically stated that the pilfering of Russia's most precious assets must stop. He surmised that Russia's natural resources would prop up its economy for at least the first half of the twenty-first century but required foreign investment and the state's strong guiding hand.[10]

Katya claimed that Putin did a deal with Yeltsin and his family: If they supported his candidacy for president, Putin would not prosecute them for corruption. She said that Yeltsin and his daughters, Tanya and Elena, were connected to a colossal bribery scandal involving the construction company Mabetex, based in Lugano, Switzerland. There were also charges that they had been gifted mansions from Russian oligarchs. Katya had no doubt that

---

10   Steven Lee Myers, *The New Tsar: The Rise and Reign of Vladimir Putin*, Knopf, 2015.

it was all true; after all, Yeltsin did try to extract large profits from Star's Sukhoi Log JV.

Katya continued, "When Russia's pro-Communist prosecutor general, Yury Skuratov, attempted to investigate these allegations, a tape surfaced showing him having sex with two prostitutes. Yeltsin immediately fired Skuratov over the scandal. Tanya told me her dad had no choice but to do the deal with the devil himself."

On his first day in office, as acting Russian president, Putin pardoned Yeltsin for any possible misdeeds and granted him total immunity from prosecution (or even from being searched and questioned) for any and all actions committed while in office. Yeltsin also received a life pension and a state dacha.[11]

Katya also told me that Putin had inherited Yeltsin's St. Petersburg "mafia"—my beloved Andrei and the other officers of the Chartwell Bank, headed by Berezovsky, who strongly campaigned for Putin's presidency.

---

11   David Winston, "From Yeltsin to Putin," Hoover Institution, published April 1, 2000, https://www.hoover.org/research/yeltsin-putin.

CHAPTER FORTY-SEVEN

Could It Be?

On May 29, 1998, Ian and I celebrated my birthday in Byron Bay, spending a few blissful days at our country estate in Ewingsdale. On our last day, we had lunch at a seaside café. Casually, I brought up the payment for my Star shares, which Ian had kept promising were coming from his secret trust fund in Switzerland, which held—he claimed—US$464 million.

To my amazement, he took out his checkbook and wrote me a check for the sum of US$630,000 (A$929,200) from his Aspen bank account. I couldn't believe my eyes.

"Is that real?" I couldn't help asking.

"Of course it is, my darling. I love you, and I don't want us to fight over this any longer. I want a life with you, and I want you to be happy. I only ask one thing," he added.

"Which is?"

"I've dated it July 29, so please don't bank it till I tell you."

I felt the usual sharp pain in my stomach.

"Why?"

"I need to make sure my Swiss trustees have transferred the latest lot of funds to my Aspen account. That's all. I assure you, my love, this time it won't be a problem. I just need a couple of months."

I really wanted to believe him. I so desperately wanted to be happy with this man, especially on what would be our last night together for a while. As usual, Ian was going back to Lambruk.

June was spent looking after Lachie and waiting for my money from Ian. Having quality time with my son was the only thing that kept me going. The thing that nagged at me constantly was that Ian hadn't settled on my shares when they were valued at over A$2.2 million. I wished I could put this behind me, but I couldn't!

On July 29, the National Bank rejected Ian's check. It was obvious by this time that Ian had no intention of paying me for my Star shares, even at his "discounted" price.

However, the two of us had talked many times about buying a home together. I'd stayed out of sight while Ian was still married. But now that he was divorced from Bobby, it didn't matter anymore if we were living together openly in Sydney. Instead of giving me cash for my shares, Ian could buy a property with me in Sydney. I thought Ian would go for this.

I started to look for an oceanfront home—and found one. It was a six-bedroom mansion on a cliff at Lurline Bay in the eastern suburbs of Sydney, overlooking the ocean, with a wet-edge pool, spa, and tennis court. The owner was celebrity lawyer John Gerathy, whose marriage had broken up. The price tag was A$3.1 million. I let Ian know I'd found a beautiful home for us, showed him a photo of it, and suggested we buy it together. The A$929,200 he owed me for my shares could be settled, I suggested, if I contributed this toward buying the house, and he put in the balance of just over A$2 million.

Ian seemed delighted and thought the house looked wonderful. "Let's go ahead. Arrange a viewing," he said.

I did. The house was even more breathtaking inside. We met Gerathy and made an offer of A$3 million, which he accepted.

I couldn't wait for us to move to our beautiful new home. Ian said he'd provide the deposit money and the balance of the settlement funds, as agreed. But he didn't want his name on the title deed for tax purposes, he said. It would be put in my name only.

A few days after we'd shaken hands on the deal with John Gerathy, Ian was gone again. When the 10 percent deposit didn't arrive, I rang him. As a result of our conversation, I reluctantly agreed to pay using funds from the recent sale of my Byron Bay beach house, on the condition Ian that would pay the stamp duty and the settlement funds.

Ian swore this wouldn't be a problem because he'd signed contracts with a company called Davnet Inc. for the sale of the Argyle Winery in Oregon. The winery had sold for US$10 million, he claimed.

On September 30, to my immense joy, we formally exchanged contracts on Lurline Bay. Ian was there. He guaranteed to pay the stamp duty, due December 31, 1998, and settle on January 18, 1999. He left Sydney the same afternoon, to go back to Lambruk. He called me from Tullamarine airport in Melbourne.

"Darling, I really need your help with something," he said. "I'm doing a business deal. I told you about it—finding reservoirs of water in the countryside surrounding Lambruk in Castlemaine—and I urgently need seventy-five thousand Australian. I can't wait for the funds to come from overseas. Can you lend me the money? I'll pay it back in seven days with thirty percent interest."

I was still on top of the world over Lurline Bay. So, I agreed.

I never did get this money back, though. When I asked Ian to give it back to me, he denied I had ever lent it to him. I also found out later that the money was for a holding deposit on a swish Sydney harborside apartment—but not for me.

Ian arrived back in Sydney a few days before Christmas. On his last afternoon in Sydney, we were walking hand in hand on our way to John Gerathy's new Sydney waterfront apartment at Finger Wharf at Woolloomooloo (a posh harborside development) to celebrate his new purchase—and ours. Unexpectedly, we bumped into some friends of Ian's, a couple called the Greens, whom I'd met briefly once before. Ian ripped his hand away from mine.

"Hi. You know Ludmila," he said.

We chatted with them for several minutes before continuing on our way. A few hours later, driving a silent Ian to the airport, I asked him what the matter was.

"Oh, nothing. It's just that the Greens are Bobby's best friends, and the wife would have called Bobby already and told her they bumped into us at the wharf."

"So what?"

"Look, if Bobby finds out that I funded Lurline Bay for you, she would reopen the settlement proceedings, as I only declared assets of ten million dollars Australian," replied Ian.

"The house is in my name. Just tell her that I paid for it," I suggested.

"She knows you don't have that type of money."

"Bullshit. She has no idea what Labstaff is worth, Ian!"

"I don't want Bobby to know my business."

"This won't affect the settlement in any way, though?" I asked after a few minutes.

"Not at all. Don't worry, darling," he said reassuringly and put his hand on my knee. But it was too late. A nagging fear—had he really divorced Bobby?—surfaced. I dismissed the thought; only a monster could play me like that. However, I waved him off at the airport still feeling anxious.

On December 30, I rang Ian in a panic, as the money for the stamp duty hadn't appeared. He swore the funds would be in my account, before adding that he was on his way to Sydney for a huge New Year's Eve celebration with me.

With no choice, I wrote a check to the State Revenue Office for A$150,494 to pay the stamp duty and gave it to our conveyancing solicitor.

I had arranged a privately catered New Year's Eve dinner party on the balcony of my waterfront apartment for twelve people, including Fran and her husband, David, and my sisters and their husbands.

Ian flew into Sydney and walked in at midday with two bottles of ice-cold Moët. He cracked open a bottle, telling me casually that the sale of the winery had been held up, so he needed an extension to settle the house. He would call Gerathy, he said, and secure a two-month extension by offering to pay interest on the balance of A$2.7 million.

We then went into the bedroom to spend a few hours together before the people who were closest to me started arriving.

The last thing I expected was the casual brutality of Ian's announcement, after we'd finished making love, that he'd promised to spend New Year's Eve at Lambruk with Angus and wouldn't be staying.

Looking back, it now seems horribly fitting that only a few days beforehand, Star had finally declared bankruptcy. The fallout from this would be monstrous. Star never recovered any of its funds from Lenzoloto JSC, and many shareholders lost their money. Some people would lose a fortune. Eventually, Star's losses from its Russian venture were officially put at around A$180 million.

Malcolm and Ian, though, came out of it with many millions of dollars each, because they'd sold their shares at the right time. But there I was, still battling to get my money from the man who, unbeknownst to me, had already sold Pan Pacific, pocketing more millions, and who, ten minutes after getting out of our bed on that devastating afternoon, was gone.

On January 2, 1999, my stamp duty check for the Lurline Bay house was dishonored. No money had arrived from Ian, and he was nowhere to be found.

Ian resurfaced a week later and said he had negotiated a deal with the State Revenue Office to pay interest until the stamp duty was paid in full. Gerathy was happy to wait another two months for settlement, as long as I moved into the house under license, since he didn't want the property to remain empty.

I enjoyed a blissful six months in this magnificent mansion, as Gerathy had agreed to two more extensions, but finally, in early July 1999, Ian failed to produce any funds on the last settlement date. In his usual poor form, he disappeared that day and no one could contact him, not even his lawyers. Gerathy had no choice but to give me notice to vacate, saying, "I'm sorry, but it's all over, rover. I believe Ian has conned us both. He never had the money." These words cut through my heart like a sharp dagger.

The Lurline Bay purchase contract was terminated. Gerathy decided to have the house auctioned. I lost my 10 percent deposit in the amount of A$300,000 and the extra $35,000 in interest that I had also paid and was in danger of being sued for the difference if the house didn't sell at the contracted price.

I was desperate to find Ian and called Tess, his executive assistant of over fifteen years.

"Tess, do you know where Ian is?"

"Yes, he's in Oregon."

"Did the winery sale to Davnet fall through?"

"Ludmila, it was never a real deal. Chris MacNee owns Davnet. They made it look like there was a contract in place to push up the price being offered to them by real buyers."

"You're fucking kidding me!"

Ian finally surfaced again at the end of July. He'd been trying to push through the sale of the winery, he said. He claimed that the Davnet deal had fallen through because Chris had failed to raise the funds to purchase the winery. "Chris really let me down," he claimed emphatically.

It was now clear that I was dealing with a pathological liar.

"Ian, why can't you fund the Lurline Bay property from your Swiss bank as you first promised? It's about to go to auction."

"Okay, let me tell you the truth. The funds are so black that to bring them into Australia would cost me sixty-six cents on the dollar, so the house would end up costing nine million instead of three, and it's not worth that much. I have been trying to negotiate a better deal, and if that happens, we will go to the auction. But for now, the funds have to come from the sale of the winery, which is a legitimate transaction. Brian Croser wouldn't have it any other way."

At this point, I decided to protect Lachlan and myself—just as Malcolm had advised me to do. I made an appointment with family lawyers Vagg & Associates.

All of Ian's assets were offshore, and Lambruk was triple-mortgaged. Nevertheless, I wanted to find out about my rights and get advice on how to force Ian to buy the Lurline Bay home.

After I told Ron Vagg the whole story, he said I had rights in both the de facto court, in relation to our de facto marriage and Lachie, and the Supreme Court in relation to my Star Mining shares.

CHAPTER FORTY-EIGHT

Court—and Finally the Whole Truth About Ian

On August 16 I commenced proceedings under the De Facto Relationships Act of 1994 against Ian MacNee. My claim, which included payment for the Star shares, the A$335,000 I'd paid to Gerathy, the A$75,000 loan, and child support, totaled A$10 million.

Ian got in touch and asked me to meet him at the waterfront Sydney Cove Oyster Bar at Circular Quay East, which had been our special spot.

Gone was the charming man who'd declared for so long that he loved me.

"Ludmila, if you take me to court over this, I'll kill you."

"You'll kill me?"

"I won't, but they will."

He further qualified that "they" were the Russian mafia partners in his Swiss bank.

"Who? Andrei? Michael? Or Berezovsky himself?"

Ian did not answer me.

I got up from the table and left in sheer disgust.

My only remaining asset was Labstaff. Luckily, it was doing well, so Fran and I sold it to Kelly Services for A$1 million cash. I ended up with A$450,000, which funded my case against Ian.

Meanwhile, thankfully, the Lurline Bay property fetched A$3.1 million at auction. In 2015 the property would be resold for A$10.5 million.

Everything with Ian had been smoke and mirrors. His capacity for lying and fraud seemed limitless. But the moment when my heart broke into millions of microscopic pieces came in January 2000, when Ron Vagg asked me in his office one day if I was sure that Ian wasn't still married.

"He said he divorced in November 1996. Why do you ask?" I replied.

"Because I have this feeling he may be still married. It would explain some of his behavior," said Ron.

Stunned, I suggested he ring Ian's lawyer, Sue, who surely would know.

"Good idea," said Ron, and dialed her.

He asked the question, listened to the answer, thanked Sue, and put down the phone.

Ron didn't need to tell me what she'd said. I could read it in his face.

Everything around me seemed to shatter. It was as if I were seeing Ron's office through broken glass. I was filled with such hatred toward Ian that I wanted to kill him.

Ron managed to calm me down. He told me that I was dealing with someone who was obviously an accomplished con man—a sociopath with a demonic ability to convince anyone of anything. And yet, as Ron also wisely reminded me, not everything was rotten. "No matter what has happened, you have a beautiful son. Never forget that," he said.

It was true, and it helped restore my sanity. Nevertheless, after leaving Ron's office, I collapsed on the steps of his building and sat there with my hands over my eyes, oblivious to everyone walking past. Ian had played me again. This time he deserved a standing ovation. I would never live a normal life; never fall in love again; never be happy. I had no more strength left.

And then, something inside me snapped. I decided I would beat Ian at his own game, even if I had to become *him*. I would become as ruthless as he was, and I would win.

Ultimately, I realized the only way I would ever get back everything that Ian owed me was to let him think we might still have a future together. And in one way we did have a future, of course, because of Lachie.

On January 28, 2000, the Supreme Court finally ordered Ian to provide A$2,644,133 to finance the purchase of another home for Lachlan and me, and to pay me A$929,200 directly.

But it wasn't until August 24 of that year, after much more torment, that Ian legitimately sold the Oregon winery for US$10 million and settled me. The sum of A$2,644,133 was transferred into a joint account requiring both Ian's and my signature at the Commonwealth Bank of Australia (CBA), and A$929,200 was transferred into my personal account. Ian had insisted on the CBA, as his good friend, Larry Terrence, was the bank manager there.

Even though the money for the home was in the bank, I knew that Ian would try every dirty trick in the book not to let this money, or me, go. I had to stay one step ahead of him if I was to secure a permanent home for Lachie and myself.

Trying to disentangle myself from Ian MacNee was an exhausting and nerve-racking journey. My health deteriorated badly. I began having multiple panic attacks in the middle of the night, and more than once I was on the verge of calling an ambulance. Migraines became a weekly occurrence. Not surprisingly, I became deeply depressed. Only Lachlan kept me sane.

On September 21, I had a meeting with my accountant and long-term friend, Wayne. He pointed out that the CBA joint account with the balance of A$2,644,133 would earn about A$12,600 per month in interest, taxed at the very high rate of 48 percent. This meant a huge tax bill. Wayne suggested we lend the funds to my company, Mick's Holdings P/L, which had huge operating losses resulting from the restaurant. I managed to flog off the restaurant for a mere A$80,000 (it became known as Cheeky Monkeys and in 2021 was purchased by Justin Hemmes for a staggering A$13.5 million). Mick's Holdings could then claim the interest against its operating losses, avoiding the huge tax bill. It was a brilliant idea. All I had to do was persuade Ian.

This took some time, but after some argument, he finally agreed, and the funds were transferred to a new Mick's Holdings account at the CBA bank, also requiring both our signatures. He even sent a message saying that this was a smart move and that he looked forward to us working together to secure Lachie's future.

In late March 2001, I found a brand-new, stunning, ultramodern mansion overhanging the Spit Bridge at Seaforth (a beautiful harborside suburb in Sydney's north) with an infinity pool and spa. The price tag was A$2.5 million. Every room had breathtaking 180-degree views over Sydney's dazzling Middle Harbour.

Ian inspected the house and couldn't fault it. He negotiated a price of A$1.97 million with the vendor. The exchange of contracts was set for April 11.

The morning of the exchange, Ian flew in from Lambruk. I'd arranged to meet him and the real estate agent at one of the restaurants on the harbor, a five-minute walk from the house. I offered to go with Ian to the CBA bank to get the bank check for the deposit, but he told me he'd pick up the check from his mate Larry

Terrence on the way in from the airport. Alarm bells immediately went off in my head.

When I arrived at the café, Ian was waiting at the table with a bottle of Moët. The real estate agent turned up ten minutes later. She placed the contract in front of us. I gave Ian the pen.

"Time to sign, darling," I said a bit too loudly, trying to hide my anxiety.

He signed. Then I signed. Ian reached into his suit pocket and handed a check for A$197,000 to the agent. I looked at the check and saw that it was from the Mick's Holdings CBA account—and gulped some champagne in huge relief because it wasn't one of Ian's rubber checks from an obscure overseas account.

The contracts were successfully exchanged. Ian left the café and went straight back to the airport to return to Lambruk.

Settlement was set for Friday the 11th of May.

On May 5, the vendor let me know he'd been delayed in London on business and asked if settlement could be postponed for a week, to May 18. Ian agreed to the new date.

On May 8, the vendor called me again and said he could now settle on the 14th. Was this time enough for me to organize the checks for settlement? It was!

I immediately called Meg Simpson, my go-to person at the CBA Bank, who had invested the funds into bank bills in the name of Mick's Holdings, upon our earlier instructions. I asked her how long it would take to pull the funds out of bank bills in preparation for settlement.

"Three days," she replied.

"Do it right now," I told her, before checking what authority she needed to do this.

"You're the sole director of Mick's Holdings, aren't you?" asked Meg.

"Yes, but Mick's Holdings account at the CBA needs both our signatures. Ian's and mine."

Meg then explained that the investment account she'd invested the funds through didn't need both signatures, and that I could authorize her to transfer the funds to any other Mick's Holdings account. "Just send me the written instructions by fax," she added.

"Can I transfer the funds to a Mick's Holdings account with another bank, say, St. George bank?"

"Of course you can."

I couldn't believe my luck. I was certain that Ian, like me, had no idea that when the A$2,644,312 was invested into bank bills, it was actually transferred into a new Mick's Holdings investment account.

Ian still thought the settlement was set for the 18th.

I faxed Meg, authorizing her to cash in A$1,755,000, the amount needed for settlement. Then, once the funds were in my Mick's Holdings account at St. George, I would organize the bank checks. We were using my solicitor, who hadn't even met Ian, so no problem there.

Monday, May 14 arrived. Settlement was set down for 11 a.m. I collected the bank checks at St. George in the city at 9:30 a.m. and, half an hour later, handed the checks to my lawyer. "Please call me the minute it's over," I said.

I went to the nearest bar and waited anxiously.

At 11:30 a.m. he called me.

"It's all done!"

I was overwhelmed with emotion. No matter what happened now, Lachlan and I had a beautiful home, and we would always be financially secure. I'd done it!

A couple of hours later, I got home and called Ian at Lambruk.

"Guess what, darling? I have some wonderful news!"

"What, little girl?"

"We have settled on the Seaforth property."

There was a deathly silence on the other end of the phone.

Ian flew to Sydney the next day. We met at the Establishment Hotel in George Street at 4 p.m. Ian was already there, seated at the bar, with a bottle of Moët and two glasses, when I walked in—and looked thunderous. After a few civil glasses of the Moët, it got ugly. Ian demanded a full explanation of why the house had settled early. My convoluted response enraged him even more. He angrily spat out that his dearest wish was to have been at the settlement. He then demanded the key to the house to "inspect" the property. I screamed that I would give him a key if his wife approved.

Our terrible fight ended when I fled the bar into the street, with Ian in pursuit. We kept fighting on the pavement until I finally managed to get away from him and scrambled into a cab.

Lachie and I moved into our beautiful new home in May 2001, days before my forty-first birthday. For a few hours that day—for the first time in many months—I was truly happy.

Then I received an unwelcome call from Ian in Lambruk.

"I am flying to Sydney and would like to visit the house."

My heart sank. Would I ever be rid of him?

Ian tried to wear me down with a barrage of emails and phone calls. He kept demanding a key and his own room in the new house. I said sure—if Bobby and Angus agreed, he could have a room and a key.

Sometime earlier, Bill O'Neill, Ian's onetime closest friend, confidant, and financial adviser, had gotten back in touch with me, and we were now in regular contact by phone. Bill let me know that he was suing Ian for A$500,000 in unpaid wages and had served Ian with a summons to appear in the district court to recover his money. My first question was about Bobby.

"Ian told me that he had divorced her, which I now know was a lie. But was their marriage ever in trouble?"

"No, not that I ever saw. I have a video I can show you taken a couple of years ago in Aspen of us playing golf together and attending an Independence Day party that evening. They were the 'it' couple of Aspen."

"You are kidding me!" I exclaimed in disgust.

Bill continued, "Remember in 1996 when Ian said he was in South Africa to meet with JCI but then disappeared and no one could find him?"

"Yes, I was frantic."

"Well, after his JCI meeting, he took Bobby on an African safari for her fiftieth birthday. That's why he disappeared from the face of the earth."

"What a prick! What a con man!"

"He also told me that you had lent him seventy-five thousand Australian."

"Yes, he said it was for some urgent business deal to find water near Lambruk."

"Ludmila, he used it as a deposit on a harborside apartment for Bobby—the same time you were trying to settle on the Lurline Bay house."

"For fuck's sake, he is unbelievable!" I cried out in anguish.

"I remember Bobby having a meltdown when she found out about Lachie's existence. She badgered Ian for giving Lachlan the MacNee name. Ian told her that he hadn't and that you forged his signature on the birth certificate."

"That's a total lie! You can't forge a name on a birth certificate. The signature has to be witnessed by a JP."

"Ludmila, it gets much worse. I presume he talked to you about his mysterious Swiss fund."

"Yes, often. What do you know about it?" I asked.

"It's called Cirrus Trust, and it's in Liechtenstein," replied Bill. "The trust owns twenty-five percent of a private Swiss bank. Ian's share was worth four hundred sixty-four million US in 1996, prior to obtaining its trading license in October 2000."

"Why then didn't he settle on the Lurline Bay property we bought together?"

Bill said that the trustees who controlled the funds in Switzerland would never allow the money to be brought into Australia.

"Because it's tax-free?"

"Yes. And for other reasons I can't discuss over the phone," came the cryptic reply.

But he didn't tell me the whole story until late in 2001.

On November 9 that year, Bill turned up at the door with a bottle of Moët and asked if we could sit outside by the waterfall feature because my house was almost definitely bugged. Russia all over again!

I followed him into the little courtyard, and there, in his direct fashion, Bill told me he'd been in contact with someone who worked for the Australian Security Intelligence Organisation (ASIO). There was a file on Ian that had been active for five years, coded G6.

I sat, stunned, as Bill dropped bombshell after bombshell, starting with Base Resources Ltd., the company Ian had owned in Malaysia. Ian once told me that Base Resources Ltd. had oil wells in Malaysia and that he'd sold it for US$10 million. Ian's partner there was in fact a front man for a Malaysian drug syndicate, and Ian himself, Bill went on, had been deeply involved in the drug world in Malaysia, and in Colombia.

Ian's mining activities were a front for his other activities. He laundered money for the drug syndicates through his Swiss bank. He had three passports—Australian, Maldivian, and Swiss. The Colombian mafia had tried to kill him just two weeks before, after he took their money and didn't perform.

Then came the biggest bombshell of all. The whole reason he'd gone into Russia was because he was trying to manufacture synthetic cocaine in Russian laboratories "in cahoots" with the Russian mafia. Star Mining was simply a front—a reason to spend so much time in Russia.

Bill even knew the identity of Nadya, the Ukrainian woman in the limousine. I'd told Bill the story, and how Ian had said afterward she was involved with his gold mining project in Kazakhstan. Bill claimed she worked for the mafia and was involved in Ian's cocaine business. Bill then alleged that Ian was producing synthetic cocaine in Russian laboratories, including those belonging to the Ministry of Atomic Energy in Moscow and Kazakhstan, with Nadya and Lebedev, two of the world's leading nuclear scientists. Bill further revealed that Ian's rich Chinese partners in Crusader had also been involved in the beginning; that was why they were so interested in a quick deal at the border with Norilsk Nickel—the deal offered to Greg and me on our first visit to Russia by Arbi and Ica (Chechen mafia). Ian and the Chinese had planned to export the nickel and platinum tailings across the Russian border to a Chinese refinery. The synthetic cocaine would've been smuggled out with the tailings and then sold internationally as a legal alternative to cocaine, marketed as designer drugs or "bath salts."

The main shock was the synthetic cocaine. Synthetic cocaine refers to a class of chemically engineered substances designed to mimic the effects of cocaine. Results can vary greatly depending on the specific chemical formula used. In some cases, synthetic cocaine has caused overdoses, organ damage, and death. This in itself made what Ian was doing criminal.

This revelation that Ian had used me and Malcolm and everyone else—even Yeltsin!—as cover for his cocaine business seemed unbelievable. But the story also cleared up so much of the mystery and unanswered questions that had surrounded Ian from the start. I had to concede something else too. The Russians, and specifically Shokhin, had got it right about Ian's money all along. It *was* drug money!

Bill then broke the news that Ian was seriously ill from cancer. Too ill, the authorities suspected, to continue with his international drug activities, although they were keeping him under constant surveillance all the same.

Two days before Christmas 2001, Bill returned. Once again, we went outside to talk. He told me that the CIA had questioned Ian in Aspen over three days early in 1997. They wanted the names of everyone he was dealing with in Russia. They'd also wanted to know about Chartwell Bank.

The Chinese mafia had threatened Ian over money he owed them, and the Israeli police were apparently now after Ian as well. That very year, some Saudi nationals had deposited large sums of money in Ian's Swiss bank, which had then invested this money in the financial markets, making huge returns. There were even rumors that these funds were used to fund terrorists.

I told Bill that I remembered Ian telling me how easy the Arabs were to deal with, as they never complained when the fund sustained temporary losses. Could Ian have had something to do with 9/11? This was too much for me to fathom.

Throughout 2002, bigger and bigger cracks started appearing in Ian's life. More people began pursuing him for money owed to them. Even S. Y. Hui commenced proceedings against Ian in the Hong Kong courts.

Bill O'Neill kept me up to date as everything unfolded through his connections with the ASIO, although in dramatic contrast to Ian's, my own life was beginning to stabilize. I suffered from extreme anxiety after ten years of Ian's coercive behavior and had no desire to socialize, go out, or entertain; I led a quiet existence. I just wanted to sit in my beautiful house in Seaforth and raise Lachie. But while I enjoyed my peaceful nights at home, reading, watching movies, ordering home delivery meals, and swimming in my pool, I wondered whether this would be the pattern for the rest of my life.

Bill eventually decided to join S. Y. Hui and others in an attempt to bankrupt Ian and seize his assets, and on November 24, 2002, an article appeared in the *Financial Review*: "Miner faces bankruptcy petition."[12]

---

12   Trevor Sykes, "Miner faces bankruptcy petition," *Australian Financial Review*, November 24, 2002, https://www.afr.com/politics/miner-faces-bankruptcy-petition-20031124-jv1zy.

Former high-flying mining entrepreneur Ian MacNee is facing a bankruptcy petition in the Australian High Court in Sydney today. The case could be a huge embarrassment to MacNee, who tried to raise money for a company called Wedderburn Mining earlier this year. MacNee became a high-flyer a decade ago when he was one of the directors along with Malcolm Turnbull and Neville Wran of Star Mining. . . .

Now MDC Investments of Hong Kong is claiming a debt of A$951,071.34 in settlement of outstanding claims arising from transactions in Star Mining shares. . . .

Today, MDC will apply for a sequestration order under which it can seize his assets. None of this information appears to have been given to potential subscribers in Wedderburn, which MacNee has been trying to float since January 2003, . . . [but the float] now appears to have been dropped. One of its prime assets was exploration licence 4214 at Moliagul, which is prospective for gold.

CHAPTER FORTY-NINE

The Secret Life of a Sociopath

In late 2002, I decided to consult a psychiatrist and chose to see Rob Hampshire, the celebrity psychiatrist I'd met at Malcolm's fortieth birthday party on October 22, 1994, mainly because he knew Bill, Ian, and the whole Russian saga well. Rob immediately diagnosed Ian as a narcissistic sociopath. He explained that sociopathy is a mental health condition in which a person has no moral compass and cannot differentiate between right and wrong. A sociopath sees others as impersonal objects or possessions to be manipulated to satisfy their own narcissistic needs without any regard for the hurtful consequences of their selfish actions.

Rob continued, "Sadly, these people are capable of ripping off their mothers, their kids, and their romantic partners. They have difficulty meeting financial responsibilities and have delusions of grandeur."

Rob concluded that I was suffering from post-traumatic stress disorder, which would require both drugs and therapy. "I propose you tell me everything that happened from the very beginning. We will go over each episode until you can recall it without feeling physically sick. I will also prescribe Prozac, an antidepressant to lessen your depression and anxiety."

And so, for the next few months I worked with Rob, recalling my whole life with Ian in minute detail. I felt sick, I vomited, I perspired, I cried, but finally came out feeling much happier and stronger. However, it took another five years to heal completely. Hearing of Ian's death in 2008 was a great release. I was totally free of him at last.

During this period, Bill and I also met constantly and exchanged more details of our lives since meeting Ian. Most of what Bill told me about Ian was deeply disturbing, and I had to process it all with Rob.

Bill then sent me a copy of the draft of his responding affidavit, "BILL O'NEILL VS IAN STEWART MACNEE. DISTRICT COURT 2002; Bill O'Neill's Draft Response to Ian Stewart MacNee's claim of Duress," a version of which he subsequently filed with the district court against Ian in his case to recover wages in the amount of A$500,000. The response contained a biography of Ian's life and was a shocking insight. It detailed Ian's relationship with Bill, me, his wife, and others. I have included a few excerpts, with Bill's permission.

***

Bill O'Neill's initial relationships with Ian Stewart MacNee

Whilst working at Morgan Grenfell as head of Corporate Finance in 1978, I met Ian Stewart MacNee ("ISM"), who was involved in mining ventures, some of them in a listed entity, Base Resources. ISM wanted to expand operations and invited me to join the board of Base Resources, which I did. Then ISM sold control of Base to Lee Ming Tee ("LMT"), one of ISM's associates in Hong Kong, whom I regarded as a corporate outlaw, so I resigned. Base expanded and became Giant Resources. Giant was sold to Pioneer Concrete, losing a few hundred million on a Canadian gold mine owned by Giant. LMT has been charged with fraud in Hong Kong.

ISM asked me to find a new listed entity and I acquired Central Mining, an Adelaide based small mining company listed on the Australian Stock Exchange (ASX), in 1987. ISM was chairman and another individual, Graeme Ellis ("GE") who was a director and ran the company, invited me onto the board of Central.

ISM was in Hong Kong, running a listed entity called Crusader, listed on the HK exchange. I then discovered that Crusader's main shareholder was none other than LMT via a secret web of nominees and Crusader operated an alluvial gold mine in the Amazon, Brazil. There was gold there; it had been extracted, but not much reached the head office.

ISM had been using the services of Ludmila Melnikoff ("LM") in Russia to acquire an interest in a large old alluvial gold mine in Russia (Lenzoloto) in Siberia, Russia, on the basis of the supposed expertise in Brazil. Lenzoloto also held a fully explored (at what would have cost A$100 million) but undeveloped gold deposit, called Sukhoi Log, containing proven reserves of 60 million ounces of gold, a gross value of A$24 billion.

ISM with the help of LM had negotiated with Yeltsin the rights to buy 34 percent of Lenzoloto and develop the gold deposit. LM was born in Australia of Russian parents, so spoke fluent Russian. Her mother was also a good friend of a famous Russian poet called Katya Shevelova, who was close to Yeltsin and introduced LM to Yeltsin.

ISM acquired the share in Lenzoloto via a company, Star Technology Ltd. ("ST") he incorporated with LM, who had a small interest. ISM held his share of ST through a chain of his offshore companies. He then decided to sell ST to Central, thereby listing ST on the Australian Stock Exchange (ASX).

Needing capital for Central to buy ST and develop the Russian gold deposit he raised about A$80 million through a merchant bank, Turnbull & Partners, resulting in ST being issued 200 million Central shares and a cash payment of $A8 million. ISM received 98.5 percent of this and LM received 1.5 percent. Central changed its name to Star Mining ("Star") and at that stage I resigned as Director so Turnbull could be appointed, and Wran became Star's Chairman. Star completed a bankable mining feasibility study at a cost of some A$15 million. Star eventually arranged US$750 million in development funding from Standard Bank of South Africa.

When the development of the gold deposit was looking positive, the Russians started an investigation into the past "privatisation" and joint venture of Lenzoloto and Star. They claimed that the past privatisation did not meet the new rules for privatisations and although it was retrospective, it allowed the Russians to get back control of the vast gold deposit.

During this period, ISM sent a famous fax to GE setting out that he was bribing Zhirinovsky, the head of the Russian Liberal Democratic Party and a presidential candidate, by putting A$600,000 from Star's bank account into Zhirinovsky's private Swiss Bank Account. ISM outlined in the fax that no-one would know about it, as the A$600,000 would be buried in Star's cost for the mining feasibility study. This bribe was to stop the investigation or ensure a "favorable" outcome for Star and I was informed that the Australian Minister of Finance ordered ASIC to investigate this matter.

Despite this payment, the Russian Government took back the interest that Star had in the gold project, leaving Star with virtually nothing. Star's share price collapsed and lost its money followed by the resignations of Wran, Turnbull and ISM, but all three had managed to sell their Star shares before Star's collapse.

ISM asked me to help him with other gold interests in Kazakhstan, a former Soviet Union republic, rich in gold. ISM's partner was a famous Russian nuclear scientist, called Lebedev. I was to do the financial evaluation of the mining prospects and arrange the capital raisings and public issues on respective stock exchanges to develop these deposits into profitable mining operations. I was to be paid US$10,000 a month for my services by ISM.

I also assisted ISM in his personal finances and became a board member of ISM's Australian company, Coherent Resources. I was to provide advice on ISM's interest in the Argyle Wine Company in Oregon, USA, a joint venture with Brian Croser's Petaluma Wines in South Australia. ISM sold his interest to Petaluma about two years ago for a net of A$20 million.

Summarized excerpt of Bill's Affidavit related to ISM's wife and family

Whilst ISM was married to his first wife, he met and had an affair with RM [Bobby]. ISM eventually divorced his wife, crying poor, resulting in his wife not receiving anything in the settlement.

ISM and RM married in late '70s. They had two homes, an expansive estate called Lambruk in Fyerstown, near Castlemaine in Victoria, Australia, and an apartment at the Noosa Springs Golfing Resort Noosa Heads, Queensland, Australia. They also had a place in Aspen, Colorado, USA, that ISM sold about two years ago for US$3 million. RM owned an apartment in Macquarie St., Sydney, Australia, but also sold it two years ago for about $A1 million.

RM and ISM had one son, Angus, currently nineteen years old. ISM had two children by the previous marriage, a son Chris, living in the UK, and a daughter, Cathy, who lives at Mangrove Mountain, Central Coast of NSW, on a property that is owned by ISM. Needless to say, ISM's relationship with them isn't positive due to him breaking every commitment made and using this to benefit himself. Some examples of this include borrowing US$250,000 from Chris under the guise of pending repossession of ISM's Aspen home by the bank, and on receiving the funds, purchasing a brand-new top-of-the-range Porsche. Another instance was transferring the 350-acre Mangrove Mountain property to Chris, who inherited a A$1 million mortgage and was worried about servicing the loan. These strategies were used to hide ISM's assets and affected his children's mental health.

RM and ISM lived in Aspen 50 percent and Lambruk 50 percent of the time. RM managed Lambruk, and the property expenses were large. ISM set up a "Lambruk Special" bank account with A$10 million, and both ISM and RM were signatories. In 1999, ISM stated this amount was to generate enough income to meet expenses and that he had also transferred Lambruk to RM. ISM explained that RM had hired detectives and was upset about the "LM situation" and was threatening divorce. He did this to placate RM and to evade declaring assets in a settlement. He added that he was now keeping all his documents in a safe.

LM later told me that this is when ISM told her that he had reached an amicable property settlement with RM and had divorced her, which was a lie. All ISM did was transfer Lambruk to RM and set up a A$10 million trust for her.

RM was suspicious about the existence of his funds in the Swiss bank as ISM was very secretive about this. However, he had stated to both LM and I that this amounted to US$464 million held in a discretionary trust managed by a team of Swiss bankers, earning about 20 percent annual income that ISM lived off tax-free.

Later ISM told me he could not use those funds in Australia as RM was watching all the bank accounts and still threatening divorce. He added, "LM is suing me under a paternity case so they wanted to know all his assets."

ISM then began pleading poor to RM, the same tactics that worked with his first wife, always saying that he had no money in front of RM, however, when travelling, he always flew first class, drank Dom Pérignon, dined in the best restaurants and stayed in 5-star hotels. He paid for these and other expenses by credit card, which was then paid by his Swiss bankers.

During an Easter weekend in 1999, whilst attending a wedding, RM confided in me that she was an emotional wreck. At dinner that night, RM found out about ISM's and LM's child. Angus, ISM and RM's son, was there and didn't know about ISM's other son. He subsequently found out about his half brother through a press article.

From that moment, I started investigating ISM's activities and contacting parties that he had undertaken business with. The results were very negative about the honesty of ISM.

Ludmila Melnikoff ("LM")

I was aware of the role of LM in the negotiations with Yeltsin and the Russian Government to acquire the interest in the Siberian gold project, as I was director of Central Mining at the time, later to be called Star Mining.

I first met LM at a Central Mining AGM in 1992 when she was introduced to me. We spoke about Star Mining and the Russian gold project for about fifteen minutes.

The next incident regarding LM was at a Central Mining Board meeting when I commented to ISM that I had heard a stock market rumour from Rupert Steel, a partner at Warburg's Bank. Rupert asked, "I heard that LM is coming back to Australia, so will that affect Central and its negotiations regarding the gold project?" He further added, "The reason she is coming back is because she is pregnant, and the rumour is that ISM is the father". I repeated this to ISM in a joking manner and he literally exploded and said, "What a vicious, malicious lie. How can people make up these dreadful things?" I thought nothing more of it.

A few years later, LM called me one night. She introduced herself saying, "Remember me, we met a few years ago at the Central AGM", which I clearly recalled. She then said that she and ISM were living together as he had divorced his wife, RM, and that they had been living together for some time in Byron Bay and then moved to Double Bay, an elite harbourside suburb in Sydney. This was a surprise to me.

LM then stated that ISM and LM were buying an oceanfront property at Lurline Bay, an upper-class suburb, to live in together. LM said when ISM and she moved in, they would invite me and my wife around for dinner. The cost of the house was A$3 million, and LM had put down the deposit herself of A$300,000. The balance of A$2.7 million was to be paid by ISM from the upcoming sale of his Oregon Winery, priced at A$20 million.

Sometime later, ISM stated that the sale of the winery had been delayed so he had hoped to settle Lurline Bay with funds from the Swiss bank, but there were problems in getting the balance of A$2.7 million into the country. ISM always deflected the blame on someone or something else. LM had moved into the house and undertaken some renovations at LM's cost, and now the vendor was demanding a settlement or he was going to cancel the contract and evict LM and her son. ISM had promised numerous settlement dates but had failed to deliver the funds. LM was pleading with me to talk to ISM and push him to settle on Lurline Bay.

I contacted ISM, cautiously, and outlined the situation. ISM commented that LM was under strain and had matters confused but was in fact buying a place for herself and the son to live in. He was having trouble getting the money out of Switzerland as RM was still talking about a divorce and had hired detectives again. ISM said the vendor wanted assurance that he could settle and requested a letter from a bank stating that ISM will settle. Then he wanted me to write a letter of assurance, and I baulked at this as legally this could be construed as a guarantee. I provided a basic non-binding character reference, that the vendor refused to accept. He cancelled the contract, evicted LM and her son, and kept the A$300,000 deposit that LM had paid. LM was not happy!

I subsequently found out that LM owned ten percent of ST, but, prior to Central's acquisition of ST, ISM had convinced her to swap her direct ten percent holding in ST with an equal value of Pan Pacific shares—one of ISM's offshore companies which owned thirty percent of ST. So, the majority of her interest in the Russian gold mine (worth about A$3 million) was in Pan Pacific, controlled by ISM. Wanting to buy LM's Star Mining shares in Pan Pacific, a contract was drawn up, the shares sold for A$2.8 million, but ISM failed to pay these funds to LM. LM threatened legal action to recover monies owed. As a compromise, ISM agreed to purchase the Lurline Bay property in LM's name as repayment for her shares.

After ISM failed to settle on the Lurline Bay property, LM commenced legal proceedings against ISM in the Supreme Court of NSW. As a further compromise to LM, ISM exchanged on another house in Dover Heights for A$2.65 million. ISM wrote a check for A$265,000, being the deposit, on a Lambruk Special Account check, that his wife operated. The check was dishonored. The vendor sued ISM and LM. The reason that LM was being sued is that she was a trustee of The Sydney Bay Trust—a trust set up to buy the Dover Heights property, for her and the son, Lachlan, to live in. ISM promised to indemnify LM for all court costs but did not. This cost LM a considerable amount. The case was finally settled after ISM wore down the vendor with the usual abuse of legal process. Ironically, ISM used the same lawyers in this case (before they sued him for non-payment of their fees).

Following the deceptions of the Lurline Bay and Dover Heights property purchases, LM started legal action to recover her money. This amounted to about $2.8 million for the Star shares, A$300,000 for the Lurline Bay loss of deposit, and additional amounts for child support. It was not a paternity case although a family property settlement claim was thrown in as well.

During my case against ISM, I contacted LM to see if she could help me in my case against ISM, by confirming that ISM had employed me on a formal basis and not the speculative success basis that ISM was trying to claim as a defence. We arranged to meet and discuss the situation.

LM outlined that she was prohibited from discussing anything about ISM's business activities under a confidentiality agreement that was part of the settlement over the court case she had with ISM. I commented, "Over the paternity suit". She asked, "What paternity suit?" It was then that LM told her side of the story.

Lachlan, the son, was in fact ISM's. LM produced photos of ISM at the birth, showed me copies of the birth certificate with ISM named as the father. LM and ISM had been living together for years, and ISM had bought a house in Byron Bay where they had lived for some time. It was later sold for some A$1.4 million, but LM did not see a cent.

ISM has not paid child support. LM had complained to Child Welfare and ISM has been investigated by the ATO to determine his ability to pay. Last year he had a taxable income of A$22,000. ISM again failed to pay the child support, claiming he had money, and has asked LM to lie to the child welfare department.

An out of court settlement was agreed with a tight confidentiality agreement. Again, ISM had applied a tactic of ongoing legal harassment to LM to make her give up her legal action. LM stated that she was on the verge of breaking down as a result of this. LM could reveal that ISM placed about A$2.65 million into the Sydney Bay Trust, originally set up to purchase the Dover Heights home for her and their son, Lachlan. This money came from the sale of his Oregon Winery and both LM and ISM were joint trustees. Part of the money in the amount of A$1.975 million was used to purchase a home in Seaforth in Sydney, Australia. Both LM and ISM had rights to reside in the Avona Crescent trust property until their deaths, upon which Lachlan was to inherit the trust's property. The balance was invested. Even though the funds were originally LM's, ISM managed to turn the settlement into funds in trust for his son Lachlan.

After the settlement, LM discovered that ISM was still married to RM and had lied about the divorce, so she broke off the relationship. She moved into Avona Crescent with Lachlan. In June 2001 LM rang me in a very upset state. ISM had been demanding that he stay with LM at Avona Crescent whenever he was in Sydney. He claimed that as he owned half the house (he did not, just a trustee) he could stay there and presumably make advances to LM. She denied him access and he made numerous threats which have included death threats. She stated that she was applying for an Apprehended Violence Order (AVO) to protect herself. She said she had compiled an application and wanted me to accompany her to Manly Police station whilst she made her statement and handing over her documentation. I was there purely for moral support. A full AVO was issued.

On a later occasion, on November 30, 2001, LM transferred some of the remaining funds from the trust's bank account at Commonwealth Bank, Bondi Junction, to a high earning investment account. These funds were to pay for living expenses and house maintenance, as per the trust deed. The Bank Manager was a friend of ISM's. When LM transferred the money into the investment account, the Bank Manager told ISM and proceeded to cancel the transfer and place the funds in the amount of A$480,000 into ISM's personal bank account, as instructed by ISM. LM rang me in tears, pleading with me to help. I drafted faxes and sent them to an old friend of mine, CEO of the Bank, requesting that the matter be investigated. The Bank Manager was sacked and the funds returned to LM.

The same Bank Manager then got a job at a home loan company and was the party that signed a loan commitment to ISM for the A$1.1 million security deposit to be placed with the District

Court to enable ISM to continue his defence against me. The loan was provided to ISM by a company called Mango Media. ISM had originally claimed that I was engaged on a speculative success fee basis only, and not a wage, so was not owed any money, but I won that case. Consequently, ISM signed Consent Orders agreeing to pay my wages of A$500,000 and my legals costs, but failed to comply and instead initiated a case against me claiming he signed the Orders "under duress". I later found out that all of ISM's mining deals in Russia were a front for his "other activities".

LM recently contacted me to enquire about the progress of my case. LM informed me that she had a full breakdown over the ISM matter but had now recovered fully. Prior to this the mere mention of the ISM name would result in LM breaking down in tears.

During a number of earlier conversations with LM, I quizzed her as to the number of occasions that ISM was staying with her in Double Bay and Byron Bay. It turned out to be considerable. LM and I then reconstructed events to work out how he did this. Every time he went to the US, at least once a month, ISM would fly up from Melbourne in the morning and I would pick him up at Sydney Airport. He did not have luggage, claiming that he had booked it in at Melbourne all the way to the USA. We would conduct business in the morning and I would drive him to Sydney International Airport. On some occasions I would accompany him to have coffee and finalise a few matters. He would then pick up his papers, tickets etc and walk into the customs area as he had seat allocation and full check-in at Melbourne.

In fact, he was just walking in, stopping, waiting for me to leave and then travelling back to the domestic terminal, picking up his bags and travelling to Ballina (Byron Bay) and being picked up by LM at the airport. We compared dates to confirm this. The only way that ISM could be reached in the US was on his mobile phone, only by leaving messages. ISM was in fact constantly calling his mobile in the USA from Byron Bay, getting the messages left on it, and ringing me or RM in response. After about a week he would eventually travel to the US and then back to RM and Lambruk. In fact, after a detailed analysis it was not possible to either track him to the USA or confirm that he was ever there.

CHAPTER FIFTY

To Catch a Thief

Ian never faced the music for anything, although I did hear that his rental house in Noosa Springs Golf Resort was sprayed with bullets one night.

The attempt to bankrupt him and seize his assets had mixed results. Lambruk was repossessed by Ian's creditors, including Bill O'Neill and the ANZ and Westpac banks, but priority was given to a creditor called Mango Media, which held a first mortgage over the property. A fire sale was held, and Lambruk was sold for A$1.75 million and its contents auctioned off. Most of the proceeds went to Mango Media and the rest to the banks. As shown in his affidavit, Bill found out later that Mango Media was a front for Ian and his Russian mafia partners in his Swiss bank.

Consequently, Ian got all the proceeds from Lambruk and avoided paying any of his real creditors, while Bill was left with a legal bill of A$600,000 and was forced to sell his two investment properties and his home.

A year passed. Then, early in 2006, Bill called me to say that his contact at ASIO had told him that Ian had metastatic cancer of the right kidney. He was dying.

A month later, Ian rang me himself with the same news and said he might only have a few months left. He was in North Sydney, he went on, and wondered if we could meet for fifteen minutes.

I was curious. What did he want to tell me?

As I drove to North Sydney, I was surprised by how forlorn I felt. Despite everything, it was shocking to think that Lachie's father would soon be dead.

He was waiting for me at the Firehouse Pub with a bottle of Piper champagne and two glasses.

"That's the best they have here," he said.

"That's fine."

He popped the cork.

"Ian, you look great. Are you sure you're sick?" I couldn't help saying.

"Thank you, but I assure you I am," he replied. "I went in for the operation, but the cancer had spread. I remember waking up and realizing only forty minutes had passed and knew instantly that there was nothing they could do."

"Oh, Ian, I'm very sorry."

"Don't worry about me. I look upon dying as the next adventure. I don't have many regrets but one is that we didn't do anything with Donald Trump in Russia. I told you that I met him once in Trump Tower in New York. He was with a group of Russians and was very keen to build a "Trump Tower" in Moscow. He knew about STAR and Lenzoloto and hence invited me to attend his meeting with the Russians. He was very impressive. If we had joined him, maybe the Trump Tower would have been built after all. More importantly, how are you?"

At the time I didn't think more of it as my only knowledge of Trump was from his TV show "The Apprentice" but many years later I would remember this conversation which further proved Ian's connections with the Russian mafia. It would be our last conversation, and Ian spent most of it telling me about his new company, Wedderburn.

"I've always had this knack at finding underground sources of water," he said. "I used to walk around Lambruk with a stick and find streams of underground water. So, we built wells and dams, and the water supplied the whole of Lambruk for years. Wedderburn has acquired leases to explore for water in the Australian countryside. I have no doubt we'll find water. You should buy shares in Wedderburn. You won't regret it. It will make you a lot of money."

I smiled and said it sounded like a promising idea.

Ian's mobile rang. It was Bobby wanting to know where he was.

We kept talking for a few more minutes and then left the pub together. He kissed me on the cheek and said he'd be in touch.

We parted. Ian walked off down the street—and I walked in the opposite direction.

On August 7, I received a call from Child Support, as Ian had been paying a nominal amount for Lachie.

"I am calling to notify you we have closed your account. I would like to offer you our condolences."

"What are you talking about?" I said blankly.

"Oh, you don't know? Ian MacNee passed away three days ago."

As I put down the phone, I pictured Ian the last time I saw him. Finally, I was free from this narcissistic abuser.

❖ ❖ ❖

August 2008. Out of the blue, my mobile rang. It was Malcolm. He was furious.

He said he'd been rung by someone from the ABC current affairs program *Four Corners* about an interview I'd given for a story they were doing on Malcolm. They had wanted to check one of my recollections: I'd said that the Russians adored Malcolm because of his passion and strength. As an example, I described how Malcolm had punched Mostovoy's plywood safe with his fist, being furious about the Irkutsk government's war on Star. Even though he scared the hell out of Mostovoy's secretary, he got want he wanted out of Mostovoy.

Malcolm launched into a tirade during which he called the people at *Four Corners* snakes. He denied the story I'd told them, and even when I described the whole episode to him in detail, he repeated with mounting anger that he had no memory of it.

"I really wish you'd kept your mouth shut. This is really going to fucking hurt me!" he yelled.

I burst into tears, and only then did Malcolm calm down. He said that if I wanted to talk about Russia, why didn't I write a book?

"I am," I replied.

"Great. Once you have finished, we can launch it together."

The fight was over. He asked after Lachie and then said he'd call in a couple of days and we'd have a coffee together.

His lawyers contacted *Four Corners* and threatened to sue for defamation if they included my interview. The program was aired without my interview.

Malcolm didn't ring about our coffee.

Two years passed. At about seven one evening, I was walking along Castlereagh Street in Sydney's CBD toward the car park in Martin Place on my way home from work. Martin Place was all lit up, ready for the grand *Vogue* Fashion Night Out party that evening. As I started to cross Castlereagh Street, I suddenly spotted Malcolm walking toward me.

Impeccably dressed in a beautiful, tailored suit, he looked hot. I had my work clothes on, my morning makeup was gone, and I knew I looked tired.

Our paths crossed in the middle of the street. He glanced at me briefly but kept walking. His entourage of equally beautifully dressed young people had gone on ahead.

I called out to him, "Malcolm!"

He spun around.

"It's me! Ludmila!"

He half smiled. "Oh, hi."

The walk light turned to red, and we both kept going in opposite directions, moving fast in front of the traffic.

I turned.

He did not look back.

Epilogue

After more tribulations, my life turned out for the better, as I now live life on my terms.

As for Ian's money, it all disappeared into the international "banking system." His family got nothing. I met up with Chris MacNee in 2011 for a drink in a city bar. His very words were "Dad said on his dying bed that I would get an email with details of my inheritance, but the fucker lied to me—no email ever arrived."

Regarding Malcolm, he won an Eastern Suburbs blue seat and became the leader of the Liberal Party. Then, in June 2016, just prior to the Australian election, the revelations about the Panama Papers exploded across the entire world, implicating many companies owned indirectly by presidents and the mega wealthy. Star Technology was one of those companies. Ian, Malcolm, and I were listed as directors. The Australian press was all over it. The *Australian Financial Review* carried the story on its front page.

Shortly after, Malcolm became Australia's twenty-ninth prime minister.

In April 2020, Malcolm published his book, *A Bigger Picture*. John Helmer promptly published an article on his blog titled "Malcolm Turnbull's Russia Story," in which he comments on Malcolm's book:[13]

> According to the index, he has met twenty heads of government of state. For almost all of them he expresses himself satisfied with his reciprocal personal equality; and over some, especially President Donald Trump, Turnbull thinks he's the intellectual superior. But Putin has proved to be exceptional. Just how that was, Turnbull recorded from their first meeting in 2007, when Turnbull was a junior minister. The Australian prime

---

13   John Helmer, "Malcolm Turnbull's Russia Story," *Dances with Bears*, April 1, 2020,

minister introduced Turnbull to Putin, saying "in his business career Mr Turnbull spent some time in Siberia." Turnbull reports what happened next: "A thin smile crossed Putin's lips, and he leant forward to me, asking in a soft voice, 'Really? What crimes did you commit?'"

Thus, for the first time—also for the last time the way Turnbull thinks in retrospect—did Turnbull meet his match.

AFTER NOTES

Sukhoi Log, which once "belonged" to Yeltsin, now "belongs" to Putin. Did Star Mining ever have a real chance to mine it? If Ian had continued to bribe the Russians and Yeltsin hadn't handed over his presidency to Putin in return for immunity from criminal prosecution, then maybe—even though the economic viability of mining Sukhoi Log critically depends on the world gold price.

Polyus, a Russian company backed by Putin, acquired the Sukhoi Log license on February 22, 2017. Polyus is currently the largest gold producer in Russia and one of the top ten gold mining companies in the world. It is listed on the Moscow Exchange and was listed on the London Stock Exchange until 2023 but was delisted due to sanctions imposed by the UK, USA, EU, and Australia following the Russian invasion of Ukraine. Polyus was controlled by Said Kerimov (son of Sulayman Kerimov, a Russian billionaire businessman), owning 76 percent, but for some reason he sold 30 percent of his share to Akhmet Palankoyev, a Russian politician and entrepreneur, donated 46 percent to the "Islamic Fund for support of Islamic foundations" in August 2022, and resigned as director.

Polyus announced its plans for a pilot plant at Sukhoi Log in an *Interfax* news article in December 2023, and in September 2024 it produced its first gold from ore mined at Sukhoi Log in a nearby recovery plant and is building infrastructure at Sukhoi Log itself and aims to start building a recovery plant there in 2025.

In early 2022, Russia pegged its currency, the ruble, to gold, and 5,000 rubles will now buy an ounce of pure gold. The plan was to shift the currency away from a pegged value and into the gold standard itself so the ruble would become a credible gold substitute at a fixed rate.

Imagine the global response to the first national currency of the twenty-first century backed by physical gold! At a stroke, Russia could reposition itself as a globally relevant economy, virtually guarantee international investor interest, and reestablish its currency as a store of value. And it could do all this *without violating sanctions*. Consider the response from the US and EU, both suffering four-decade-high inflation, both crippled by debt and awash in freshly printed currency. A new Russian gold standard would represent an economic coup over the West. All without firing a single shot.[14] This would also weaken, if not destroy, the US dollar, which I believe is Putin's strategy. It seems that invading Ukraine was all part of his master plan.

But Putin needs a lot more gold to complete this process—so what is Putin's intention for Sukhoi Log? We now know that Sukhoi Log contains 5,669 tons of silver on top of the 4,220 tons of gold.[15] Huge stuff—enough to alter the economic balance of the

---

14   Peter Reagan, "Russia's gold stockpile proving to be a safe haven," *Bullion.Directory* precious metals analysis, Financial Market Strategist at Birch Gold Group, 21 March 2022.

15   Eugene Gerden, "Russian Polyus accelerates development of Sukhoi Log gold mine," Resource World, October 2024, https://resourceworld.com/russian-polyus-accelerates-development-of-sukhoi-log-gold-mine/; Star was given the official reserve data in 1996 which showed these figures.

modern world! Putin has built a nuclear bunker the size of a city in the Altai Mountains, near the Irkutsk region in Siberia. Sukhoi Log is just 3,000 kilometers away. Underground tunnels, thousands of kilometers long and constructed by German diggers, run in all directions from the bunker.

So, is Sukhoi Log Putin's "golden checkmate" in his game against the West?

Ludmila (second from right) with fellow students in Uzbekistan in 1980

Ludmila (at back of group) with fellow students in Uzbekistan in 1980

Meeting with President Yeltsin in December 1990. From left to right: Katya Shevelova, Ian MacNee, President Yeltsin, Ludmila

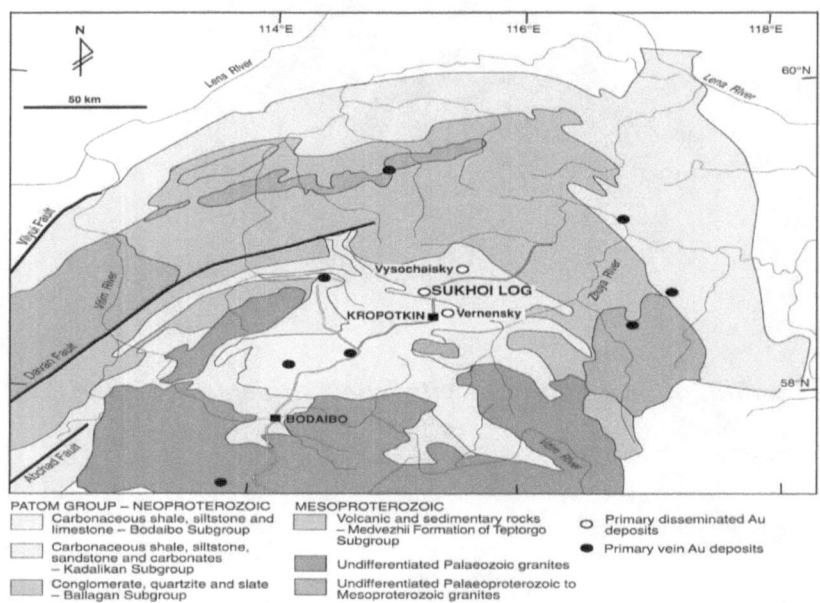

Sukhoi Log graphic created by Star geologist Bryce Wood

Sukhoi Log graphic created by Star geologist Bryce Wood

CERTIFICATE OF INCUMBENCY

We, **MOSSACK FONSECA & CO. (B.V.I.) LTD.**, Registered Agent of **STAR TECHNOLOGY SYSTEMS LIMITED** (the "Company"), an International Business Company existing under the Laws of the British Virgin Islands, do hereby certify that:

1. The Company was incorporated as an International Business Company numbered 23797 on 8th January, 1990.

2. The directors, shareholders and officers of the Company are:

   Directors
   - Christopher Stewart MacNee
   - Ian Stewart MacNee
   - Graeme Allen Ellis
   - Neville Kenneth Wran
   - Malcolm Bligh Turnbull
   - Ludmila Melnikoff
   - HUI Sik Yin, Alfred (Alternate)
   - John Alan Thomas (Alternate)

   Shareholder   Star Mining Corporation N.L.   30,000 shares held
                  (frmly-Central Mining Corporation N.L.)

   Officers   L.A. Secretaries Limited

3. Insofar as is evidenced by documents filed at the Registered Office, there are no proceedings pending or threatened against the Company, and that no action has been taken to wind-up the Company or to appoint a receiver or manager.

4. The Company does not maintain a Register of Mortages and Charges pursuant to Section 70A of the International Business Companies Act.

Dated this 15th day of June, 1995.

MOSSACK FONSECA & CO. (B.V.I.) LTD.
Registered Agent

Star Mining Certificate of Incumbency, 1995

At the Lenzoloto cabin in Bodaibo, May 1992. From left to right: John Thomas, Ian Martens, Ian MacNee, Ludmila, Terry Willstead, Chris MacNee, Bryce Wood, and Ivor Borovik

At Lenzoloto cabin in Bodaibo, May 1992. From left to right: Bryce Wood, Ian MacNee, local Russian guy, and John Thomas

Ludmila and Greg Moore with a bag of beluga caviar by the Caspian Sea, Russia, in 1990

Ludmila and her secretary Masha at the Lenzoloto cabin in Bodaibo, May 1992

Ludmila at the famous Moscow Central Market in 1992

Ludmila (second from the right), Arbi (third from the right), and Ica (fourth from the right) dining with Arbi's family in Grozny, in August 1990

www.ingramcontent.com/pod-product-compliance
Lightning Source LLC
LaVergne TN
LVHW091540070526
838199LV00002B/144